CURIOUS JOURNEY

ORIGINS OF THE NEW AGE

A TRAVELER'S GUIDE
TO THE UNKNOWN

Robert Hunter presents an excellent case that there is way more to what's going on in this world than most of us have any idea. Knowledge is power, and the knowledge he presents is stunning.

Marianne Williamson
Author of *The Age of Miracles, The Gift of Change, Healing the Soul of America,* and numerous other bestsellers

· · · · · · · · · · · · · · · · ·

A Curious Journey is a literary tour de force spanning the experiences, formulations, and applications of spiritual seekers, and cultures, throughout the ages. What is especially laudable is how Author Robert Charles Hunter describes the vast scope of such highly complex material in a very clear, concise and down-to-earth manner; sometimes enthralled, sometimes tongue in cheek, sometimes incredulous, often humorous. This book is a "must" read for anyone embarking on their own *Curious Journey,* as well as anyone who is seeking a comprehensive history of the permutations of spiritual thinking."

Arthur Kornhaber, M.D.
Author of *Spirit* (1986 St. Martin's Press)
Founder and president of the Foundation for Grandparenting
www.grandparenting.org

· · · · · · · · · · · · · · · · ·

Rarely will you find a 'cool cucumber' entrepreneur and successful business maven like Robert Charles Hunter researching and writing a biting and brilliant tableau of New Age, Old Age, Metaphysics, Folklore and Mysteries, including Astrology and Numerology, that teaches and transforms skeptics and main line religious conservatives like *A Curious Journey.* Hunter insinuates his own spiritual growth with his discoveries and makes it possible for each of us to unearth ancient and current truths that we didn't know existed. If you want to cajole your family and friends who will learn to be more open to what can free them from innate prejudice against spiritual wisdom, buy them this book. I'd suggest that you buy it by the caseload and stimulate your whole neighborhood.

Albert Clayton Gaulden
Author of *Signs and Wonders* and *You're Not Who You Think You Are*
Founding Director, the Sedona Intensive™

· · · · · · · · · · · · · · · · ·

Since I met my husband at the crossroads of our mutual quest, I have been privileged to witness his brilliant observations and share his profound descriptions of discoveries and wonderous miracles . . .

Diane Ladd
Author of *Spiraling Through the School of Life*
Actress, Director, Screenwriter, Producer and winner of 23 International awards including 3 Academy Award™ Nominations and the British Academy Award

CURIOUS JOURNEY

ORIGINS OF THE NEW AGE

A TRAVELER'S GUIDE
TO THE UNKNOWN

BY

ROBERT CHARLES HUNTER
©2008

ILLUSTRATIONS BY KARISSA DINGUS

EXXCELL
PRESS

This first edition published by Exxcell Press
Los Angeles & Nashville

Printed in the United States of America

Library of Congress Cataloging-in-Publication Data:

Hunter, Robert Charles
Curious Journey / Robert Charles Hunter
Includes bibliographical references
ISBN 978-0-9817920-0-2

Acknowledgements

My heartfelt THANKS and gratitude go to

SK for turning light to life.

My mother for giving me birth.

My father for giving me hope.

Smokey for opening my mind.

My children Amy, Brandon, and Ej
for insight and opening my pen.

Albert for opening my eyes.

Laura for the insight into the liberal heart and mind.

Glenda for opening the esoteric door.

Gurudev for showing me the simplicity of wisdom.

Arthur for bridging my mind and feelings.

Bob and his crew at The Visibility Company
for taking me to print.

And to the literally hundreds of individuals throughout
my life who have taken their time to teach my heart, my
mind, and my soul; to help me see their point of view;
to help me grow physically, mentally, and spiritually
and understand the diversity of our world.

And most of all, for my soul mate, Diane who touches
my body, mind, and spirit with a gentleness I relish, an
insight I cherish, and a love that I believe can't perish.

**To all of you, I appreciate the gift you've given me,
for I could not be me without YOU.**

TABLE OF CONTENTS

PREFACE

I come from a world of three-piece suits, endless corporate meetings, and straight-laced business presentations. That which is tangible, marketable, and ultimately profitable rules the universe where I thrived for decades.

But something was missing. I knew there was more to life than climbing the corporate ladder, but I knew little of self-exploration, spiritual realms, and that-which-lies-beyond-whatever. Indeed, I was suspicious but intrigued about anything "Woo-Woo," as such concepts are classified by skeptics and those who don't have an open mind.

Anything "New Age" was, and usually still is, given the cold shoulder by corporate America. I was guilty too. But during my journey — which isn't yet over — I've learned there is room for a different, more inquisitive approach, even in the boardroom.

I believe delving into New Age concepts reveals another world that's right before our eyes. It's much like someone from the past or far distant future handling a simple kitchen can-opener: They'd probably be fascinated by it but they wouldn't have a clue what it's for – until they discover a can. Then they can associate the two and probably figure out how the opener works. Only then can they appreciate the technology, the thinking, and ultimately the culture of its inventor.

That's diversity in its purest form. I've found a holistic view of any situation, problem, or plan more understandable when we realize we never have the entire picture — we just have our perspective of a slice in time. When we understand what is, then we can better comprehend what can be.

• • • • •

A successful businessman, I spent 23 years with PepsiCo, Inc., which back then was a Fortune 15 company. When the powers-that-be decided to sell PepsiCo Food Systems, the very lucrative division I led since its inception, I chose to retire at age 50.

Early retirement was one of the goals I set in my early 20s, so the change in direction wasn't unwelcome. During my successful working years, I provided a very good living for my family, but my reason for being on the planet gnawed at me. What was I doing to contribute to mankind's progress? It was a question that begged my mind for a long time.

My early childhood was a world of logic. My young mind was oriented to *cause and effect* and that played out daily. Get outside the acceptable routine—that is, anything out of my strict mother's rules and expectations—and some form of punishment was just around the corner. School reinforced that logic: do well and nobody gets hurt. Step out of bounds and it's a trip to the principal's office or worse: a conference with the parents.

My dad was an engineer and flexible in his approach to both me and discipline. He was fairly easy-going, teaching me about his world without a lot of rigidity. I do recall a few occasions when my responses to scolding caused him to chuckle out loud when he was "enforcing" the rules.

My mother, on the other hand, was the enforcer. She had a tough life, growing up in East Prussia (northern Poland) during World War II. Even the name Prussia sounds tough to me. In 1943, her family thought they had seen the worst of the war, but conditions deteriorated. At age 17, my mother found herself running from the Germans, hiding from the Russians, and dodging American bombs as she and her mother struggled to get to Berlin on foot. I believe these encounters had an incredible impact on her mindset, creating certain prejudices and establishing discipline as a life-or-death tool; if you don't obey, you die! A simple philosophy, but she came by it honestly. I truly believe you can't really know someone unless you know how they grew up. Those early experiences can't help but influence how we all make decisions.

So, "strict" was the norm through elementary school—dress, chores, study time, and play were all prescribed and carefully monitored by Mom. I was clearly set on the straight and narrow.

My world crashed in on me when I was 12. Dad died, joining the forty percent of people whose first sign of a heart attack is sudden death. My grief fomented anger and disobedience rather than sorrow. And with my changes in behavior, Mom's discipline rained down on me. I was confused. I just didn't understand why my dad had to leave this world. We had so many plans!

I was asking questions no one could answer. While I didn't know the word *patronized*, I certainly was. There were no straight answers, only clichés and talking around the topic of death and whatever hereafter there might be. Raised Lutheran, I was supposed to have *faith*. Not easy.

When I was 15, my mother met and married a wonderful man. Smokey didn't patronize me. He spoke to me like a real person, human to human, and surprisingly, man to man. We talked a lot and often. Nothing was off base, not even the previously off-limit question of "Why are we here?" Our talks helped me gain perspective. They stripped away some of my anger at losing my Dad, tempered the prejudices learned from my mother, and eventually, whittled away at the chip on my shoulder.

Graduating from high school in 1966, I was fortunate enough to be awarded a scholarship at a new "free enterprise" college in southeastern New Mexico, the College of Artesia. The scholarship covered everything: tuition, room, board, books, and even a job for spending money. I graduated in May of 1969 with a B.S. in Biological Science, with enough credits to give me a pre-med qualification, a business major, and an art minor.

I was setting myself up for several career choices including business, medicine, or art. Even with these options before me, I had the opportunity to head in a completely different direction. In 1968, I signed an option to play football for the Dallas Cowboys as a punter. I had two more trimesters of college before graduation and to the Cowboys' credit, I was encouraged to get my degree and we'd talk the following year.

During that interim, they signed an exceptional punter and while Smokey encouraged me to pursue the possibilities, I opted to work in what now was a family business for my stepdad. His expansion of a specialized local truck line to a regional general commodities carrier brought with it issues and opportunities. He needed my help and it felt great to be needed.

I started to fulfill my pent-up desire to "do it all." By the time July of '69 rolled around, I'd gotten married, had a pilot's license, and was skydiving, drag racing, and pushing motorcycles to their limit in desert motocross and hill-climbs. I was 21 and by golly, no one could stop me from doing anything!

By the time I was 25, it was sell the family business, divorce, another marriage, and let's see how big business works. Making progress, making money; I was very successful by most measures.

In 1981, I was in my early 30s. Together with some incredible people, I led the inception and expansion of a test project that was to become PepsiCo Food Systems, a business with nearly $4 billion in sales that was sold in August of 1997 for $830 million. Throughout this time, I believed satisfaction was just around the corner. But I didn't find it on the job.

In my quest for fulfillment along the way, I sought alternatives. On my 35th birthday, I resolved to leave enough of "me" for my children and grandchildren to understand who I was and what made me tick. Writing was the avenue I chose: vignettes, essays, editorials, and ultimately books. Satisfied that I was at least leaving them a glimpse of who I was, I still had an emptiness in not knowing exactly how I could help humanity.

Time passed, and I had three wonderful kids, but after 24 years of marriage, another divorce. I was still wondering about all the things we're supposed to have faith in, and finding little contentment in what I'd done. Is that all there is?

As an adjunct to my work at PepsiCo, I held leadership positions in numerous non-profits, seeking to make this world a better place. It was rewarding to see the good my fellow man could leverage in helping those who were less fortunate. It felt good, but still a void was eating at me. Where would I find my contribution? I wanted to impact this world for a higher good, but I didn't know how I would do it.

So there I was. Almost fifty years old, divorced, retired, and seeking to find a greater purpose. Just like when my Dad died, there were no clear answers. We study, we work, we gain some level of success, but it's never enough – we're wrapped up in making more money, getting bigger/faster cars, smaller electronics, second-third-fourth homes, and looking for the sense of accomplishment that those things should bring. But it's short-lived. What good are we doing besides providing a boost to the economy when we buy more "stuff?" How will we be remembered by future generations? Did we leave a mark, or just an obscure smear?

In late 1997, my latest contribution to the economy and newest economic smudge was a new Ferrari 350 convertible. Early the next year, I planned a trip that would last months, driving around the country and spending time in unfamiliar environs. I wanted to observe and capture the nuances of the people, their work, and their lives. Before my trip, I planned to head to Sedona, Arizona to visit with Albert Clayton Gaulden, astrologer, writer, and raconteur. Four years earlier, he'd given me an astrology reading that came true in spades. That fueled my curiosity and I was eager to question him on his methods and insights.

He convinced me to visit him and go through his personal growth program, The Sedona Intensive™, to learn a lot more about myself. I soon arrived in Red Rock country.

Albert tailored my week from what he knew of me and my astrology. I learned about healers, inner child counselors, massage therapists, American Indian medicine ceremonies, astrology, and most importantly, myself. I found baggage I didn't know I was carrying about my father, my mother, and even me. I learned that "a clearing" is getting in touch with yourself, your inner child, your body, and your emotions. I discovered awakenings that literally launched me to another level of living I didn't realize possible. Not everything I learned rang true to me, but my eyes were opened. Yet humanity and my obligations still gnawed at the edges of my mind.

Coincidentally that week, on Wednesday at dinner, I met a wonderful woman who was going to change my life—Diane Ladd, the actress and film icon. I had no idea who she was when we first met. Of course, I promptly made quite an impression with sparkling and charming questions such as, "So, what do you do?" Nice thing about BIG mistakes, you only make them once!

Before the week was done, I explored another new horizon—time in Diane's world. Interestingly, Diane had a house in Sedona as well as in Beverly Hills where she spent most of her time. She hadn't planned to come that week, but was she compelled by a strong urge to bring her entourage to Sedona. She tells the story of our meeting in her book *Spiraling through the School of Life* (Hay House).

As my new-found self pondered my immediate future and how I'd begin my "trek around America," Diane said she'd be in New York doing a show for Sally Jesse Raphael, and she invited me to see the taping. I said I'd be there.

Long story short, we met there, saw a bazillion plays, and fell in love. Our meeting meant I never took that driving trip across the country, but I found a different adventure. We've been together ever since, marrying on Valentine's Day, 1999.

We've both been on a path of constant learning and loving every minute.

Diane knows about *stuff.* She's led such an insightful life, delving into medicine, healing, and miracles. Oh, and Diane knows about the New Age. She was researching esoteric teachings before it was vogue. She pegged my astrological sun sign as well as my rising sign in the first hour we met. How'd she do that? I was intrigued.

Diane is an amazing window into the human soul and that which lies beyond. As I have watched her, I've been taken aback by her sensitivity, impressed by her grasp of abstract ideas, and awed by her understanding of humanity. She's my daily inspiration in a world too full of scrambling to nowhere, hurrying to be late, and posturing for those that don't matter.

Still, I was a bit dubious of her perception of what's outside our present reality, and I sought to better understand. Therein, the seed for this book took root. I saw the opportunity to get some concepts important to me on paper, perhaps even sparking a flame in someone else who thirsts for answers in a sometimes too-logical world.

● ● ● ● ●

I'm still thirsting.

Consider this: Have you ever been thinking about someone and they call? Or a package arrives from them? That's synchronicity. Many say it happens a lot in our world. If it's happened to you, you've already stepped into the land of the New Age.

There are things in this world we have yet to conceive, yet to imagine, yet to experience. It's surprising how many times we believe we know a fact, then it's disproved or improved upon over the next few years. Our minds can barely handle what we have today. Witness the Zoloft® generation: stressed out and depressed, turning to pharmaceuticals for relief.

So where can we find answers?

Perhaps not here, but what I offer is a starting point—a closer look at some of the "Woo-Woo" areas—to make you more aware of the world's capabilities. And by the way, this isn't the definitive word on anything. It's only a springboard.

I've used endnotes so you can refer to the sources I've come across when you find something that interests you. Look up the reference and make up your own mind. My fondest hope is that you'll read a section of this book that sparks your curiosity to find out more. Then you can decide for yourself if it's "Woo-Woo," entertainment, hogwash, or something substantive that begs more time. Feel free to say "Pshaw," "Oh, brother," or "Wow," right out loud as you read; see if you don't feel better!

INTRODUCTION

You've been there. A cocktail party, a backyard barbeque, intermission at the opera, lounging around the community pool. You're just within earshot of a small group, and someone is telling a tale with such passion that you just have to listen in. You edge a bit closer, noting that the audience is hanging on every word bubbling off the speaker's tongue. They're all rapt with attentive curiosity.

"... and then, with all this gold on me, the necklaces, bracelets, sashes, all dripping with magnificent gems, the priests escort me up this incredible stairway above throngs of cheering people. At the top I see my throne and pause before I sit. The gleam in the eyes of the priests turns sinister as they draw ceremonial daggers and move my way – they're going to *sacrifice ME!* I run as fast as I can, down the back side of the pyramid, chased by the priests and a number of guards. The roar of the crowd is deafening as I stumble to a path through the jungle, the overgrowth snagging me as if it heeded the priests' bidding. They're getting closer! I'm tossing off the heavy jewelry, running as fast as I can, stumbling, my insides wrenched with fear ... and then I came out of it. It was the best regression I've had so far!"

Huh? It happens!

Or, "... I reached out to shake her hand, then, WHAM, I went psychic and saw she was going to be in an accident. I warned her to be careful on the way home. When I saw her at the hospital later, she said, 'I was being careful, it was just like a hand reached down and threw me from the car as it skidded over the cliff.' I'm just so glad she got out!"

You gotta be kidding me! Just a coincidence!

Or, "... then I heard a voice, just like someone was leaning over my shoulder to whisper in my ear, that said, "Go to New York. I did and that's when I met Frank. We've been together ever since!"

Gimmie a break! Welcome to Southern California and the world of Woo-Woo!

I know you've walked in on these conversations or at least overheard something similar. This kind of unknown or related phenomena has grown in popularity and acceptance with TV programs like *Medium* and *The Ghost Whisperer* and with movies like *The Sixth Sense*. These stories explore, or, at least expose events or occurrences we can't explain, don't believe, or have trouble comprehending. Because of more widespread exposure, we find people are more willing to share their experiences, their interpretations, and maybe, their beliefs, more openly than ever before.

Well, friend, you've just been exposed to what many call the New Age. But what exactly is the New Age? How does it work, and why are so many people talking about it? Has it always been there and perhaps you just didn't notice? What's involved? Is it a religion, a cult, or just something that happens as you grow older?

I'm not sure. But I do know that many different names are tagged on any person who steps beyond the tangible arena we perceive as socially acceptable to mainstream society. It is a New Age, but there's still a ragged edge that a lot of people don't readily accept. It's just too new.

The New Age can mean many things to many people, but the masses seem to hold to a singular message about so-called New Agers: they're waaaaay different, out there, and maybe even strange! In my experience, New Agers can be intriguing and more often than not, their stories hit close to home with some of our own experiences.

How so? Well, you must remember what it's like to be a beginner – to attempt something new that perhaps others can do well but you've never tried. Or more challenging yet, chancing something that no one else has done. I still wonder who ate the first oyster!

To all things New Age, I showed up as a beginner, just like you. But even as a beginner, I was continuously probing the unknown, whether through a teacher or by my own curiosity. I vividly recall that curiosity getting me into quite a predicament when I was just four years old.

I loved smelling flowers and poking things with sticks. In a bush at the corner of my grandmother's rural house I discovered a heretofore unseen flower. It was gray, with a flat face and many holes, a lotus-pod looking plant, only much smaller. I noticed "things" bobbing up and down in most of the holes and like the curious child I was, poked at it with my ever-present stick.

In a flash, the "bobbing things" united and turned their attention to me, systematically stinging my legs, arms, body, and face. I learned quickly to recognize wasps' nests and show due respect. This experience represented my first lesson in using care to investigate the unknown.

Like you do, I used my senses to add to my knowledge base. If I could see it, it was there. If I could touch it, it was real. My curiosity continued throughout my childhood and as my horizons expanded, I began to lose the need to see, touch, hear, smell, or taste to comprehend and believe the world around me. As my thinking-process matured I began to rely on faith. I delved into more complicated issues so that I could no longer pick apart my world with only my senses. I had to pull them apart with my mind.

I found things I could believe in that I couldn't see. Sure, I could certainly see the steel wire that represented the electric fence around the farmer's field, but I couldn't see the electricity that pulsed through it. But one touch made me a believer. These transitional experiences allowed me to better understand the role that faith plays in discovery.

Faith allows you to open doors into new territory. Faith allows you to explore worlds well beyond what sits in front of you. With faith comes greater understanding.

If you're lucky, these understandings and transitions will occur throughout your entire lifetime. They will expand your

knowledge with possibilities of which you were previously unaware.

All of us "buy" something beyond our comprehension or
understanding. It's the fundamental basis of hope, deities, and
religions, whether it's the wish to draw a fourth ace at penny-
ante poker or the expectation of life in the hereafter. I guess
that particular "purchase" qualifies someone as hopeful on that
topic. Two or more "hopefuls" may qualify you as someone
delving into the New Age.

I'm only going to scratch the surface in this book. My design is to reveal some of the origins of the New Age; those
things people talk about today that were generated by some
event or discovery and have been passed down through the
generations. You see, New Age beliefs and studies aren't all
that new. They had their beginnings with the onset of thinking,
believing, and trying to explain our existence on this planet.
It goes beyond the physical.

When we encounter something we don't understand, we
usually explain it through reference to what we know and what
others will understand. My favorite depiction of this idea is a
cartoon I ran across in the 1960's, during the time of prolifer-
ating UFO sightings. The cartoon showed two Seminole Indians standing in the Florida Everglades, surrounded by stately
trees dripping with hanging moss, with water nearby. The Indian Brave points to a biplane just above the trees on the horizon. The Medicine Man, clad in his regalia, stoically stares at
the Brave and simply says, "Swamp Gas," the then popular explanation for UFOs seen in the low-lying terrain around
Florida.

Like the Seminoles in the cartoon, we rationalize things
that don't fit into our understanding. We grope to fit new things
we don't understand into our world view.

Now, I have my own set of beliefs about a supreme being
that influences and governs the things I do. That has *nothing*
to do with the insight I hope to provide you. I'm not here to
preach what I believe. Instead, I hope to provoke some introspective thinking on what *is* and what *is possible*. If we have

an open mind, we have fertile ground for nourishing a concept and letting our intelligence and experience enable it to grow to fruition. Or, alternatively, your open mind could decide the concept is a weed that needs to be uprooted and cast aside. It's your choice, because after all, it's your garden.

My intent is to expose you, the reader, to that which I have stumbled across, been exposed to, or learned. And a lot that I've come to understand and believe. I don't buy into all these concepts, but I do think they are worthy of further critical thinking. Or at least dreaming.

Read. Think about what you read and how it fits with your current thinking. Challenge the status quo with at least an open mind. That's the core of diversity. Then decide if it's possible, probable, or true. Expose yourself to things outside the droning of your everyday world.

This exposure should prompt you to further consider a topic, or it could convince you outright that it's weird, bizarre, outlandish and that it doesn't merit further thought. OR it could reveal you've just climbed another step in the learning process. You, after all, are the ultimate judge of you!

Enjoy!

CHAPTER 1

METAPHYSICS

Obfuscate. That's what we do when we disguise, confuse or complicate a situation we can't explain clearly. Sometimes, obfuscation is the result of our difficulty conveying meaning or feelings. What we want is clarity — at least that's what we want from others, right? Most of the time? Maybe.

To be sure, concepts that are more complex lead to less clarity. When you begin defining words like metaphysics, you're bound to get different definitions from different people. Webster defines metaphysics as "abstract philosophical studies: a study of what is outside objective experience." Click onto the internet, type in "define metaphysics" and choose from more than 39,000 sites that give you their truth, their definition of metaphysics. Isn't the internet great? Fortunately, everyone gets to participate. Unfortunately, everyone gets to participate. That means what we end up with is more information than we could possibly ever read, but unfortunately there is no BS filter – anybody that can type can opine on what is, leaving you to wonder about truth, facts and the real world. But that's our point, isn't it? The real world!

So let's look at the beginnings of what people "who don't yet know" view as Woo-Woo. Interestingly, "woo" is Chinese for "fog." So "woo woo" would mean "foggy." So at least we gain a little insight to the Woo-Woo world and its origin has a basis in fact: things we don't understand can be a bit *foggy*, can't they?

So are we any better off with all this information than if we never had it? Yes! Information gives us opportunity to test, to evaluate, to explore. Let's begin from a scientific perspective.

The term *metaphysics* originally referred to the works of Aristotle around 350 BC. These works came after his writings on physics. His original work was titled *Metaphysica* and can literally be translated from the Greek as "that which comes after physics, matter or nature." So in some sectors, meta-physics looks for the *permanent reality, unchanged "being-ness" and stationary existence* as the basis for everything that shows constant change. Whoa — translation please!

In today's English metaphysics is a field of science which explores concepts such as meditation, healing, the afterlife, as-trology, and the supernatural among others. It often times de-notes enlightenment and has little to do with physics other than sharing the main concept of energy. It has close links with *parapsychology*, such as telepathy and telekinesis. There are those that use the terms interchangeably.

So-called "channeling" — communication with inter-di-mensional beings — and reincarnation are metaphysical con-cepts. While Eastern philosophies provide a wealth of information on reincarnation, mediation and health, western civilization is rich in its own contribution to metaphysics: Ka-bala, Gnosticism, early Christian sects, Native American prac-tices and Grail Mysteries.

So, as we begin sampling from the New Age buffet, I want to make clear that I'm deliberately going to select "main-stream" concepts. These are concepts that would be recogniz-able by anyone who has ever picked up a National Enquirer, Star or Globe. Let's begin with the idea that within us there are three distinct yet overlapping areas: The *Physical*, the *Mental* and the *Spiritual*. Most people seem to agree with this con-ceptualization. These areas will be different sizes and some-times one area spills into another, as depicted by Figure 1.

The *Physical* is pretty self-explanatory: it's the part of us and our environment that we can touch or feel, like our arm, the mountains or the wind. It has a presence that is tangible, eas-ily described to others and without a doubt, *is*. And, any prop-erties of a physical nature, for the most part, will follow the

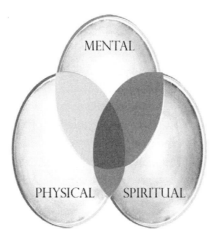

Figure 1

natural forces of physics. You know, all the laws we once studied and have long since forgotten that will constantly and consistently have a way of kicking our butts when we forget them or abuse them. Like gravity. It's always there and occasionally has surges of strength, momentarily increasing when you're leaping across a rain-filled ditch causing you to miss the safety of the other side by half a shoe.

Or, like Sir Isaac Newton's third law of physics: every action has an equal and opposite reaction — Ever encounter a cranberry juice lid that was stuck? All the force you exerted to get it open had an equal reaction when the lid released and sloshed you and everything within a radius of twelve feet with permanent, pale red stains. The laws work the same way, every time you least expect it. The only known exception to this rule is my personal experience with mustard dripping on a white shirt: the effort to get the stain on the shirt is miniscule compared to the Herculean time and effort needed to remove the stain!

The *Mental* is a bit more difficult to comprehend, but like the physical, it's tangible *some* of the time. You are aware of your thoughts and your deliberate body movements occur only through commands from your mental capacities, mostly located in your brain. You know your mental capabilities — the ones that produce rote learning like multiplication tables and reasoning faculties that enable you to solve problems. What you don't know is the limit of your capabilities.

We often hear that we only use a small portion of our brain's capacity. I believe that's true. And if it is true, then there is probably more to your mental capabilities than you are aware. Is it possible that some of us are actually able to tap into more of our mental capability than others? Are some able to access mental ability that is extraordinary? There is plenty of evidence suggesting the answer is "yes." One such New Age concept is telekinesis — the moving of tangible objects through mental application.

The third area is *Spiritual*, the most difficult to comprehend. This is like good art: hard to define, but you know it when you see it! This is the realm that deals with the soul. Most of us on this earth believe we have a soul, whatever that concept may be. A soul can be clinically described as "the immaterial essence, animating principle or actuating cause of an individual life."

Our comprehension, especially in the Western world, usually connects "soul" to religion. Soul transcends the physical chamber and therefore sparks the imagination of its very nature. Where was it before there was a body? Where does it go when there is no longer a body?

Clearly this understanding and belief in a soul requires a belief in more than just the physical. You can't touch a soul with your hands. It is definitely beyond the mental because it can't be calculated or reasoned away. The concept of a soul requires something else: faith. Faith is believing and trusting beyond what we can logically comprehend and appears to be the basis for all belief systems and religions.

Depending on how you interpret the topics we'll review, you might see the *Physical-Mental-Spiritual* relationship more like Figure 2 than Figure 1.

So within each of the planes or arenas, there are areas we'll describe and allow you to draw your own conclusions of what is and what you believe or buy. We'll pursue some of the top-

Figure 2

ics on a historical basis, others on a scientific basis. What's the difference you ask?

Well, anyone can write history. It's what was witnessed, described or imagined, then reduced to written or oral communication to recall an event, occurrence, or deed. Then we pack it into bite size chunks we can assimilate and pass on to others. This takes on the form of stories, tales, lore, writings, and within the last hundred years or so, imaging and film.

Pure science, on the other hand, follows the scientific method that requires logical proof of a conclusion. History can creep into science and that does in fact create confusion as to what is "real." As an example, science in the middle-ages, prior to the discovery of antiseptic methods, didn't bode well for abdominal wounds. A scientific diagnosis at the time probably involved the phrase "May I have your sword?"

Today, the mortality rate is significantly lower based on our understanding of science and medicine. It's the *understanding* of the science that creates history, not science itself. In my abdominal wound example, science was the same then as now: if bacteria grow unchecked in the human body, you will die. The *known* science at the time led to the history that not many survived abdominal wounds; today's history will reflect few die with immediate treatment. The reality is the same in both instances, yet understanding of the science led to different outcomes, in turn, a different history.

My point? Understand whether you're dealing with history or science. That can well help you interpret what you hear, see, and read in its context. That will allow you to draw conclusions and editorialize with better perspective. Even so, in scientific reports, as well as accurate historical observation, many times the writer feels obligated to draw conclusions that are beyond the scope of what was seen. Everyone's entitled to his or her opinion, but the fact that it is indeed just that — an opinion — should be so noted.

Obviously, metaphysics deals with historical findings as well as scientific evidence. You have to sort it out. It's like the Bible, the Koran and other religious writings; it's best to have the original so as not to be diluted through translations that differ with time and cultural interpretation. Determine if you're looking at history or science. That should give you the purest view for you to draw your own conclusions. We won't even touch ulterior motives of the authors, because that's *really* subjective.

Now we need a little background to see how and possibly why today's thinking came to be, so let's take a look at some of what may have been.

CHAPTER 2

FOLKLORE & MYSTERIES

There are a lot of folk out there and with them they bring *lore*. That's the stuff of unknown origins, having some basis in reality that's been passed down over time, probably embellished along the way making for better storytelling. Like the stories your Mom tells of Aunt Martha and her 28 cats saving the old homestead from rats. Or like the origins of the universe – the Big Bang Theory... or God creating this world in six days, complete with history that spans millions of years. Now don't get excited, I'm not challenging these stories or those who believe in them, just citing them for reference! Somewhere in the lore are stories of Lemuria, Mu and the lost continent of Atlantis — probably some of the oldest relating to the origins of this planet and its people.

To begin digging deeper into the concept of New Age, it is instructive to spend a few minutes reviewing what New Age people talk about in terms of ancient civilizations and their technical achievements. At the very least, you'll read some interesting stories while acquiring some basic exposure to popular New Age conversation.

Lemuria and Mu[1]

According to tradition, the first civilization arose 78,000 years ago on the giant continent known as Lemuria or Mu and lasted for an astonishing 52,000 years. It's said to have been destroyed by earthquakes in approximately 24,000 BC[2], sinking into the ocean. There are those who believe Lemuria is the same as The Garden of Eden and was the actual birthplace of civilization. It's claimed that from Lemuria, civilization spread to Atlantis.[3]

Supposedly, there was one language and one government. Education was the keystone of their success. Because citizens were versed in the laws of the universe and afforded training in a profession or trade, the continent prospered.

Naturalists in the nineteenth century postulated that Lemuria was a land bridge stretching across the Indian Ocean and Indonesia all the way to the Pacific Ocean and explained the presence of the lemur, a small primate found in Madagascar and the Indies. Lemuria can be interpreted as "Land of the Ancestors" — wherein lemurs derive their name, "for Indonesians long knew that man descends from the apes," according to Dr. Ansio Nunes dos Santos.[4]

So there you have it! This was ostensibly the beginning, the crawl from primordial soup, the first civilization. According to ancient lore, this was one story of how it all began, and of course there are many versions of the origin story. Research if you will.

Atlantis

Atlantis was a continent, presumably in the Atlantic Ocean where, according to Plato, an advanced civilization developed some 11,600 years ago. Plato affirms that, as the result of a huge, worldwide volcanic cataclysm, this continent sunk into the ocean, disappearing forever. Hard science rejects the actual existence of Atlantis, because so far no one's been able to find any traces of its reality.[5] Pretty conclusive!

According to "those that know," it's said that when the continent of Lemuria or Mu sank, the oceans of the world lowered drastically as water rushed into the newly formed Pacific Basin. The relatively small islands which had existed in the Atlantic during the time of the Lemurian civilization were left high and dry by the receding ocean. The newly emerged land joined the Poseid Archipelago of the Atlantic Ocean to form a small continent. This continent is called Atlantis by historians today, though its real name was Poseid.

Atlantis is believed to have taken technology to very advanced stages, well beyond what exists on our planet today. In the book "A Dweller On Two Planets," first dictated in 1884 by Phylos the Thibetan to a young Californian named Frederick Spencer Oliver, as well as in a 1940 sequel, "An Earth Dweller Returns," there is mention of such inventions and devices as air conditioners to overcome deadly and noxious vapors; airless cylinder lamps, tubes of crystal illuminated by the night side forces; electric rifles or guns employing electricity as a propulsive force (rail-guns are similar and a very new invention); mono-rail transportation; water generators, an instrument for condensing water from the atmosphere; and the Vailx, an aerial ship governed by forces of levitation and repulsion.[6]

Atlantis is the material of legends, passed down from tribe to tribe, clan to clan. As previously stated, however, there is no concrete proof — no one's found any tangible proof of its existence. Does it exist only in memories and imaginations? Was it ever? Or maybe it's truly at the bottom of an ocean, silted over by the tides of time. Think about how difficult it is to find ships that sank at known locations in relatively shallow water. Here are ships only a few hundred years old, if that, and they're covered with sand, silt and coral, obscuring them from all but the most sophisticated gadgets we have today. But they're there. Once real. Now recumbent in their ocean graves, complacent with never being found. So imagine the silt, the coral, the sand that can accumulate in 10,000 years. Whatever was there is certainly deeper now!

Rama Empire

Fortunately, the ancient books of India's Rama Empire have been preserved, unlike those of other civilizations. Many ancient nations are now either desert wastelands, swallowed by thick jungle or literally at the bottom of some ocean. Yet India, despite devastation by wars and invasion, managed to maintain a large part of its ancient history.

For a long time, Indian civilization was believed to date

from circa 500 BC, only about 200 years prior to Alexander the Great's invasion of the subcontinent. In the past century, however, the extremely sophisticated cities of Mohenjo Daro (Mound of the Dead) and Harappa (Clearing your Throat City? Just kidding!) have been discovered in the Indus Valley of modern-day Pakistan.

The discoveries of these cities forced archaeologists to revise the dates for the origin of Indian civilization back thousands of years. A wonder to modern-day researchers, the cities were highly developed and caused leading archaeologists to believe that they were conceived as a whole before they were built: a remarkable early example of city planning. This clearly demonstrates there are no ancestral connections to Los Angeles and the surrounding areas! Even more remarkable is that the plumbing-sewage system throughout the large city is superior to that found in Pakistan, India, and most Asian countries today.

Osirian Civilization

It is said that at the time of Atlantis and Rama, the Mediterranean was a large and fertile valley. These people, pre-dating dynastic Egypt, were known as the Osirian Civilization. The Nile River flowed out of Africa, as it does today, and was called the River Styx. However, instead of flowing into the Mediterranean Sea at the Nile Delta in northern Egypt, it continued into the valley, and then turned westward to flow into the deepest part of the Mediterranean Valley where it created a large lake that then flowed out between Malta and Sicily, south of Sardinia into the Atlantic at Gibraltar (the Pillars of Hercules). When Atlantis was destroyed in a devastating upheaval, this cataclysmic change in the Atlantic slowly flooded the Mediterranean Basin, destroying the Osirian's great cities and forcing them to move to higher ground. This theory helps explain the strange megalithic remains found throughout the Mediterranean. Perhaps their name stems from other civilizations asking "Oh, sir! Oh, sir! Where're you from?"

It is an archaeological fact that there are more than 200

known sunken cities in the Mediterranean. Egyptian civilization, along with the Minoan and Mycenaean in Crete and Greece are, in theory, remnants of this great, ancient culture. The civilization built huge earthquake-proof megalithic structures and had electricity and other conveniences common during the time of Atlantis. Like Atlantis and Rama, they had airships and other modes of transport, often electrical in nature. The mysterious cart tracks of Malta, which go over cliffs and under water, may well be part of some ancient Osirian tram-line, possibly taking quarried stone to cities that are now submerged. Probably the best example of the high technology of the Osirians is the amazing platform found at Ba'albek, Lebanon. The main platform is composed of the largest hewn rocks in the world, the famous *ashlars* of Ba'albek. Some of the individual stones are 82 feet long and 15 feet thick and are estimated to weigh between 1,200 and 1,500 tons each!

So we have evidence and we have lore. I buy the rocks, but airships? I need more data!!

Uiger Civilization

Many ancient cities are said to have existed at the time of Atlantis and Rama in the Uiger civilization of the Gobi Desert. Though the Gobi is now a parched land-locked desert, these cities were ocean ports. Edgar Cayce, an American psychic who has had a significant influence on the current New Age movement, once said that elevators would be discovered in a lost city in the Gobi Desert, and while this has not happened yet, it may not be out of the question.

Vimanas — or flying machines in Vedic Indian literature — and other advanced devices are said to have been in use in the Uiger area. The famous Russian explorer Nicholas Roerich reported seeing a flying disc over northern Tibet in the 1930s.

Significantly, it is claimed that the Elders of Lemuria, known as the Thirteenth School, moved their headquarters prior to the cataclysm to the uninhabited plateau of Central Asia that we now call Tibet. Here they supposedly established a library and school known as The Great White Brotherhood.[7]

For instance, the great Chinese Philosopher Lao Tzu, born in 604 BC, talked frequently of Ancient Masters and their profound wisdom. He wrote the famous book — arguably the most popular Chinese-language book ever written — Tao Te Ching. When he finally left China, near the close of his very long life, he journeyed west to the legendary land of Hsi Wang Mu. According to the ancient Chinese, this was the headquarters of the Ancient Ones. Could this have been The Great White Brotherhood and the Thirteenth School of Mu?

Another civilization with advanced technology disappears from the face of the earth. Fact or fiction? How do they do it? One can only wonder!

Tiahuanaco

As in Mu and Atlantis, construction in South America was on megalithic scale with polygonal construction techniques designed to make the massive walls earthquake-proof. Homes and communal buildings were built out of megalithic blocks of stone. Because of the high regard the culture had for the well being of future generations and the value they placed upon the gradual, sustained growth of the community, structures were built to last for thousands of years.

The famous ruins of Tiahuanaco are massive megalithic constructions that were tossed about like toy building blocks. What kind of cataclysmic upheaval could have done such a thing? Here is the kind of construction meant to last for thousands of years; yet, the 100-ton blocks have been torn asunder by mighty geological forces.[8]

Tiahuanaco is in the Bolivian Andes at 12,500 feet above sea-level, located some 15 miles from the shores of Lake Titicaca. As with many other sacred sites on the planet, it remains an enigma. Researchers can only speculate on its origins and purpose of the stone markers bearing only clues to humanity's creational story.

Tiahuanaco was the capital of the Pre-Inca Civilization. This could be the oldest city in the world, thought by some to be built by an extraterrestrial race that created the Nazca Lines as well. More about the Lines and aliens later!

Interestingly, Tiahuanaco was a seaport at one time, although the nearest body of water is Lake Titicaca some 12 miles away. On the rock cliffs near the piers and wharfs of the port area of the ruins are yellow-white calcareous deposits forming long, straight lines indicating pre-historic water levels. The surrounding area is covered with millions of fossilized sea-shells.

Oceanic creatures live to this day in abundance in the salty waters of the lake. What seems to be the original seashore is much higher in one place than in another. The port of Tiahuanaco, called Puma Punku or "Door of the Puma," is an area filled with enormous stone blocks scattered hither and yon like matchsticks, and weighing between 100 and 150 tons! One block still in place weighs an estimated 440 tons! How were these blocks quarried? How did the builders handle such huge blocks? And what tremendous forces tumbled and scattered these gigantic stones so easily about the site? Many of the blocks are held together by large copper clamps shaped like an "I," rather than interlocking shapes found at other nearby ruins.

Tiahuanaco was the center of a powerful, self-sustaining empire. Some of the docks and piers in this area are so large that hundreds of ships could dock at one time. Lake Titicaca, ten miles away, is nearly 100 feet lower than the ruined docks. Big yachts and nowhere to go!

Around the turn of the 20th century, Bolivian scholar Arthur Broznansky began a fifty year study of the ruins of Tiahuanaco. Using astronomical information, he concluded that the city was constructed more than 17,000 years ago, long before any civilization was supposed to have existed. He called Tiahuanaco the "Cradle of Civilization."[9] Just like kids, they leave their room a mess . . . and these were evidently very strong kids with the unanswered disarray of the rocks!

Mayan Civilization

Originating in the Yucatan around 2600 BC, the Mayans rose to prominence around AD 250 in present-day southern

Mexico, Guatemala, northern Belize, and western Honduras. Building on the inherited inventions and ideas of earlier civilizations, the Maya developed astronomy, calendar systems and hieroglyphic writing. The Maya were noted as well for elaborate and highly decorated ceremonial architecture, including temple-pyramids, palaces and observatories, all built without metal tools. They were also skilled farmers, clearing large sections of tropical rain forest and, where groundwater was scarce, building sizeable underground reservoirs for the storage of rainwater. The Maya were equally skilled as weavers and potters. They cleared routes through jungles and swamps to foster extensive trade networks with distant peoples.[10]

The ancient Mayans were also brilliant astronomers and mathematicians whose early cities lived in agrarian harmony with earth. They built canals and hydroponic garden cities throughout the ancient Yucatan Peninsula. Some of the Mayan glyphs were allegedly radionic-type insect control devices that broadcast an etheric vibration of the targeted pest.[11] Perhaps our world's first bug-light!

Mayan pyramids are found from Central America to as far away as the Indonesian island of Java. The pyramid of Sukuh, on the slopes of Mount Lawu near Surakarta, would match any in the jungles of Central America. The pyramid is in fact virtually identical to the pyramids found at the ancient Mayan site at Uaxactun, near Tikal. How does that happen?

Around 300 BC, the Maya adopted a hierarchical system of government with rule by nobles and kings. This civilization developed into highly structured kingdoms during their Classic period, 200-900 AD. Their society consisted of many independent states, each with a rural farming community and large urban sites built around ceremonial centers. It started to decline around AD 900 when, for reasons still largely a mystery, the southern Maya abandoned their cities. When the northern Maya were integrated into the Toltec society by AD 1200, the Maya dynasty finally came to a close, although some peripheral centers continued to thrive until the Spanish Conquest in the early sixteenth century.[12]

Edgar Cayce, whom we'll talk about later, mentions the Mayas and their technology in one of his readings:

"As for a description of the manner of construction of the stone: we find it was a large cylindrical glass (as would be termed today); cut with facets in such manner that the capstone on top of it made for centralizing the power or force that concentrated between the end of the cylinder and the capstone itself. As indicated, the records as to ways of constructing same are in three places in the earth, as it stands today: in the sunken portion of Atlantis, or Poseidia, where a portion of the temples may yet be discovered under the slime of ages of sea water, near what is known as Bimini, off the coast of Florida. And (secondly) in the temple records that were in Egypt, where the entity acted later in cooperation with others towards preserving the records that came from the land where these had been kept. Also (thirdly) in records that were carried to what is now Yucatan, in America, where these stones (which they know so little about) are now, during the last few months, being uncovered."

It is believed that an ancient Hall of Records resides somewhere in the Mayan region, probably beneath an existing pyramid complex, in an underground tunnel and chamber system. Some sources say that this repository of ancient knowledge is kept in quartz crystals that are of exceptional quality and capable of holding large amounts of information in the similar manner as a modern CD.[13] So there's more than clarity in these crystals!

Ancient China

Ancient China, known as Han China, is said to have come, like all civilizations, from the huge Pacific continent Mu. The ancient Chinese are known for their sky-chariots, their geomancy, and the jade manufacture that they shared with the Mayas. Indeed, the ancient histories of the Chinese and the Mayas seem indelibly linked.

Anthropologists make a good case for a Taoist influence coming to Central America by showing Shang dynasty symbols and motifs — the yin-yang is the most famous, but there are many more — and then relating them to known Mayan art and sculpture. Jade was of particular importance to the Shang Chinese. So far, the source of Chinese jade has not been pinpointed. Much of it may have come from Central America. Even the source of Central American jade is a mystery and many ancient jade mines are believed to be still undiscovered. Anthropologists suggest that Chinese voyages to Mexico, between 500-300 BC, may have been related to Taoist trade in magic mushrooms or drugs of longevity.

The ancient Chinese are often said to be the originators of every invention from toilet paper, earthquake detectors, paper money, cannon, rocket technology, printing methods, and thousands of other clever and high-tech items. In 1959, archaeologists in China discovered belt buckles made out of aluminum thousands of years ago; aluminum is generally processed from bauxite with electricity![14] So how did they do it and also as important, how did they disseminate their technology to other parts of the world so long ago? The mystery remains!

Ancient Ethiopia and Israel

From such ancient texts as the Bible and the Ethiopian book Kebra Negast, we have tales of the high technology of ancient Ethiopia and Israel. The temple at Jerusalem is said to have been founded upon three gigantic ashlars — hewn stone — similar to those at Ba'albek, Lebanon. Today, the revered Temple of Solomon and Muslim Dome of the Rock Mosque exist on this site. Their foundations apparently reach back to the Osirian civilization.

Like much of the later Phoenician construction, the building at the Temple to hold the Ark of the Covenant and the tem-

ples in Ethiopia are the last of the megalithic stone constructions. The massive Temple Mount, built by King Solomon on
the ruins of earlier megalithic temple, was made to house the
ancient relic, the Ark of the Covenant.

The Ark is said to have been an electrical generator box
which housed several sacred objects, including a solid gold
statue from earlier cultures that is called the Holy of Holies.
This box and gold statue were said to have been removed from
the King's Chamber in the Great Pyramid in Egypt by Moses
during the period of the Exodus. Many scholars believe that
the Ark of the Covenant, as well as other ancient artifacts, was
actually electrical devices, some of which were worshipped in
temples as oracles. The Bible recounts how certain unautho-
rized persons would touch the Ark and be electrocuted.[15] Such
shocking history!

The Aroi Sun Kingdom of the Pacific

The last on the list of ancient civilizations is that of the virtually unknown ancient culture, the Aroi Sun Kingdom of the
Pacific. When the lost continent of Mu sank, the Pacific was
later repopulated by a racial mixture of all civilizations, coming from Rama, China, Africa and the Americas. An advanced
island nation, with larger areas of land than are currently in the
Pacific, grew up around Polynesia, Melanesia and Micronesia. Ancient legends in Polynesia attribute this remarkable civilization to the Aroi Kingdom that existed many thousands of
years before the European rediscovery of the Pacific. The Aroi
allegedly built many of the megalithic pyramids, platforms,
arches, roads and statues throughout the central Pacific.

When some of the more than 400 gravel hills on New
Caledonia were excavated in the 1960s, cement columns of
lime and shell composition were carbon dated by Yale and the
New Caledonia Museum as having been made between 5120
BC and 10,950 BC. These weird cement columns can be found
in the southern part of New Caledonia and on the Isle of Pines.

According to the Easter Islanders, the statues of the islands
walked or levitated in order to move in a clock-wise spiral

around the island. On the island of Pohnpei, the Micronesians claim that the stones of the eleven-square-mile city were levitated into place.

The Polynesians of New Zealand, Easter Island, Hawaii and Tahiti all believe that their ancestors had the ability of flight and would travel through the air from island to island. Was this the Air Atlantis flight that stopped in Malta, Ba'albek and Rama destined for the remote but popular convention center at Easter Island? If not, how did they move about so prodigiously and more importantly, how did they move the gigantic rock formations?

So, the ancient civilizations may have had a number of attributes in common among themselves, but the most evident is the lack of historical records other than glyphs which are open to interpretation. And some, like Lemuria and Atlantis, not even a trace can even be found! Not to say that folks haven't tried. Many have spent significant portions, some their entire adult life seeking the secrets of these civilizations. Perhaps someday we'll know — who knows, maybe we'll uncover an old Air Atlantis vacation-getaway poster and schedule!

Much of what's written about the prehistoric civilizations stems from not only found artifacts but also the lore that surrounds those artifacts and constructions. Is the lore product of fertile imaginations winding yarns or do they have basis in witnessed fact?

Another challenge to the rational mind is the coincidence of cultures, supposedly without contact with the world beyond their own boundaries, evolving to the same structure in the same time frames. Look at the Mayans, developing their central population centers within walls where nobility, clerics and warriors lived, while the bulk of the people lived outside the walls where they cultivated crops and kept livestock. During that construction period, between 500 and 1000 AD, numerous models along this style are evidenced throughout the Mayan world in what is now Mexico and Central America.

At the same time in Europe, without any substantiated communication, castles and fiefdoms grew in the same model:

Nobles, religious leaders and knights inside the castle structure; farmers and herders outside the walls. In both instances, the "Inside the Wall" guys protected the "Outside the Wall" folks because that's where there food supply was!

Coincidence and yet no evidence of contact in any way. Do you think it is imbedded in the human genetic map that during our growth toward humanitarian ends we coincidentally saw two separate groups in Europe and Central America "evolve" at the same time to literally the same social structures? Or, was there a higher essence that shared a master plan between these cultures? How can we know for sure?

Additionally, there is lore that's a little farther "out there" like nature spirits, sprites, elves, gnomes, fairies and devas. These perhaps are the precursors to gods and deities that arose from ancient cultures, giving way to mythology as mankind honed their god image and sorted the wheat from the chaff in what ultimately becomes religion.

Nature Spirits

Ancients believed that all life is made of four magical elements: Earth, Air, Fire, and Water. These elements correspond to the four directions of our physical world, the four winds, and the four quarters of the universe.

Think of them as four states of matter — solid, liquid, gas, and plasma — and you're close to understanding the concept of elements. *Elementals* are the inhabitants of these elements. They are nature spirits who have no definite form, but are believed to be forces in nature whose activity can result in storms, earthquakes, unpredictable ocean currents, and the like. Some believed elementals lacked souls and sought sexual union with humans so they could acquire one. Folklore of many countries contains tales of such unions. Hercules, Achilles, Plato, Alexander the Great, and Julius Caesar were said to be children of Elementals.[16]

The concept of everything in nature having a life essence is the basis for much of the lore surrounding nature spirits. Kathleen Jenks, Ph.D., provides some background as she delineates nature spirits from other deities: "… I view goddesses and gods as generalists, and nature spirits as specialists. It should be noted that some scholars argue that all gods and goddesses began as nature spirits … for example, (there) was once a powerful mountain storm-spirit, El-Shaddai, who seems to have begun as a friend to local desert tribesmen; then he gradually took over the functions and powers of other nature spirits until he became the deity of an entire people. This is a familiar pattern in worldwide religions. Many Greek gods (e.g., Pan and Hermes) fit this same model — as their power-base of devotees increased, so too did their own fame until they finally assumed the status of gods.

"If *all* deities began as nature spirits, however, there's a serious flaw in the process because many nature spirits are exceedingly kind and patient whereas many deities are wrathful, vengeful, ambitious, and autocratic. So it does not seem possible that all deities necessarily began as nature spirits."[17]

There are those who believe that animals choose to dwell with your own spirit and stay with you throughout your lifetime. Many believe that you do not choose what animal you are spiritually connected to, that they choose you.

Others believe that you choose your totem and they in turn also choose you. For instance, you may have always been fascinated by bears and one day you may find that you have been surrounded by the spirit of the bear your entire life. Ultimately, you may find that you posses the same strengths and weaknesses of your animal guide and that you need to learn the life lessons that these animals also learned.[18] We'll touch on this more later and you can find the animal in you!

Then we have the *devas.* According to Joshua David Stone, "there are three types of devas:

1. All elementals working with the etheric doubles of humankind and all elementals working with the etheric bodies of inanimate objects. The "violet devas" (evolve through feeling, education of humankind) are on an evolutionary path. The elementals are on the 'involutionary' path, their goal being to evolve into the deva

kingdom with the violet color.

2. The fairies and elves ... (are) the elementals who work with the vegetables, fruits and all the verdure that covers the earth's surface. Also connected with this group-devas of magnetization that are connected to stones, talismans and the sacred spots of the Earth.

3. There is one last groups of devas ... (those) in this group ... found around the habitations of the masters who live on the Earth. ...this group works with the elementals of the air and sea, the sylphs, the water fairies, and the devas who guard human beings."[19]

So, what about *fairies* or the "little people?" Well, let's take a look at their genesis. Charles Perrault provides us with their origins: "The word Fairy is derived from the ancient "faunoe o fatuoe" which, in the pagan mythology, were creatures endowed with power of foretelling the future and ruling the human events." The word Fairy also comes from "fatigue," which in Middle Ages was synonymous with "wild woman," that is woman of woods, waters and, in general, of the natural world.

Fairies are so prevalent in mythical culture that it's natural to wonder about their origin. The Little People are said to be the dispossessed early tribes of the British Isles. They faded away into uninhabited places, growing smaller and smaller with time as they were forgotten and passed into legend. The Irish believe that the fairies are a previously conquered society, People of the Goddess Dana, who were driven into hiding when the Celts invaded Ireland. The Pagan gods of the Tuatha, skilled in building and magic, went underground to live in the tombs and mounds they had built. Hidden from sight, they grew smaller in the popular imagination until they turned into fairies.

Charles Perrault, in his book, *The Origin of Fairies*, describes fairies this way: "Other cultures believe that fairies are the souls of the dead, people not good enough to enter Heaven yet not bad enough for Hell. They wander the Nether land in between and are occasionally seen by humans. Along a similar theme, fairies are also believed to be angels that had been cast out of Heaven. Some fell into the sea and some onto the land, where they would do no harm if left alone. In Wales, fairies are thought to be a race of invisible spiritual beings living in a world of their own. Some people also believe that fairies were originally local gods or nature spirits that dwindled in majesty and size over time."[20]

Gnomes are dwarf fairies. Thomas Brown provides the following fantasy account: "Gnomes appear to be quite old because they mature very early, though their average life span is around a thousand years. They reach maturity in about a hundred years, at which time they stand about 12 inches tall and look well past middle age... they are kind-hearted and will always aid sick or frightened animals."[21] The Dutch book "Gnomes" by Will Huygen, since translated into English is the best known book on the subject.

In ceremonial magic, Gnomes are not only the archetypal earth elementals of the north who are called upon to witness all rituals, but in the Order of the Golden Dawn they are known as one of the four "Essential Spiritual Beings" who are called upon to "praise God" during a ritual known as the Benedicite Omnia Opera. Gnomes can help you protect yourself and your pets and lend their energy to any number of magical purposes, especially healing spells, at which they excel. They may also be willing to teach you some secrets of medicinal herbalism. Gnomes love to dance to raise energy and might be persuaded to lend this energy to rituals celebrating the deities, especially the Gods and Goddesses of the woodlands.[22] I suppose one could say these are "little gnome facts!"

Amy Brown offers information on other types of "little folk." Sprites are of the same ilk, "...more playful nature spirits, and are not likely to inhabit anything but trees, a pond, or any other place that's serene and cool. Sprites were charged with changing the colors of the leaves on the trees in autumn.

"The *Leprechaun* is an Irish fairy; a small, old man with a cocked hat and a leather apron. According to legend, leprechauns are aloof and unfriendly, live alone, and pass the time making shoes. Leprechauns are the self-appointed guardians of ancient treasure left by the Danes when they moved through Ireland which they hide in crocks or pots. If caught by a human, he will promise great wealth if allowed to go free. A Leprechaun carries two leather pouches. In one is a silver shilling, a magical coin that returns to his purse each time it is paid out. In the other pouch, he carries a bright gold coin. This coin turns to leaves or ashes once the Leprechaun has parted with it!

"*Elves*, in Germanic mythology, are usually represented as tiny people. They are said to dwell in forests, in the sea, and in the air. Although they can be friendly to man, they are more frequently vengeful and mischievous.

"*Pixies* are cheerful and mischievous. They often take the form of a hedgehog. They are also well known for their pranks and they adore music and dancing.

"The *sylphs* are the air spirits. They have the highest vibratory rate of the four elements: air, earth, fire, water. They live hundreds of years, often reaching one thousand, never seeming to get old, and are said to live on the tops of mountains, varying in size from as large as a human to much smaller. They are usually seen with wings, looking like cherubs or fairies. Because of their connection to air, which is associated with the mental aspect, one of their functions is to help humans receive inspiration. The sylphs are drawn to those who use their minds, particularly those on creative arts. Rarely do they associate with others, but when they do, they usually form bonds that last for life."[23] So, the deva-fairy-gnome thing is a little "out there" for most of us, but we've all heard of them through children's stories and, of course, fairy tales. But there are some folks who readily believe in these creatures and even talk to them. Each to their own!

We've touched on a bit of lore and probably a bit of fantasy with the nature spirits. They fit in, around, or after man's awareness of the environment and its impact on him. Somewhere in the primordial soup distillation process came the need to have deities, gods or supreme beings and it seems that nature spirits moved that train of thinking along the tracks to full-fledged mythology and real religions.

This now gives us the foundation to move from lore to concrete evidence in our past. Relics provide us with depictions of our past, even if the hieroglyphics and Sanskrit isn't easily translated and sometimes leave us with more questions than answers. At least we've got "messages" left by cultures that spawned today's baseline for history. Maybe in this New Age, we'll sort out exactly what those cultures wanted to pass along!

Chapter 2 Endnotes

[1]   Childress, David Hatcher, *10 Ancient Civilizations with Advanced Technology*

[2]   ibid.

[3]   dos Santos, Ansio Nunes: continuing references to atlan.org/*FAQ*

[4]   ibid., dos Santos

[5]   ibid., dos Santos

[6]   op. cit., Childress

[7]   The Great White Brotherhood by no means relates to color of skin; it relates to nearing the creator, the White Light.

[8]   op. cit., Childress

[9]   Crystal, Ellie: *Tiahuanaco*

[10]   Canadian Museum of Civilization: *Maya Civilization*

[11]   op. cit., Childress

[12]   op. cit., Canadian Museum of Civilization

[13]   op. cit., Childress

[14]   ibid., Childress

[15]   ibid., Childress

[16]   Campbell, Wayne, *Basics of Magick: Elementals*

[17]   Jenks, Kathleen, *Author's Notes*

[18]   Unknown: Website, *Animal Guides*

[19]   Stone, Joshua David, *Devas*

[20]   Perrault, Charles, *The Origin of Fairies*

[21]   Brown, Thomas, *Gnomes*

[22]   ibid., Brown, Thomas

[23]   Brown, Amy, *Fairies* et. al.

CHAPTER 3

HISTORIC RELICS

History, while not always recorded, leaves us with a signature of what's happened in the past — I guess that's why they call it history! Regardless of what we as humans do, we leave a trace of where we've been, whether it's the cities, roads and machines we've created or merely the footprints on a forest path or along the beach. We leave our handiwork. We're also good at leaving our trash, but that's another story.

There have clearly been magnificent minds and artists on this planet for thousands of years, pushing the envelope of understanding and creating a physical manifestation of what's in their mind's eye. Many of those interpretations have stood the test of time and we view them today as antiquities in museums and private collections. And some are just too colossal to relegate to a building or even a confined viewing space. Take for example, Machu Picchu and the Lines of Nazca, as well as the Great Pyramid and Sphinx.

But history is not always recorded in books or on tablets. Sometimes the record is only an artifact, leaving its origins a mystery to be pondered throughout the ages. We have massive examples of handiwork. Handiwork that took both thought and skill and probably an inconceivable amount of time and effort to accomplish. Handiwork that has no written record, sometimes simply lore, oftentimes only conjectures as to its creation. And, it seems, always confusion.

It's recorded only in the fact that it is here for all to see. For all to marvel at the achievement, to ponder the minds that shaped the concept, consider the effort it took to bring to fruition, and reflect on the brilliance that enables the structure to endure. That's the recorded history I want to now touch upon, giving you the opportunity to know perhaps a bit more about items you've probably heard about and maybe have even visited. Moreover, it's the prospect of challenging your thinking to consider, in your own mind, how these magnificent artifacts came to be. Perhaps you've wondered how these marvels actually were achieved; and maybe you've even found yourself wondering whether man had some superhuman assistance in their creation.

Whoa! Now were getting into conjecture. But that's what the New Age is all about — challenging what *is* to understand what can *be*. Let's put this conjecture into the framework of a few specific creations that have caused many generations to wonder with you.

The Great Pyramid

Certainly one of the most recognized landmarks today is one of the Seven Wonders of the World, the Great Pyramid of Khufu or Cheops on the Giza Plateau. The Egyptian pyramid was believed to have been built by 100,000 workers over a 20-year period around 2560 BC.

Theories about how the massive structural blocks were moved in order to create these pyramids abound. They range from ramps and rollers to wet Tafla — a kind of clay used to slide blocks into place — but there is no incontrovertible evidence on any particular theory about how the structure was built.

The well-known structure consists of approximately two million blocks of stone, each weighing at least two tons. To put this enormity into perspective, the same stones could be reassembled into a ten-foot high, one-foot thick wall completely surrounding France. Don't get any ideas here, it's just an illustration! Interior stones fit so well that a playing card won't fit between them. The exterior of the blocks was covered by a casing of stones, providing a smooth and reflective surface though it has eroded over time.

Great Pyramid [1]

When it was built, the Great Pyramid was 481 feet high, but has lost 30 feet of that over the years. It was the tallest structure on Earth for more than 43 centuries.[2]

The base is level within less than one inch, and the lengths of the sides are equal to within 1¾ inches. Talk about precision — my house, built with modern construction techniques and precision tools, has more variance in one wall than all the deviations noted on the Great Pyramid. And the heaviest blocks of granite used to roof the Kings Chambers were estimated to weigh between 50 and 80 tons each.[3]

Now, the real question: Why were the pyramids built? We've all heard the widely held belief they were constructed for the Pharaohs as a resting place to start their mystic after-life journeys. The only problem with that theory is that no body has been found in the Great Pyramid, nor any evidence of one ever being there. The fact that there are no hieroglyphics on the inner walls substantiates that claim. Perhaps the Pyramid was an observatory for studying the stars; perhaps it was a place of cult worship, or a structure conceived and built by a long-gone civilization about which we know nothing.[4]

According to Zecharia Sitchin in his book *Stairway to Heaven*, the Pyramids of Giza were healing chambers. At one time, Napoleon was said to have spent the night in the Great

Pyramid and emerged "pale and dazed." When questioned about the experience, he replied, "You wouldn't believe me if I told you." And beyond its purpose, do we really even know *when* the Great Pyramid was built?

The controversy continues about the construction of the pyramids — sixty ton blocks fit together with precision that doesn't exist today. David Pratt in an article on the pyramids states:

"The Pyramid is an unrivaled feat of engineering and craftsmanship. It is aligned with the four cardinal points more accurately than any contemporary structure, including the Meridian Building at Greenwich Observatory in London. The 350-foot-long descending passage is so straight that it deviates from a central axis by less than a quarter of an inch from side to side and only one tenth of an inch up and down — comparable with the best laser-controlled drilling being done today. The casing stones, some of which weighed over 16 tons, are so perfectly shaped and squared that the mortar-filled joint between them is just one-fiftieth of an inch — the thickness of a human nail. Egyptologist Sir Flinders Petrie described such phenomenal precision as "the finest opticians' work;" work of this calibre is *beyond the capabilities* of modern technology. The casing stones show no tool marks and the corners are not even slightly chipped. The granite coffer in the King's Chamber is cut out of a solid block of hard red granite — so precisely that its external volume is exactly twice its internal volume … the evidence shows that the Egyptians would have to have possessed ultra-modern tools, including tubular drills that could cut granite 500 times faster than modern drills."[5]

If that doesn't get you thinking, then consider the following geometric proportions represented in the Great Pyramid that indicate a precision and knowledge of Earth and the Solar System beyond anything available to the Egyptians. Here are author Wynn Free's proportions that challenge coincidence:

- The base of the Great Pyramid times 43,200 equals the equatorial circumference of Earth, with better than 1% accuracy.
- The height times 43,200 equals the polar radius accurate to 0.2%. It would seem that whoever built the pyramids knew that Earth wasn't a perfect sphere, for there were different measures for the equatorial and polar circumferences.
- 4320 is the number of years for Earth to move through two zodiacal signs, or one sixth of the precession of the equinoxes.
- The three main pyramids at Giza mimic the stars of Orion's Belt in size and arrangement, as they would have appeared in 10,450 BC.
- If the Nile is represented by the Milky Way, then the position of the three Pyramids in relationship to the Nile reflects exactly the position of Orion's belt relative to the Milky Way during the time of solstice in 10,500 BC.
- Each of the Pyramid's four walls, when measured as a straight line, is 9,131 inches long, for a total of 36,524 inches. The exact length of the solar year is 365.24 days.
- The Great Pyramid's perimeter/height ratio is exactly $2\pi - pi$. The π constant in mathematics was not discovered until much later.
- The Pyramid is located at the exact center of the Earth's landmass. Its East-West axis lies exactly on the longest land parallel — passing through Africa, Asia, and America. The longest land meridian, through Asia, Africa, Europe, and Antarctica, also passes right through the Pyramid.
- The sides of the Pyramid are very slightly and evenly bowed in, or concave, the effect discovered around 1940 by a pilot taking aerial photos. Today's laser instruments show that all of these perfectly cut and intentionally bowed blocks precisely duplicate the curvature of the earth.

Another key observation is the fact that the pyramids built for the fifth dynasty kings, just a few decades after those at Giza, are vastly inferior in materials and workmanship. A down-market Pharaoh doing things on the cheap? Why were construction skills lost? Or did the Giza construction crews have help?

There is thinking that the Egyptian gods weren't mythical beings, but in reality, extraterrestrials with extraordinary powers.[6] How could the Egyptians have built the pyramids with slave labor, especially the Great Pyramid using stones with tolerances that we can't replicate even today? Did they have help in both design and construction? Where are the tools or their depiction of their use? Are the proportions coincidental or are they an attempt at communicating critical information? Perhaps some day we'll know, but for now, we can only question what we see and what others believe.

The Sphinx

Also in Egypt, the Sphinx is carved out of indigenous rock; it's 241 feet long and is 65 feet high, facing east toward the equinox. While Egyptologists believe that it was built in 2500 BC in the time of pharaoh Chephren of Khafre, there are no inscriptions that identify Khafre with the Sphinx. It's not realistic that such a great monument painstakingly carved out of solid rock would not have been celebrated, yet there is no mention regarding its construction.

Great Sphinx[7]

While the wind and sand have left horizontal erosion marks on the Sphinx, there are also vertical marks indicating water erosion. That would have had to happen long before 2500 BC, as the arid climate since that time has been well documented. It would seem that the Sphinx and the Great Pyramid were constructed about the same time, much earlier than the 2500 BC date.

Research done by Robert Buvaul and Graham Hancock indicates that if the position of the stars were regressed to 10,500 B.C., the inclined shaft in the Great Pyramid would be aligned with the south meridian toward a group of stars in the constellation Orion. This also happens to be the golden age ancient Egyptians called *Zep Tepi* — The First Time — of Osiris. Osiris was another name for Orion. The shaft in the pyramid appeared to indicate "here is Osiris."

So, if the theory was correct and the Sphinx was constructed around that time, it also coincides with the first time of Leo — the lion constellation Leo would have risen before dawn on the day of the spring or vernal equinox. The Sphinx, then, is perfectly aligned with its own image on the horizon at his "own" time. Did the builders of the Sphinx put some blueprint into motion that was to be completed much later by the construction of the pyramids? Were there "master astronomers" in Giza throughout the ages responsible for this scheme? And if so, where did they come from? The book *Keeper of Genesis* reveals the full investigation by Buvaul and Hancock and appears to be the "tour de force" on the age of the Sphinx.[8]

So the mystery continues. The water erosion lines could indicate heavy rains such as those possible between 10,500 and 2500 BC, but not afterwards — it was too arid by that time. Did the Egyptians have help? Did extraterrestrials provide the astronomy and technology to carve the rock? This was significant work to say the least. Do you believe it was done with hammer and chisel? Perhaps the New Age may bring answers, but for the moment, we don't know.

Easter Island

Easter Island is by any measure, the world's most isolated inhabited island and probably the most mysterious. Easter Island is in the Pacific Ocean, roughly halfway between Chile and Tahiti, well south of Hawaii. The closest inhabited land is 1,260 miles away — tiny Pitcairn Island where the mutineers of the H.M.S. Bounty settled in 1790.

Archaeological evidence indicates Polynesians discovered the island around 400 AD. In 1722, a Dutch explorer, Jacob Roggeveen, sighted and landed on the island on Easter Sunday, hence the name, Easter Island. He discovered three distinct groups of people, dark skinned, red skinned and very pale skinned people with red hair.

Consensus has it that its people are of Polynesian descent, but anthropologists have argued the true origins of these people, some claiming that ancient South-American mariners settled the island first. Many early explorers found a scattered population with almost no culture they could recall and no links to the outside world. Slave traders found Easter islanders easy prey during the 19th century which further depleted any recall of their tenuous culture, history and ancestors.

Mention Easter Island and the first image that pops into your mind is huge, carved stone figures dotting the coastline and landscape. These massive, indigenous stone statues are called Moai and are seen all over the island in different shapes, sizes and stages of completion, some even unfinished at the quarry site. Many are buried up to their shoulders and appear to be disembodied heads.

They are carved from the island's volcanic rock which is softer and lighter than most other rock, but even the smallest Moai weigh several tons, with some estimated to weigh as much as 80 to 90 tons. There is no clear explanation for the Moai, but research together with accumulated lore indicates they were carved by the ancestors of the present inhabitants. Theories are numerous without definitive resolution.

The generally accepted presumption is that these majestic stone statues were built to honor Polynesian gods and deified

Moais on Easter Island [9]

ancestors such as chiefs as well as other figures important in the island's history. Most of them are attributed to the 14th and 15th centuries, although some may have been erected as long ago as the 10th Century. Their function, it is believed, was to look out over a village or gravesite as a protector, but could have also served as status symbols for villages or clans.

By most accounts, all of the Moai were toppled in tribal wars about 250 years ago. They were excavated and photographed for the first time by Thor Heyerdahl in the 1950's. A reconstruction program then began to restore the Moai to their original orientation and positions.

There are a number of religious sites on the island and one of the most interesting is Ahu Akivi, a sanctuary and celestial observatory built about 1500 AD. It was the first serious restoration accomplished on Easter Island by archaeologists William Mulloy and Gonzalo Figueroa, with excellent results. As in the case of many religious structures on Easter Island, it's situated with astronomical precision: its seven statues look toward the precise point where the sun sets during the equinox. How did they do that? How did they know?

Ahu Akivi is an unusual site in several respects. A low ahu — a ceremonial shrine — supports seven statues all similar in height and style. The shrine is located far inland and the statues were built to face the ocean. This is the only site on the island where this was done. The statues were discovered knocked off the ahu, lying face down in the ground. In 1960, Archeologist William Mulloy's team spent several months raising the statues to their original positions.

Folklore holds that its seven Moai represent the seven young explorers that the Polynesian King Hotu Matu'a dispatched from across the seas, probably from the Marquesas Islands, to find this new homeland for him and his people. These seven stone giants may well symbolize those seven explorers, but no one knows for sure, just as no one knows what exactly the Moai really represent.

The seven at Ahu Akivi each stand about sixteen feet high and weigh about eighteen tons. The tallest Moai on the island exceed thirty feet, with many in the range of 12 to 20 feet. Even the occasional tiny Moai are at least six feet high. Many of the Island's hundreds of Moai are erected at sites miles from the quarry where they were carved.

It's almost certain that all but a few of the Moai were carved at Rano Raraku, a volcanic cone with a crater lake. It's a decidedly eerie spot. Scattered all around the Rano Raraku quarry are 394 Moai in every stage of creation. Some are fallen and some appear to have only heads, although they are really full figures that have been nearly buried over the centuries. For reasons that remain a mystery, it appears that the workers at Rano Raraku laid down their tools one day in the middle of a multitude of projects and the carving and excavation abruptly ceased.

As significant a feat the carving process might have been, the real question is how could so few people move so many statues even a couple of feet, let alone several miles — and without breaking them? And once they did move them, how did they get them upright? Even today, using cranes and other powerful machinery, it would be an interesting challenge!

So how were they moved? As you would expect, there are several theories.

Many of the indigenous Rapa Nui people believe that the statues were moved and erected by *mana*, a magical force best described as levitation, a concept you hear frequently in South Seas lore. Great kings of a long-gone era simply used their *mana* to command the Moai to move to the distant sites and stand there. The people also believed that the Moai also possessed *mana*, which was instilled at the time their white coral eyes were put in place. Their *mana* was used to protect the people of the island. Today none of the genuine coral eyes remain so *mana*, it is said, is no more.

Other, more practical — maybe — theories postulate that perhaps men slid the Moai from the quarry to their destinations on the island on layers of yams and sweet potatoes. A slippery theory at best!

Thor Heyerdahl, whose books *Kon-Tiki* and *Aku-Aku* stirred great interest in Easter Island, conducted an experiment showing that an upright stone statue could be moved using ropes, tilting and swiveling it along. But the test was conducted on a flat surface over only a short distance and so this theory isn't considered plausible. So, the generally accepted belief is that the statues were transported on sledges or log rollers and then levered erect using piles of stones and long logs.

Then we have the "furthest out" theory, the intervention of extraterrestrials. Erich Von Däniken suggests that a small group of "intelligent beings" were stranded there and taught the natives to make robot-like statues. This links with theories that Easter Island was once part of a lost civilization. We'll have more on these theories in a later chapter on aliens — suffice it to say it will at least challenge your thinking if not your inner compass!

Another mystery of Easter Island is Rongo-rongo, a hieroglyphic script found on a number of tablets. For more than a hundred years, controversy has raged over the meaning and source of these enigmatic characters. There are only 21 known tablets in existence, scattered in museums and private collections. Tiny, remarkably regular glyphs, about one centimeter high, highly stylized and formalized, are carved in shallow grooves running the length of the tablets. Lore has it that scribes used obsidian flakes or shark teeth to cut the glyphs and that writing was brought by the first colonists led by Hotu Matua.

The direction of writing is unique. Starting from the left hand bottom corner, you proceed from left to right and, at the end of the line; you turn the tablet around before you start reading the next line. So, the orientation of the hieroglyphs is reversed every other line: imagine a book in which every other line is printed back-to-front and upside-down. That's how the tablets are written!

Comparison and analysis of the tablets bearing the same text indicate that the writing apparently followed rules. All that has been deciphered some two to three lines of the tablet commonly called *Mamari*. It clearly deals with the moon and there appear to be several versions of the ancient lunar calendar of Easter Island on it. We'll have to wait to understand the content.[10] Who knows, maybe the aliens can help us!

There is no clear history, no clear understanding of why or how the statues of Easter Island came to be; only lore and archeological estimates. Nor is there any credible evidence of how such massive, heavy statues were moved about the island with a population of significantly fewer than one thousand people. In fact, population estimates prior to 400 AD indicate only a few hundred people inhabiting the island. Even with the supposition that at one time, the population may have been around 9,000, there is serious doubt that sufficient food was available to sustain life for this many people unless supplies were supplemented by outsiders.[11] Add to that the similarity of the ahu stone masonry closely resembling the style found in Peru, one has to ask, "How were such an isolated, thinly populated people able to accomplish these extraordinary feats? And who helped them?" It certainly makes one wonder!

Machu Picchu

Machu Picchu was revered as a sacred place long before the Incas built their ceremonial site in the early 1400's. Nine thousand sixty feet above sea level in the Andes of Peru, Incans built hundreds of stone structures, their ruins "rediscovered" in 1911 by archaeologist Hiram Bingham of Yale University. It's one of the most beautiful and enigmatic ancient sites in the world with little evidence of its ancient beginnings.

Legend and myth have added to Machu Picchu's mystique making it a "must see" for those interested in ancient sites; and especially those interested in ancient sites with purported high energy or magnetism. Whatever its origins, the Inca turned the five square mile site into an extraordinary high altitude city. Unseen from below and completely self-contained with natural springs and surrounding agricultural terraces sufficient to feed its population, there is evidence that Machu Picchu was utilized as a secret ceremonial Incan city. Two thousand feet above the rumbling Urubamba River, the cloud shrouded ruins of palaces, baths, temples, storage rooms and houses survive the ages, remarkably preserved.

The structures, carved from the gray granite of the mountain top are wonders, reflecting both architectural and aesthetic genius. Many of the building blocks weigh fifty tons or more yet are so precisely sculpted and fitted together without mortar that a thin knife blade can't be inserted between the joints. It's been suggested that the same methods and skills used to fit the stone blocks of the Egyptian Pyramids were probably used here, begging the question, "How was that knowledge transferred? Or was it coincidentally discovered by two civi-

Machu Picchu [12]

lizations separated by thousands of miles of ocean and thousands of years?

Little is known of the social or religious use of the site during Inca times although there is conjecture that the site may
have been a sanctuary for the training of priestesses or brides
for the Incan nobility. From a practical perspective, it appears
that Machu Picchu functioned as an astronomical observatory.

The Intihuatana stone — meaning "Hitching Post of the
Sun" has proved to be a precise indicator of the two equinoxes
and other noteworthy celestial periods. The Intihuatana is designed to "hitch" the sun at the two equinoxes — not at the solstice as sometimes reported in tourist and New Age literature.
At midday on March 21st and September 21st, the sun stands
directly above the pillar, creating no shadow at all. At this precise moment the sun "sits with all his might upon the pillar"
and is for the moment, "tied" to the rock. It was at this precise
time the Incas held ceremonies at the stone in which they "tied
the sun" to prevent the sun's northward travel in the sky,
thereby ensuring they would move back to warmer days.

Legend has it that when sensitive people touch their fore-
heads to the stone, the Intihuatana opens their vision to the
spirit world, affording them access to understand spirits around
them. Intihuatana stones were the supremely sacred and the
Spaniards systematically searched for and destroyed the stones
throughout the Inca Empire. By breaking the stones at an Incan
shrine, the Inca believed that the deities of the place died or
departed. Fortunately, the Spaniards never found Machu Picchu thus the Intihuatana stone and its resident spirits remain
in their original position.[13]

While Hiram Bingham found many objects of stone,
bronze, ceramic and obsidian, he found no gold or silver. Not
having found Machu Picchu, the Spaniards were not responsible for stealing the gold and silver that probably was in the city.
The Spaniards always took great pains to visit every inhabited
settlement in Peru and record it in detail before relieving it of
everything worth taking, but there's not a single reference to
Machu Picchu in any Spanish chronicles. Peruvian scholar, Dr.

Victor Angles Vargas believes the city died toward the end of the fifteenth century, before the Spaniards arrived. Why the Inca left is still a mystery.

There are, as you would imagine, a number of theories. Wars between rival Inca tribes were common, often bloody, some resulting in the annihilation of entire communities. For example, when the Incan ruler, Wayna Capac defeated the tribe of the Caranques, he ordered the execution of all survivors. The citizens of Machu Picchu may well have met their fate this way.

Another possibility is that a novice priest defiled one of the sacred Virgins of the Sun. Garcilaso de Vega, the son of a Spaniard and an Inca princess, wrote exhaustive commentaries on Inca customs. According to him, anyone found guilty of sexually violating an "ajilla" was not only put to death himself, but their servants, relatives and neighbors as well as inhabitants of the same town and all their cattle were all killed. Could this have been the fate of the inhabitants of Machu Picchu?

Or, perhaps it was an epidemic, common enough even in modern times. For example, in the 1940s, malaria decimated the population of an area near Machu Picchu. Perhaps the ancients suffered a similar fate. In Hiram Bingham's exploration of the city, a rich woman's skeleton reflected evidence of syphilis and was unlikely to have been alone in her affliction. Perhaps the city was ravaged by a plague so terrible it was permanently quarantined by the authorities.

There are no records, evidence or substantiation of why the Inca abandoned this sacred city, only conjecture. The enigmatic Incas knew neither the wheel nor any written language. Today, they remain an enigma; how could a civilization build a city whose citadel is such an amazing achievement in urban planning, civil engineering, architecture and especially stonemasonry [14] without knowing either the wheel or any written language?

Discovery in and around Machu Picchu continues, even today. As reported in November of 2003, a team led by Briton Hugh Thomson and American Gary Zeigler used infrared aerial photography to penetrate the dense forest canopy in hopes of making other discoveries. They found ruins at Llactapata, less than three kilometers from Machu Picchu. The site was mentioned by Hiram Bingham in 1912, but the location was vague and has lain undisturbed until the 2003 discovery. The site covers several square kilometers and contains houses and a solar temple in the same alignment with the Pleiades and the June sunrise solstice as Machu Picchu. Not only was Llactapata a probable ceremonial site in its own right, excavations indicate it might have served as a granary and dormitory for Machu Picchu.[15]

Where did the Inca gain their insight, skills, and desire to build Machu Picchu? Did they have help? If so, where did it come from and why is there no record? And why did the Inca leave?

Nazca Lines

Larger than life artifacts unfold across the Nazca plains in Peru — the famous Nazca Lines. They look like a giant map or signs left by ancients, perhaps directing or warning those that can see them from the air. The Lines include straight lines ranging from one to ten feet wide and four to five miles in length. There are also geometric and crude figures formed by one continuous line, drawn as if a pen is not lifted from the page. They are in fact, an enigma.

There is no who, when or why these Lines were created. Since their discovery, the Nazca Lines have inspired extraordinary explanations as to their origin and use: ancient gods, a landing strip for aliens, a celestial calendar, astronomy rituals or simply a map of underground water supplies[16] are some of the theories.

The mysterious Plains of Nazca lie some 300 miles south of Lima, Peru. The Plains take their name from the highly developed civilization of the Nazca who thrived here around 800 AD. Situated in one of the driest deserts of the world, the conditions perfectly preserve the Lines made by the removal of darker stones from the lighter colored earth. As they were removed, the stones were stacked up in piles along the perimeter, thus adding depth and a more definitive delineation to the Lines which average from a few inches to never more than a foot deep. The flat, stony ground curtails the effect of the wind and with no dust or sand to cover the plain along with little rain, the Lines stay drawn.[17]

The Nazca Lines were first spotted by commercial airlines as they began flying across the Peruvian desert in the 1920's: passengers reported seeing "primitive landing strips" on the ground below. The Lines were "rediscovered" by Paul Kosok in 1929 and were studied by a number of archaeologists over the years, but it was Maria Reiche, a German mathematician, who attracted attention to the Nazca Plains. She moved there in 1932, living in a one room bungalow next to the major drawings, dedicating her life to the mysterious lines and figures that spread some thirty two miles along the desert and up the foothill slopes of the Andes. Reiche died in 1998 at the age of 95 and is buried in the arid valley she loved so well.

The Lines appear to be of two kinds of colossal designs: geometric and figures of things such as spiders, flowers and birds. All made in the same fashion, they are best viewed from aircraft. Interesting that the creators of these lines could maintain the perspective of their design, isn't it?

Many of the Lines are geometric: angles, triangles, spirals, rectangles and wavy lines, while others form concentric circles converging with or emanating from a outcropping. Other Lines are indiscriminate and seem to have no pattern at all. They are scattered, seemingly at random, over the desolate plain, intersecting for no apparent reason.

The other category of design includes figures, like plants, flowers, a candelabra, a whale, a hummingbird, a monkey and a lizard among the many different outlines across the desert plain. Others are "The Man with a Hat" and "The Executioner" which appears to be the most primitive. These figures are very similar to the small petroglyphs found in the rocky areas of the region. One curious design is of two enormous hands, one normal and the other with only four fingers. Anthropomorphic figures, while relatively few, are situated on the slopes and prompt much conjecture, the most well-known being "The As-tronaut," a figure about a hundred feet long, discovered by Ed-uardo Herran in 1982. Is this a depiction of visitors from above?

Theories abound on the origin of the Lines. It's believed that they show the rising direction of the important stars and planetary events like sun solstices. Designs like the spider and the monkey possibly show star constellations like Orion and Ursa Major. The foremost issue is not knowing when the lines were made: the earth's position within our galaxy gives us a perspective of the stars at that particular time. As our solar system travels through time and space, the orientation of all celestial bodies with earth changes, giving us a different position for any specific star.

Maria Reiche led a determined effort to discredit theories of extraterrestrial visitors. Her premise has been to argue that the Nazca Indians constructed the Lines relatively recently — somewhere between 300 BC and 800 AD. Supporting this possibility, some scientists have put forward ingenious ideas on how the geoglyphs could theoretically have been designed from the ground. The more important evidence, however, is that which attempts to link the Lines definitively to the Nazcan culture.

Unfortunately, neither of the two key pieces of evidence survives close scrutiny. The first is a series of radiocarbon dates, based on ceramic and wood remains left at the Lines by the Nazcan people. The claim is this proves that the Nazcans constructed the Lines. However, the dating of these materials only verifies that the Nazcans lived in the area and may have already existed when the Nazcan culture emerged. The second piece of evidence is the alleged resemblance of the Nazca geoglyphs to certain features found on Nazcan pottery. This is important because it potentially offers substance that the Nazcans either designed the images or at least viewed them from the air.

In 1968, a study by the National Geographic Society determined that, while some of the Nazca Lines did point to the positions of the sun, moon and certain stars two thousand years ago, it was no more than could be expected by mere chance. In

1973, Dr. Gerald Hawkins studied 186 lines with a computer program finding only 20 percent had any astronomical orientation, again, no more than would occur by pure chance.

In 1980, Georg Petersen pointed out that Reiche's theory did not explain the different lengths and widths of the lines. More recently, Johan Reinhard noted that the surrounding mountains provide a much more effective tool for the Nazcans to use as a solar calendar; the lines would thus have been quite superfluous to them if used for that purpose.

Theories, both plausible and farfetched, from serious researchers are well documented. Conjecture is extensive. Many explorers speculate the lines have significant meaning, from astronomic calendars, Nazcan zodiacs, precipitation measurement systems, subterranean water flow markers, analytic geometric codes, clan signs, population control — when you're working, you can't make children? — to places for ritual ceremonies, magic lines from a cat cult, evidence of visitors from other stars, or a secret code linking other unexplained geological constructions around the world.[18]

The size and number of these enormous designs clearly suggest a long and arduous task. More importantly, how did the builders maintain a perspective of what they were building if they didn't have a way to view the work in progress? We may never know how these incredible lines were made, but they certainly conjure many thoughts about broader thinking beings that weren't satisfied sitting around on their sofas waiting for the next growing season!

Stonehenge

Stonehenge is located about two miles west of Amesbury in Wiltshire, approximately ninety miles west of London in the United Kingdom. The stones we see today, unfortunately, show Stonehenge in ruin. Many of the original stones have fallen or been removed over time for construction or road repair. Serious damage to some of the smaller bluestones by visitors prior to 1978 is evident and prehistoric carvings on the larger *sarsen* stones — a very hard sand stone eroded by glaciers — show significant wear.

Stonehenge has watched the seasons change thousands of times over. It monitors the heavens, phases of the moon but more so the annual trek of the sun. While most of the year sunrise can't be seen from the center of the structure, the longest day of the year — June 21st, the summer solstice — finds the rising sun appearing behind one of the main stones, creating the illusion that it's balancing on the stone. As the rising sun creeps up the length of the rock, called the "Heel Stone," it creates a shadow that extends deep into the heart of a horseshoe comprised of five pairs of sarsen stone pillars with large slabs of stone laid across the top. Just as the sun clears the horizon, it appears to hover momentarily on the tip of the Heel Stone. A few days later, the sun will appear once again, but this time it will begin to move to the right of the heel stone. The same phenomenon is repeated during the winter solstice in the opposite direction at sunset. Both are indicators of a change of season.[19]

Stonehenge is clearly a construction and engineering feat, demanding vast amounts of both labor and time. The first phase appears to have been a large earthen bank and ditch arrangement, called a henge, probably constructed around 3000 BC. It's believed the ditch was dug with tools made from the antlers of red deer and wood. The underlying chalk was

Stonehenge [20]

loosened with picks and shoveled with the tools created from the shoulder blades of cattle, then loaded into baskets and carried away.

About 2000 BC, the inner stone circle, comprised of about 80 small bluestones, was begun but abandoned before completion. The stones used in that first circle are believed to be from the Prescelly Mountains, roughly 240 miles away at the southwestern tip of Wales. These bluestones weigh up to four tons each, presenting quite a transportation challenge. A logical theory speculates "the stones were dragged by roller and sledge from the inland mountains to the headwaters of Milford Haven, where they were loaded onto rafts, barges or boats and sailed along the south coast of Wales, then up the Rivers Avon and Frome to a point near present-day Frome in Somerset. From this point, so the theory goes, the stones were hauled overland, again, to a place near Warminster in Wiltshire, approximately six miles away. From there, it's back into the pool for a slow float down the River Wylye to Salisbury, then up the Salisbury Avon to West Amesbury, leaving a two mile drag from West Amesbury to the Stonehenge site."[21]

The giant sarsen stones forming the outer circle weigh as much as fifty tons each. Their origin, Marlborough Downs — roughly twenty miles to the north — presents an even greater dilemma than that of moving the bluestones. Most of the route is relatively easy going, but at the steepest part of the course, at Redhorn Hill, work studies estimate that at least six hundred men would have been needed just to get each stone up the path!

Once positioned on site, a sarsen stone was prepared for stone lintels along its top. It was then dragged until the bottom was over the opening of the hole, then it's believed massive levers were inserted under the stone and raised it until it slid into the hole. The stone was then mostly upright, standing on about a thirty degree angle from the ground. Ropes were attached to the top, then teams of men pulled from the opposite side to bring it full upright and then secured it by filling the trench around its base with small, round stones.[22] The stone pillar was then allowed to settle in safely before work proceeded.

It was some time, perhaps years after erecting the pillars, before the setting of the lentils began. There is only speculation how the actual lifting was performed, but the commonly accepted theory is perhaps the only logical explanation as to how the builders achieved their task. It's believed the lentil stones were "jacked" up and into their final resting places using a lattice-work of logs. A stone was wedged onto a single log, then another log wedged under the opposite side, parallel to the first. Next, the stone was wedged up and another log was inserted underneath, perpendicular to the first set. The process was repeated and continued until the stone had been raised to the top of its pillars, where it was finally rocked into place. It's estimated that a lattice tower would require about a mile of six-inch diameter logs cut into twenty-foot lengths, notched like a log cabin wall. Imagine the work involved in hauling just the wood alone![23] The lintels were lowered into place and secured vertically by mortise and tenon joints and horizontally by tongue and groove joints. Stonehenge was probably finished around 1500 BC, taking more than three hundred years to complete. Tenacious people, those Brits!

So who are the resolute folks that built Stonehenge? That question remains largely unanswered, even today. The construction has been attributed to many ancient peoples throughout the years, the most often, the Druids. The antiquary, John Aubrey, posed this erroneous connection about three hundred years ago based on writings by Julius Caesar and other Roman writers telling of a Celtic priesthood that flourished around the time of their first conquest in 55 BC. However, by that time, the stones had been standing for more than 2,000 years and probably already in ruins. More importantly, the Druids supposedly worshipped in forest temples and had no need for stone structures!

Our search for a more appropriate hypothesis leaves us with this best guess: it seems that the Stonehenge site was begun by people during the late Neolithic period — around 3000 BC — and continued by people from a new economy arising at this time. These "new" people, called "Beaker Folk" because of their use of pottery drinking vessels, used metal implements and were more communal than their ancestors were. There are those who think they may have been immigrants from the European continent, but that argument isn't supported by any archaeological evidence. It's more likely that they were indigenous people doing the same old things but doing them in new ways.

Situated in a vast plain surrounded by hundreds of burial mounds, Stonehenge is truly impressive even from afar. Its awe increases as you approach it. We can only speculate as to its purpose, but clearly, many spent incredible effort to craft it into a reality. The educated guesses as to its purpose include a temple, an astronomical calendar, a religious construction, or interestingly, a sexually symbolic site.[24]

Whatever its origin, its purpose and its history, it is food for thought. What people formulated plans and then led hundreds over the course of centuries to construct Stonehenge? Did extraterrestrials help in planning or in actual relocation of the huge stones? How will we ever know?

Recorded or at least repeated history affords us a concise, sometimes flavored view of the past. It clarifies challenging questions about our earth, its people and how they interrelated. Archeology offers us a window into history as well. Comparatives with recorded history reinforce and refine thinking about past cultures. Standing alone, archeology gives us our only perspective on ancient peoples and cultures, enabling our minds to fill in the blanks.

I believe there are just too many "holes" in our record of history and archeology to properly represent *exactly* what happened at any given time. I firmly believe masses of humanity worked together to do amazing things, build incredible monuments and develop methods that catapulted their civilizations to where we are today.

BUT, there are so may unexplained phenomena that challenge both the logical and emotional mind. How did so few people move such massive stones without stumbling over one another? Why were images portrayed in the way they were? Who looks like a tiki god? Why do hieroglyphics and drawings depict flying people and craft? Why can't we explain why massive monuments and designs exist on this earth or how they came to be?

Well, for all the things we can't explain, we say they're impossible or improbable. Or we turn it into a religion! Explain it away through faith in something grander than we can comprehend. Or if you're not into gods, perhaps you're pulled into the supernatural.

If you move away from lore and beyond religion, you may be moving into woo — the fog. Too much woo can clearly launch you into the New Age. And when you start considering New Age, you're certainly going to begin considering traditional religions. Let's take a closer look at how religions have influenced thinking throughout our world as we look to gods and angels.

Chapter 3 Endnotes

[1] Jupiterimages Corporation, ©2008, *The Great Pyramid*
[2] Ashmawy, Alaa K., *The Great Pyramid of Giza*
[3] Bayuk, Andrew, *The Great Pyramid of Khufu*
[4] op. cit., *The Great Pyramid of Giza*
[5] Free, Wynn, *The Reincarnation of Edgar Cayce*
[6] ibid., *The Reincarnation of Edgar Cayce*
[7] Jupiterimages Corporation, ©2008, *The Great Sphinx*
[8] Waldron, Ian, *The Sphinx*
[9] Jupiterimages Corporation, ©2008, *Moais on Easter Island*
[10] Crystal, Ellie, *Easter Island*
[11] Fisher, Diana, *Easter Island Population*
[12] Jupiterimages Corporation, ©2008, *Machu Picchu*
[13] Gray, Martin, *Machu Picchu*
[14] Crystal, Ellie, *Machu Picchu*
[15] Lovell, Jeremy, The Globe and Mail, *Explorers in Peru Find Lost Inca City*
[16] Crystal, Ellie, *Nazca Lines*
[17] Ladatco Tours, *Nasca Lines*
[18] op. cit., *Nazca Lines*
[19] Dimitrakopoulos, Sandra, *Stonehenge*
[20] Jupiterimages Corporation, ©2008, *Stonehenge*
[21] Fox, Seth, managing editor, Britania.com, *Stonehenge*
[22] ibid., *Stonehenge*
[23] Pomona College, *Construction*
[24] op. cit., *Stonehenge*

CHAPTER 4

GODS AND ANGELS

"God, please make it go away!" A prayer for relief, probably as old as mankind, made as floodwaters rose, as fires chewed the forest, as windstorms sucked life from the land. Or as manmade afflictions like sieges chipped away at castle walls. Or, on a more personal level, a migraine pounded at the base of the petitioner's skull. It seems mankind pleads for divine intervention when it can no longer cope, seeking a higher power to deal with that which they cannot.

It's the basis of religions: the hope of divine intervention for a better, brighter, and longer life. Religion is defined by Merriam-Webster as the service and worship of God or the supernatural. It's clear, however, that one doesn't necessarily have to serve or worship to believe in God, gods, a supernatural, or Supreme Being. When hard-pressed, even the atheist or the agnostic may implore a higher essence to intervene.

In nearly all cultures, ancient as well as today's, there's been reference to "higher beings" that have powers beyond those of mere mortals. No doubt even the earliest humans were in awe of the forces or entities that controlled weather, fire, and the heavens. Let's take a look at these higher beings — God, the gods, or however you may perceive Him, Her or Them — to see how those who came before us considered them. And perhaps we may challenge our own thinking; clearly, our present state of knowledge is not the end of the story by any means.

I don't intend to be the definitive authority on any of the religions or belief systems I'll reference throughout this chapter. I simply want to explore some of the various perceptions of how our earth came to be, along with related beliefs about which Supreme Being or Beings may have been responsible. I seek to push your envelope on understanding other's thinking and perhaps get you to dig deeper into those that interest you.

So as we delve into this topic, I believe you'll find that those things you don't sort into your "pigeon holes of understanding" can genuinely be called New Age. And as we delve deeper into what might be, Woo-Woo may well play a role!

Evolution

Where better to start than with the theory of evolution — where did we come from and how did we get to where we are today? That question has launched a thousand theories. And theories, you will recall, are based in part on scientific fact, with the resulting "story" based on interpretation of those facts. Interpretation — man's creative spin on what he "knows" — is the name of the game, and the reason there are many different theories.

Let's first start with fundamentals: How did all this begin? Most astronomers now agree the universe started with a giant explosion 13.7 billion years ago,[1] called the Big Bang. In the twentieth century, Edwin Hubble observed that the universe was expanding. This suggests that in the beginning all the galaxies were compressed into one massive yet tiny sphere, the origin of the expansion. But the Big Bang theory doesn't tell us where the "massive yet tiny sphere" came from. Didn't someone or something have to create it?

So, the Big Bang was the instant the universe began, when space and time came to be and all matter in the cosmos started to expand. At its inception, the universe was inconceivably hot, cooling quickly to one billion degrees with protons and neutrons combining to form the nuclei of a few heavier elements, most notably helium. Ground zero of the biggest explosion ever!

Approximately 300,000 years after the Big Bang, when the universe had cooled to a comfortable 3000 degrees, electrons could combine with atomic nuclei to form neutral atoms. Stars and galaxies formed about one billion years after the Big Bang and the universe has since expanded and cooled, creating conditions conducive to life as we know it. So began our universe.

There are three primary reasons for accepting the Big-Bang theory. First and most widely acknowledged, the universe is expanding. Second, the theory predicts that a quarter of the universe's total mass should be the helium formed early in the explosion; scientific observations agree on that fact. And finally, and most convincing, is the presence of the cosmic background radiation, predicted by the Big-Bang theorists well before radio astronomers chanced upon it.[2]

While this is the most widely accepted theory, there has been recent evidence and discussion that the expanding universe may be contracting in some areas giving rise to a "pulsing" rather than "expanding" theory. We'll have to wait to see what unfolds as scientists collect more data and postulate revisions. The Big Bang theory will undoubtedly be modified over time as new theories are proven factual in our evolving world.

So the universe began and expands. We can safely assume that over its thirteen-billion plus years, stars, galaxies, planets, and space debris "evolved" to where we are today. Even if you believe that life on earth was created in six days, it's hard to deny that the expanding universe has both growth and erosion. So what we see today isn't quite the same as it was a million years ago, just like your hometown isn't what it was the day you were born.

So as the universe evolved, so began our planet earth. Formed some 4.6 billion years ago, it was a lifeless, inhospitable rock, number three from the Sun. A billion years later our rock was teeming with organisms similar to blue-green algae. How did that happen? Who brewed this primordial soup? This long-standing question continues to generate fascinating conjectures and ingenious experiments, many of which center on self-replicating RNA as a critical milestone on the road to life. This challenges thinking: who or what put the chemicals or elements together to begin this process?

In the mid 1600's, most people believed that God had created mankind and other higher organisms. But it was still believed that insects, frogs, and other small creatures arose spontaneously in mud or decaying matter. Over the next two hundred years, challenges to the notion of spontaneous generation set the stage for modern discussions on the origin of life, which began in earnest in the mid-nineteenth century.

In a dramatic revelation, Louis Pasteur discredited spontaneous generation by proving that even bacteria and other microorganisms arise from parents resembling them. But the solution to one mystery begets another: How did the first generation of each species come to be?

Enter the theory of Natural Selection, proposed by Charles Darwin and Alfred Russel Wallace.[3] Since ancient times, Greek philosophers such as Anaximander had hypothesized that life developed from non-life and suggested that man descended from other animals. Darwin simply brought a new wrinkle to that old philosophy — a plausible mechanism called "Natural Selection."

Natural selection acts to preserve and accumulate minor advantageous genetic mutations. So how would that work? Suppose a member of a species developed a functional advantage over time such as growing wings and learning to fly. Its offspring would inherit that advantage and pass it on to their offspring. The inferior or disadvantaged members of the same species would gradually die out, leaving only the superior or advantaged members of the species.

Natural selection, then, is the preservation of a functional advantage that enables a species to compete better in the wild. In modern times, domestic breeding practices mimic Natural Selection, eliminating undesirable traits in livestock and other domestic animals gradually over time. Similarly, natural selection eliminates inferior species gradually, over time.[4]

As you would guess, Darwin was vigorously challenged by the religious establishment. This apparently resulted in some hedging by Darwin as he wrote the final paragraph of *The Origin of Species*: "the Creator" originally breathed life "into a few forms or into one." Then evolution took over. "From so simple a beginning endless forms most beautiful and most wonderful have been, and are being evolved."

In private correspondence, however, Darwin suggested life could have arisen through chemistry, "in some warm little pond, with all sorts of ammonia and phosphoric salts, light, heat, electricity, etc. present." Our primordial pond!

For much of the twentieth century, "origin-of-life" research has aimed to flesh out Darwin's private hypothesis: to explain how, without supernatural intervention, spontaneous interaction of the relatively simple molecules dissolved in the oceans, lakes or pools of the prebiotic world could have yielded the ultimate origin of life. So, the crux of research on the origin of life can be reduced to a simple question: What chemical reactions in this interdependent system of nucleic acids and proteins take place to create life?[5] Who helped? Was it simply a chemical/biological process evolving over millions of years that enabled man to come into being on this earth? Or did the process have help from others beyond this world?

Today the evolution discussion is alive and well. There are factions that believe in evolution and there are those that categorically reject any concept of evolutionary adaptation. So let's put it into today's context.

The discussion is primarily between groups at opposite ends of the spectrum. Those who are convinced of evolution are still opposed by those who categorically reject it. But here's something worth considering. If you believe that God or a Supreme Being is responsible for the universe, it follows that this omnipotent entity had the foresight to establish the laws of nature, physics and the universe to meet His long-range plan. So to ensure that the plan worked, and to allow adaptation to changing environments both in the universe and on this earth, the laws are the basis for allowing a living organism to adapt to the changes it encounters. Clinically speaking, can't we call this evolution?

That's really all I want to pose here. There is a *higher entity* laying out the rules in our universe. And those rules are the laws of physics, genetics, and life as we know it – all inanimate forces, organisms, plants, and animals follow those laws. Even human intelligence and thinking play a role in adapting our habitation of this planet.

We use only a small portion of our capacity according to science. Obviously the human brain has the capacity for more knowledge — look at what we take for granted in understanding how computers work when even a hundred years ago, man had difficulty comprehending the creation, much less the application, of a hand held computer.

So I believe the term *evolution* is worthy of consideration of the emergent changes underway in our world — even though your religious beliefs may conflict. I also believe that our place on this planet still affords us amazing scientific and esoteric discoveries. Just as we look back on the 1800's way of life, so will those a hundred years hence question how they could live in our age and think the way we do.

For that reason, I don't believe facts gleaned from science conflict with religious beliefs of creation. Perhaps once again we're trying too hard to be literal in translating history. Using the Bible[6] as one reference and the Big Bang theory as a scientific possibility and progress from that point forward — see Earth Timeline in the Appendix — what if:

- In the beginning "… without form and void; and darkness *was* on the face of the deep." This history *could* coincide with the original "one massive yet tiny sphere" mentioned above prior to the Big Bang. This would be more than 13.7 billion years ago. "On the first day … "Then God said, 'Let there be light.' And God saw the light …" This *could* have been the moment of the Big Bang 13.7 billion years ago.
- On the second day, "… God made the firmament." This *could* be the formation of protons and nuclei formed very quickly after the moment of the Big Bang, creating the stars, planets, asteroids and other space debris, 13.7 billion years ago. Things would need time to cool down!
- On the third day, God said, "Let the waters under the heavens be gathered together in one place, and let the dry

land appear." This *could* be the creation of the earth 3.8 billion years ago. Also on the third day, God said, "Let the earth bring forth grass, the herb *that* yields seed, *and* the fruit tree *that* yields fruit according to its kind, whose seed *is* in itself, on the earth" (emphasis supplied). This *could* be the time between 3.5 billion and 500 million years ago, as life was formed beginning with the primordial soup of amino acids, blue-green algae, and eventually plants.

- On the fourth day, God said, "Let there be lights in the firmament of the heavens to divide the day from the night; let them be for the signs and seasons, and for days and years;" This *could* be the collapse of a supernova that became our sun about 3.4 billion years ago.
- On day five, God said, "Let the waters abound with an abundance of living creatures, and let birds fly . . ." This *could* be the emergence of simple animals throughout the earth 1.5 billion to 300 million years ago.
- On day six, God said, "Let the earth bring forth the living creature according to its kind:" This *could* be the emergence of animals developing from 420 to 4 million years ago.
- Also on the sixth day, God said, "Let us make man in Our image, according to our likeness; let them have dominion over the fish of the sea, the birds of the air, and over the cattle, over all the earth ..." This *could* be the appearance of human beings 4 million to 50,000 years ago.

I'm not arguing for your total agreement, but I do ask you to consider the possibilities.

So maybe traditional belief and scientific facts don't conflict. But I still wonder how the "one massive yet tiny sphere" posited by the Big-Bang theory came to be. I also question how apparent jumps in development between "evolving" species occurred; however, I do allow that a million years is a considerable time and much could happen that we haven't discovered or can't comprehend. And I do believe that sometime between the "bipedal hominids" and modern man there was the introduction of the soul — a concept that merits further exploitation. I believe we had some help! But from whom?

So even when one accepts evolution and other scientific findings, there are still some gaps and questions, and that's where the supernatural and religion come into play. Let's begin by looking at some early practices of reaching out beyond the known, to see how ancient peoples dealt with the phenomena in the world around them, and how they rationalized their ignorance, their fears, and their evolving beliefs.

Pagans, Devas, and Shamans

So as early mankind developed, there was much he and she didn't comprehend or understand. Historically, when we don't understand something, we turn to others for explanation. When there are no others, perhaps we then conjure reasons to the best of our intellectual capacity and imagination.

Conceivably that's the origin of beliefs and practices that characterize pagans, heathens, and other polytheistic individuals. We'll briefly touch on a few definitions to set a framework of admittedly old, often misused, and understandably diverse polytheistic beliefs in the forces of nature and perhaps even the supernatural.

Initially, a *pagan* simply meant a country dweller, but as the Roman Empire declined in the fourth and fifth centuries, it came to mean "civilian" or "local." The term later was related to heathen and adopted by English-speaking Christians as a slur referring to those too rustic to embrace Christianity.

Even today, a *heathen* is defined as one who has little or no religion and delights in sensual pleasures and material goods. Taken to extremes, that could make one a *hedonist*, one who lives for pleasure as the chief goal in life. Boy, that one hits a little too close to home for some of us, doesn't it?

There are a number of pagan subdivisions that merit mention.

- *Paleo-Paganism* is the hypothetical pagan culture that's not been disrupted by other civilizations — there are none in existence today.

- *Meso-Paganism* is a group which has been influenced by a conquering culture but has been able to maintain their independent religious practices, such as Native Americans, and Australian Aborigine Bushmen.
- *Syncreto-Paganism* is a culture that's been conquered and they merge the conquering culture's religious practices into their own, such as Haitian Voodoo.
- *Neo-Paganism* is the attempt by modern people to reconnect with nature, pre-Christian religions, or other nature based spiritual paths. Neo-Druidism and Wicca are examples of such religious beliefs.[7]

Devas

In the Hindu religion, Devas are celestial beings that control the forces of nature such as fire, wind, water, and air.[8] *Deva*, a Sanskrit word for god or deity, and can be any supernatural being of high excellence.

Devas are considered nature spirits, visible only to the clairvoyant. They supposedly communicate with humans through "clairaudience" and meditation. It is believed that as humans become more in touch with the natural world, they enter into a closer relationship with Devas. For Devas are thought of as the "architects" of nature, and are assigned to every living thing, even the soil. They are believed to be the designers of all living things, controlling the energies for growth and health. Today, they are allegedly concerned over man's destruction of the environment, and are willing to work with people who strive to understand the intricacies harmonic structure of nature.[9]

Findhorn — a community begun in 1962 near the town of Forres, 30 miles from Inverness, Scotland – now the Findhorn Foundation, is dedicated to the evolution of human consciousness toward spiritual values. Community members have no formal creed or doctrine, but recognize all the world's major religions as many paths to knowing our own inner divinity.[10] In the 1970s and 1980s, gardeners in Findhorn tried consciously working with Devas to produce more succulent fruits, vegetables and herbs. They continue their work today, producing unusually potent healing oils and fragrances that are sold throughout the world.[11] Is it Devas or simply believing in what you're doing? A step or two into the New Age?

Shamans

In non-industrial societies, the *shaman* is priest, meta-physician, and healer, a bridge between the "higher" and "lower" states of existence.[12] He or she uses magic to cure the sick by divining hidden and controlling events. The shaman can supposedly move beyond his own physical body, traveling to higher levels of existence or to parallel worlds. This is accomplished through self-hypnosis, where the shaman's trance enables him or her to communicate with spirits, gain information, and make subtle changes that may affect the physical world.

One becomes a shaman either by being born with the ability, or by receiving a "call" that bestows the requisite talent or gift. A third route is through personal choice and training, but this results in a considerably less powerful shaman than those who are born or "called." Shamans include such stereotypes as witch doctors and medicine men, but activities of shamans go well beyond the dispensing of herbs and potions.

Neo-Pagan Religions
Wicca

Let's look briefly at two surviving pagan-based religions. The first is *Wicca*, an "earth religion." In Old English, *Wicca* meant necromancer or male witch, but today *Wicca* refers to the religion where initiates work in covens. "Solitary Wicca" refers to the practice of Wicca rites by individuals on their own. Wicca has a number of followers in many English-speaking countries, and seeks to connect the individual to the four cardinal elements of air, fire, water, and earth.[13] Wiccans worship "the Goddess," and almost all followers also worship "the God."

While Wicca is as old as the first pagans who dabbled in magic, it was modernized in the 1940s in Britain by Gerald Gardner. He formalized specific beliefs and practices that are used today. The idea of a supreme Mother Goddess was common in Victorian and Edwardian literature, and Gardner used these references as well as the concept of a "horned god" — related to Pan or Faunus — and reconfigured Wicca around this core. Wicca celebrates eight main holidays or *Sabbats,* which include the solstices and equinoxes. They also hold *Esbats*, rituals held at the full and new moon.[14]

Wiccans practice witchcraft, considered a learned skill, and based on the casting of spells and the practice of "magick"; the "k" distinguishes the "Science of the Magi" from all counterfeits. In older, popular usage, "witchcraft" often meant the use of black or evil magic, something Wicca does not encourage.

Wicca is described as an unending path of light, magic, love, and constant learning. Followers revere nature and see the true divine beauty of the universe, recognizing that everyone has the ability to take their fate into their own hands and choose how they use that power. They have no scripture, no prophets, and are governed by the "Wiccan Rede" which basically states, "if it harms none, do what you will."[15]

Many Wiccans hold to the "Law of Threefold Return." This is the idea that anything one does may be returned to them threefold, good deeds as well as bad ones, similar to *karma*, which we'll discuss later. While there are many differing practices, Eight Wiccan Virtues are cultivated by followers: Mirth, Reverence, Honor, Humility, Strength, Beauty, Power, and Compassion. Respect for the elements as well as all living things is the central theme in varying practices around the world.

Druids

The second religion is *Druidism*, the religion of the Celtic people that was administered by priests called Druids. Remnants exist today, known as Neo-Druidism. In ancient times,

Druids held their sacred assemblies in groves of trees, especially oaks. *Druid* means "knowing the oak tree" in Gaelic.

Little is known of the Druid religion, since their teachings were transmitted through oral tradition. Most of our information on the Druids comes from the writings of Julius Caesar, whose occupying legions observed them. Druids were apparently the keepers of traditional wisdom concerning moral philosophy, natural phenomena, and theology. None of their trusted knowledge was committed to writing but conveyed through mnemonics.

As well as leading divine worship, they officiated over public and private sacrifices, interpreted ritual questions, settled disputes and meted out punishment to those refusing to obey their rules. Doctrinally, Druids believed that after death the soul passes from one physical body to another. The Druids esteemed themselves above kings, calling themselves "creators of the universe." The question of whether the Druids built Stonehenge continues to be debated; while the Druids may not have actually constructed it, Stonehenge seems to have played a large role in their ceremonies in latter years.

The Celtic tribes spread throughout Britain, Ireland and other parts of Europe, Asia Minor, and the Balkans. Druidism was critical in holding the Celtic people together; their descendants eventually civilized a major portion of Europe and the British Isles.[16] By the first century AD, the Roman attacks against the Celts had greatly reduced the Druidic population, and Christianity led to their ultimate demise.

Whether pagan, heathen, or Druidic, religious beliefs fostered both official and religious bonds that held ancient tribes together and gave them structure and character. Now let's turn to Egyptian, Greek and Roman mythology, to see who their gods were and how they influenced their cultures.

Gods & Myths –
The Egyptians, Greeks, and Romans

In early Egypt, forces of nature were identified as supernatural beings or gods. The annual flooding of the Nile, the unchanging aridity of the surrounding desert, and the sun's daily rising and setting were all attributed to various gods. The ancient Egyptians worshipped hundreds of gods in addition to the sun-god Re, honored with festivals throughout the land.

Religion was a mainstay to Egyptian society. Each region adopted its own patron god to look after its affairs. At home, people turned to lesser gods for help with everyday problems, and used magical charms or amulets to ward off danger. There was no official hierarchy of the gods; one god or goddess might be worshipped throughout the country, while another was known only locally. Cities worshipped their own group of gods, and when a city became important, so did its gods.

Like all people, the Egyptians turned to gods to rationalize things they didn't comprehend. Once they understood and could explain something, there was no need for a god.[17] So like us today, the Egyptians relied on a higher being to deal with those things not explainable by current thinking. From the earliest cave-dweller to the Egyptians to modern day, rationalization of the unknown integrated with the discovered, gives us the incremental steps to today's belief systems — we still worship what we believe, not what we know. Perhaps this began the progression from the sun god, the moon god, the fire god and the rest. The beginning of a New Age, even then.

Myths are all that remain of ancient Greek religion — a religion whose supporters worshipped the deities known as the Olympians. Written versions of the Greek Myths date from around 800-500 BC; oral versions go back much further in time. By the time they were written down by Homer and Hesiod around 800 BC, these myths had survived 400 years of additions, deletions and changes, slowly becoming the "authentic" versions. The Greek Myths are a window into the distant past, a view of a world that existed not only in the mind of the Greek poets but also in the hearts of the humble and long-suffering inhabitants of ancient Greece.[18] As with the Egyptians and their predecessors, mythology reflected the Greeks' religion. The myths were a way to explain origins and occurrences that couldn't be rationalized with contemporary knowledge.

The Roman's gods emanated from various diverse origins. Latium, the area around Rome before it became a big city, was settled by superstitious villagers, the Latins, who believed in many gods and spirits. As Rome grew and became more powerful, interaction developed with the Greeks, who had a complex Pantheon of their own. It appears that the Roman gods were a blend of those two main influences, Latin and Greek. In many cases the Romans found there was a Latin and a Greek god for the same entity. So they combined the two into one. For example, Vulcan was the Latin god of fire and the Greeks had a god called Hephaestus, god of fire and metalworking. The Romans combined the two making them one. Paintings and statues of Vulcan typically depict him as a blacksmith.

Interestingly, the Romans were broad-minded about their gods, and were open to hearing about others' gods. Given the vastness of the Roman Empire, there were many opportunities to encounter other cultures and their gods. The Romans adopted new gods as they saw fit, like Isis, Egyptian goddess of the earth, and Mithras, Persian god of light. These were then included in their Pantheon, with temples built accordingly. A smart way to cover all your bases, don't you think?

In 312 AD, on the eve of a great battle, the Emperor Constantine had a dream in which he believed he received a sign from the God of the Christians. After trouncing his enemies, Constantine converted his entire empire to Christianity. This has obviously had a huge impact on our world ever since.[19] Constantine's role in shaping Christianity is renown, from his Edict of Milan in 313 AD to his Council of Nicaea in 325. He apparently chose to focus the populace's attention on this lifetime so as to lead them away from belief in multiple lifetimes. After all, it was easier to convince Christians that they must be saved in their current lifetime rather than atone for past lives in the future; a true turning point for the relatively new religion.

So it's safe to say that religion or belief in gods has played an important and probably on-going role in the lives of almost everyone on this planet, even when they do not realize it. As for the agnostics or atheists, they sometimes call for help from a higher level in their hour of need.

One of the most profound bumper stickers I've ever seen appeared on the back of a shabby white pickup, complete with hay bale, gun rack, and Oklahoma license plates. It read: THERE ARE NO ATHEISTS IN THE CHUTE. Too true if you've ever been on a rodeo bull for the *second* time, regardless of who you are, your mantra is "Oh God, oh God, oh God...!" You may have heard the military version of this saying; it goes something like, "There are no atheists in foxholes." No matter who we are, we look for help in all kinds of places!

Now let's take a look at so-called "mystical" religions. Let's start with Gnosticism.

Gnosticism

Theology has been called an intellectual wrapping around the spiritual kernel of a religion. If this is true, then many religions seem to be strangled and stifled by their wrappings. Gnosticism avoids this pitfall by stating its world view in myth, rather than in theology. Myths express profound truths and can be interpreted in diverse ways.

Gnosticism is believed to have predated Christianity. While most Gnostics were nominally Christians, there were also Jewish Gnostics, as well as an older pagan group that incorporated elements of Egyptian "hermetic thought," astrological teachings and Platonic views. Most of the sects professed a type of "dualism" that was decidedly Persian. Gnostics believe that all is God, for all consists of the substance of God. And because our world is corrupted, this too emanated from divine essence. This forms a duality that Gnostics take to deeper levels. Bad as well as good came from God, because God is all there is.

Predictably, this view did not sit well with traditional Christians, who routinely persecuted the Gnostics and destroyed their writings. Once Constantine converted to Christianity, Gnosticism and other "heresies" were actively suppressed, and their followers persecuted. It was during this time that the Library at Alexandria was burned to the ground. Critics claim that Constantine didn't want anyone to trace the roots of Christianity in this ancient literature.

It's said that the Gnostics included some of the finest minds of the times, but they were essentially individual thinkers with little theological consistency. Thus they were no match for the increasingly effective organization of the official church. And unlike Christians, who believe their salvation is guaranteed on the basis of faith, Gnostics had to individually "earn" their salvation, which is still a teaching of the Ageless Wisdom.

The Gnostic belief was driven underground, resurfacing in various forms throughout the Middle Ages and later. Nearly all the great Christian mystics had recognizable traces of Gnostic ideas in their beliefs. They had much in common with the thinkers and philosophers of their time.[20] When Gnostics express what they believe to be the truth, they speak with the authority of the human spirit, which is probably why the Gnostic world view could not be wiped out in spite of many centuries of persecution.[21] As with all leading-edge minds, they suffered from a lack of receptivity by the masses — not much has changed!

Gnostics hold that the world is flawed because it was created flawed. Gnosticism begins with the fundamental premise that life on earth is filled with suffering. The ancient Greeks counseled people to look to the harmony of the universe so that by admiring its grandeur they might forget their immediate burdens. But Gnostics see little value in this harmony because it still contains the cruel flaws and alienation of existence. Moreover, the Eastern idea of Karma is regarded as evidence of creation's imperfection and suffering but it only explains how the chain of suffering and imperfection works, not why such a sorrowful and destructive system exists. More on Karma later.

Let's take a look at how Gnostic duality plays out in man. Human nature mirrors this duality, containing a perishable physical and psychic component as well as a spiritual component — a fragment of the "divine spark." Death releases the divine spark, but if the soul has not done sufficient work toward Gnosis — knowledge of God and spiritual truth — the divine spark will be hurled back and re-embodied within the slavery of the physical world. As old as Gnosticism is, it qualifies as New Age!

So, those who do not attain a liberating Gnosis while here on earth will be trapped in that existence once more, through a cycle of rebirths. While Gnosticism doesn't emphasize reincarnation, it is implied that those who have not made effective contact with their transcendental origins while on earth will have to return to these sorrowful conditions. It's the "You're coming back and doing it again until you get it right" club!

Elements of Gnosticism live on today in the drive for discovering what we don't yet know.

Kabbalah

Kabbalah — also spelled Qabalah, Cabala, Qaballah, Kaballah, Kabala — is Hebrew for "that which is received" and refers to oral teachings passed from teacher to student. Kabbalah intrinsically contains mystic application of geometry, numbers, and links between the worlds of Kabbalah that develops a definitive philosophy enabling better understanding of existence and its relationship to any other existence on many levels.

It is an element of Jewish mysticism dealing with assumptions on the nature of divinity, creation, the fate of the soul, and the role humans play in the unfolding of the universe. Regarded as an esoteric offshoot of Judaism, it is a compilation of devotional, meditative and mystical practices revealed to a select few. The term "Kabbalah" was first applied to secret mystical teachings in the eleventh century by Iba Gabriol, a Spanish philosopher, and has since been synonymous with all Jewish mystical practice.[22]

Many of the principles and ideas found in the Kabbalah parallel Gnosticism, probably because both developed in the Eastern Mediterranean near the time of Christ. Both hold that important knowledge — *Gnosis*, the knowledge of God — comes not from rational thinking, but is inspired by God. Sin is regarded by both as ignorance that separates man from God.

The Kabbalistic idea that God embodies all ideas and their contradictions forms the basis for the magical laws of polarity and synthesis. Both laws are based on the assumption that all ideas and concepts contain an opposite essence, such as up and down or black and white. The law of synthesis holds that opposing or conflicting ideas will produce a new, third idea that will not be a compromise of the original two.[23]

Jewish tradition holds that when Moses received the written law from God, he also was given the oral law, the Kabbalah. As the divine Torah was studied, a secret oral tradition also arose, claiming to possess an initiated understanding of the Torah's hidden meanings and of divine powers hidden within its text. It is believed that by studying the text, one can unlock the mysteries of creation.

Jewish religion also established the influence of prophets, held to be chosen by God as his spokespersons on Kabbalah. God was seen as approachable, albeit with great fear and trembling. Practical techniques for approach were handed down from the time of the Biblical prophets, to better facilitate this communication. Studying the Torah and making rational efforts to approach God form the foundation for Kabbalistic development.[24]

The Kabbalistic *Sefer Yetzirah* or *Book of Creation* was written perhaps as early as the third century AD by Rabbi Akiba, although oral versions are said to date back to Abraham or before. The book is the framework for Kaballah, and relates God's creation of our earth by means of thirty two secret paths, ten *sephirots* — emanations that formed the cosmos — and the twenty-two characters in the Hebrew alphabet. It should be noted that Kabbalah places importance on the numerical value of letters and words, on the first and last letters of words, and on combinations of letters.[25] The sephirots, each depicting a certain aspect of God, together form The Tree of Life, a central image of Kabbalistic meditation. The tree also portrays the path the divine spirit descended into the material world as well as the path mankind must take to ascend to God.

Many differing portrayals of the Tree of Life are available, some pieces of genuine artwork, depicting the emanations or sephirots and their key roles. The first nine sephirots form three triangles with the tenth creating the foundation or base. The first triangle represents the creation impregnation of the female by the male creating the world and child, the second the development of the world and child, while the third is the adult or finished product of the world. The triangles also symbolize the human body, the first triangle is the head, the second is the torso and arms, and the third is the reproductive organs and legs — an analogy of the relation between man and God.

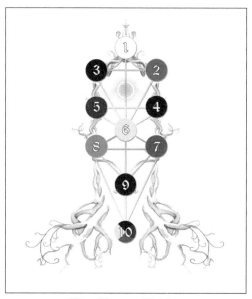

The Tree of Life [26]

The numbered sephirots above are the following:

1. Kether   Supreme Crown
2. Chokmah   Wisdom
3. Binah   Understanding
4. Chesed   Mercy, Greatness
5. Geburah   Strength, Rigor
6. Tiphareth   Beauty, Harmony
7. Netzach   Victory, Force
8. Hod   Splendor
9. Yesod   Foundation
10. Malkuth   Kingdom

Classical Kabbalah began in Provence, France in the thirteenth century and flourished in medieval Spain. While it contains elements of Gnosticism and Neo-Platonism, it's more focused on the nature and structure of all creation.

The Zohar, or Book of Splendor, was written between 1280 and 1286 by Spaniard Moses de Leon. It is considered the most important work of this period — generating the written word based on the lore of a second century rabbi, Simeon bar Yohai. The premise is ten *sefirot* emanating from the *en sof* — "ineffable infinite" — from which the universe was created and is maintained. The third important text, *The Bahir,* appeared in France around the eleventh century.

The nineteenth and twentieth centuries have seen further development of the Western Kabbalah from occultists. Links between the Kabbalah and many other philosophical, mythological and religious systems have been suggested and detailed, the most significant between the Kabbalah, astrology, and the Tarot.[27]

So, although the Kabbalah finds its origins in the Torah, it is not an intellectual discipline. It's held that mystics are not to practice it in solitude but use it to enlighten humanity. Accordingly, the Kabbalist seeks a union with God while maintaining a family, social, and communal life structured around Judaism.

The study of Kabbalah — gaining knowledge of God and all existence — can be a life's work; and it is for many. It can be used by anyone, regardless of religion or creed, to control the subtle forces around themselves and attain a true mystical union with those powers.

Theosophy

Theosophy is a combination of two words, theology and philosophy. It seems to be an appropriate word for combining religious doctrine and applied thought to a belief system. The term Theosophy, according to Helena Petrovna "Madame" Blavatsky in her book *The Key*, means "Divine Wisdom." Theosophy is thousands of years old, and comes from Alexandrian philosophers called "lovers of truth." It's a synthesis of science, religion, and philosophy, its credo being "There is no religion higher than Truth." The goal is to reconcile all religions, sects, and nations under a common system of ethics based on the eternal truths.

The Theosophical Society adopted the great moral truths inherent in the secret teachings as well as their credo in the late 1800s.[28] Genuinely a New Age belief system, Theosophy presents itself as a spiritual and cosmological system seeking to explain the Cosmos and man's role in it.

Madame Blavatsky is the recognized founder of Theosophy, formalizing its framework through her teachings. Other key figures in the popularization of Theosophy in the West in the twentieth century are Alice Bailey, who studied under a Tibetan teacher, Djwhal Khul, and Annie Besant. In Besant's writings in the 1930s and 1940s, Alice Bailey depicts our universe as a vast living being containing countless other life forms, all evolving towards higher states of consciousness.

Ancient Wisdom — whether overtly in Egypt, Greece, and perhaps the yet to be found Atlantis, or covertly in the Middle Ages among alchemists, Rosicrucians, and Freemasons — has always existed and sought to be understood by both initiates and contemporary society at large. Today, Theosophy is explained as an ever-expanding science originating in the cosmic mind of God, who can be represented by myriads of beings on many different planes of existence as well as varying levels of consciousness.

Theosophists believe in a Great Plan, which involves the entire cosmos. Here on earth, the Plan plays out via "Earth's Spiritual Hierarchy," also known as the "Great White Brotherhood." In the Great White Brotherhood, "White" is not a racial reference, but refers to the aura or halo of "the White Light of the Christ" that surrounds the saints and sages from every nation who have transcended the cycles of karma and rebirth and have ascended to a higher reality.[29]

This hierarchy is comprised of perfected men and women who have finished the cycles of reincarnation and have mastered their human and spiritual nature and the forces of three lower worlds: the physical, the emotional, and the mental. They express perfected love and wisdom and have chosen to remain on Earth to serve humanity's growth.[30]

A number of the Hierarchy are easily recognized. Buddha founded Buddhism. Master Jesus incarnated into Palestine and is credited for anchoring unconditional love in the world providing the basis for Christianity. Koot Humi incarnated as Pythagoras, one of the great teachers of Greece, and later as Francis of Assisi, a Saint in the Catholic Church.

Theosophy seeks to show the similarities in the world's religions knowing that all religions are given from the Hierarchy as teachings to humanity. The religions express the same divine truths at their core; as much as humanity is ready to assimilate at that moment. For instance, Gautama Buddha showed humanity how to gain freedom from desire by changing it to aspiration for wisdom and understanding. Jesus Christ taught us about the importance of love, forgiveness, and compassion as a way to gain peace in the world and reach the Kingdom of God.

There is the propensity toward the concept that the God of all religions is the same. In turn, the goal of all religions is also the same: to establish love and brotherhood on earth. Over the past 2000 years, we can see the effects of suffering and the progress made by humanity as strong spiritual energies flow to the planet.

Theosophy describes in great detail a number of universal laws such as the Law of Reincarnation, the Law of Evolution, and the Law of Karma. These laws govern our personal lives as well as the cosmic laws such as the Law of Love, the Law of Mercy, the Law of Periodicity, and the Law of Contrasts. Each of these bear further research and discussion, if you're interested, but for now, simply know they are contained in Theosophy's framework.

Another important facet of theosophical teaching is the Seven Rays. These are said to be divine intelligences or energies which permeate the solar system, emanating from the seven stars of Ursa Major, the Great Bear, and going to the seven stars in the Pleiades, the Seven Sisters. It is said that all living beings within this solar system are characterized by one or more of these rays.[31]

We'll delve into explanations of reincarnation as well as the Seven Rays in just a moment, but you should know that the evolution of Theosophy contains many vast concepts of energy and existence in our universe. It's an attempt to codify and elucidate notions that comprise our existence. It satisfies the scientific demand for hypothesis and proof, provides the basis for religious belief based on empirical love and a oneness with God. It also affords a platform for thought and formulating a belief system that withstands the challenge of humanity's thought process.

Reincarnation

The concept of reincarnation probably dates beyond antiquity, but it's the Egyptians where we first see evidence of a belief in reincarnation. They believed that the soul energy lived on beyond physical death and went to the next world or life.

Pythagoras, the Greek philosopher and mathematician, taught that the soul was immortal and only resided in the body, enabling it to survive bodily death. He expanded on that concept and held that a series of rebirths occurs with the soul resting and purifying itself between death and rebirth.

Plato, another Greek philosopher, shared Pythagoras' view that man's soul was eternal, pre-existent, and wholly spiritual. But he held a different view of the progress during a lifetime. Plato believed that souls became impure during a body's lifetime with little former life knowledge and if the body does "good" and eliminates impurities, it will eventually return to its pre-existent state. However, if the soul deteriorates during its bodily cohabitation, it will end up in a place of eternal damnation. This could be the origin of both the concept of *karma* and the Christian concept of Hell.

Both Greek and Roman scholars were surprised by the fact that Druids, the priestly caste of the Celts, believed in reincarnation. This probably contributed to the fact noted by Julius Caesar that the Celts were formidable warriors, absolutely unafraid of death.

There is little evidence of reincarnation among the early Hebrew people but it later became part of Kabbalistic teaching. Interestingly, the Bible quotes Christ's early followers as asking him if he "was Elijah who had come before."[32] The Gnostics believed in reincarnation, and even the Christian Saint Gregory, Bishop of Nyssa, is quoted as saying, "It is absolutely necessary that the soul shall be healed and purified, and if it doesn't take place in one life on earth, it must be accomplished in future earthly lives."

Such teachings were later repudiated by mainstream Christianity: in 533 AD reincarnation was declared a heresy by the Council of Constantinople. This stance was based on the teachings about death and judgment in orthodox Christian doctrine, which declare that man has just one life in which to merit either eternal reward or damnation. There are those who believe such a doctrine strengthened the Church and its hold on its membership.

Western belief surrounding reincarnation revolves around man reincarnates to higher spiritual levels of life. If a higher level isn't attained, then man must repeat the cycle until he does.

Karma

Karma is a Sanskrit word roughly meaning act or deed. In several eastern religions, it comprises the entire cycle of *cause and effect*. Karma is the sum of all an individual has done and is currently doing. Those deeds affect present and future experiences, and ultimately make one responsible for their own life. When the concept of reincarnation is incorporated, karma extends throughout past, present, and future lives.

Karma is innate to India; The Law of Karma is central to Hinduism, Sikhism, Buddhism, and Jainism, all of which were formed in India. There are a few variations, based on religion or theology:

• *Hinduism*
Karma is not fate, because man has free will to create his own destiny. According to the Vedas, if we sow goodness or evil, so shall we reap. Karma is the totality of our actions and their respective reactions in this and previous lives, all determining our future. Karma doesn't return immediately but may accumulate and return unexpectedly in this or other lives.

Karma is not punishment or retribution, simply an extended expression of natural acts. Karma is not only personal, but extends to societal groups like nations and their people.

• *Buddhism*
While the Law of Karma is cause and effect, only intentional actions are karmic. Its effect can also influence an action, thereby the chain of causation continues *ad infinitum.*

Karma comes in two flavors: good and bad. Good leads to positive and pleasurable experiences while bad leads to suffering and low rebirth, perhaps in Hell or as an animal.

There is also a liberating karma, neither good nor bad. It allows an individual to break an uncontrolled cycle of rebirth leading to suffering. To generate liberating karma, one must develop powerful concentration through an ethical self discipline.

• *Theosophy*
The idea of karma was popularized through the work of the Theosophical Society. They also promote a metaphysical concept called omni-karma, which concerns the "omniverse," a space that contains all of the universes. Omni-karma includes concepts such as souls, psychic

energy, synchronicity — the concept that when things happen at the same time, they are related — and premises from quantum and theoretical physics. Karma here isn't about good and evil deeds, but about positive and negative energies: being creative and solving problems is positive; sadness and fear are negative.

• *Western Interpretations*
While karma per se is not a component of western religions, a spiritual person ultimately believes that virtue is rewarded and sin creates suffering; this belief can lead them to a belief in karma.

New Age thinking sometimes flippantly equates karma with good or bad luck. However, bad luck doesn't necessarily evolve from one's own karma; some of it may stem from someone else's karma, or collective karma, as when a person dies in a war or a car accident.

The basic ethical purpose of karma is to behave and act responsibly. Good deeds bring good, bad deeds are destined to bring bad. Karma isn't salvation, but it does serve a purpose in the concept of God's relation to good works, such as in Christianity or any other religion that has an omnipotent judge.[33]

So what goes around, comes around. Karma appears to be the cumulative burden of good and bad deeds that each of us carry with us — what we sometimes refer to as baggage. And if you believe in reincarnation, you could be bringing some heavy-duty stuff into this life that you have to rectify. All of us could be better, so we must strive to make the good outweigh the bad. A good start is to help others!

The Seven Rays

The Tibetan Master Djwhal Khul is our primary source of information on the Rays, through the writings of Theosophist Alice Bailey. The Seven Rays deal with components of the universe and its influence on one's character, potential, and development. As described earlier in this chapter, energies emanating from Ursa Major and the Pleiades are believed to permeate our solar system, with the result that every living thing is comprised of one or more of the Seven Rays. Given the possible permutations of combining seven rays in the physical/etheric body, the astral body, and mental body, each having its own mix of Seven Rays, every individual is unique.

Until the last century, the Seven Ray system was known and taught only to a limited few disciples and scholars of Ageless Wisdom. Much of the doctrine of the Seven Rays is contained in all the great philosophies and religions, but it's not been freely revealed or discussed.

Why? The rationale can be captured by the phrase, "When the student is ready, the teacher will appear." As the world speeds toward the future at an accelerating pace, it appears that humanity is on the threshold of a great awakening.

The doctrine of the Seven Rays is clearly linked to astrology, which historically progressed in two arenas: *exoteric*, which is available for the general public; and *esoteric*, which is understandable by only an enlightened inner circle. The Rays have been largely hidden from the world, available only through esoteric teachings.

So, the once-secret Rays are revealed and nuances taught through Alice Bailey's books based on the Tibetan Master's words. Djwhal Khul says a ray is the name for a particular discreet force or type of energy with emphasis on the quality that force exhibits, but not on the form which it creates. So it doesn't affect the form as much as it affects the form's behavior. It's not how you look, it's how you act!

In tune with modern physics, which states that everything is energy, the Seven-Rays hypothesis holds that all energy within a form is septenate or comprised of seven discrete archetypal streams. Those seven streams are considered the vibrations within matter, space, and form that define all objects, beings, and events in their manifestation, or the way they appear. They combine and interweave to create all the complex systems we know as reality. Their influence is found within the grandest interstellar spectacle and the minutest mundane occurrence. The Rays strike a chord in our consciousness that is closer to us than breath, yet as elusive as the cosmos. To understand the Rays is a great challenge.

The challenge is demonstrated by the fact that, as we are able to comprehend today, these seven primordial energies are beyond exact depiction in words.[34] Describing these energies in our own mind is similar to being able to see only a narrow band of light — visible light — in the entire spectrum of light; we know there's more there, but we can't see, touch, or easily feel it.

So the teachers of the Seven Rays have developed a depiction — different from a definition! — of each of the Seven Rays. As with everything in our universe, there are pluses and minuses, or as Phillip Lindsay, a student and teacher of Ageless Wisdom and Esoteric Astrology, calls them, virtues and vices. Each energy can cause a positive or negative action, because, after all, we do have free will. And as is the case with most science-based writings, there is a structure and a category for the energies described.

So what are the Seven Rays? Let's list a few of their virtues and vices:

Virtues	Vices
One: *Will/Power*	
Strong, Courageous,	Ruthless, Cold,
Large-Minded, Truthful	Arrogant, Cruel
Two: *Love/Wisdom*	
Calm, Enduring,	Fearful, Indifferent,
Patient, Serene	Love of Being Loved
Three: *Active Intelligence*	
Intellectual, Sincere,	Devious, Obstinate,
Cautious, a Planner	Critical, Inaccurate
Four: *Harmony through Conflict*	
Affectionate, Devoted,	Self-Centered, Moody,
Generous, Sympathetic	Extravagant, Cowardly

Five: *Concrete Science*

Accurate, Perseveres,   Narrow, Harsh, Proud,
Rational, Upright   Lacks Sympathy

Six: *Devotion/Idealism*

Tender, Loyal, Loving,   Selfish, Jealous,
Intuitive, Reverent   Fanatical, Deceptive

Seven: *Ceremonial Order/Magic*

Detailed, Courteous,   Bigoted, Opinionated,
Practical, Strong.   Judges Superficially

And as you would guess, many jobs and careers can align with the Rays. Here is a list of occupations that might be attractive to a specific Ray.

Ray One   Leaders, Executives, Managers, Explorers, Dictators

Ray Two   Teachers, Scholars, Philanthropists, Healers, Servers, Humanists

Ray Three Philosophers, Economists, Historians, Business People, Mathematicians, Astrologers

Ray Four   Artists, Architects, Psychologists, Musicians, Mediators, Poets

Ray Five   Scientists, Researchers, Engineers, Analysts, Inventors

Ray Six   Ministers, Missionaries, Orators, Crusaders, Zealots, Mystics

Ray Seven Builders, Administrators, Designers, Magicians, Revolutionaries.[35]

The Ray teaching purports to give us an energy picture of creation and life at all levels of being. It provides an explanation of the interrelationship of all things material and spiritual, ultimately claiming a "oneness" of everything in the universe. These ray energies provide a practical understanding in the psychological framework of individuals, groups, and even countries. The premise of inherent impulse, the immediate need, and the prescribed path of evolution of beings toward their creator provides a compelling path to understanding our universe.[36]

Followers, students, teachers, and masters see the Seven Rays as an interpretation of our universe, its creator, and the hierarchy of evolving laws governing our world, the people around us, and ultimately ourselves. It provides structure, it offers explanation, requires an open mind, and delivers new horizons.

The Seven Rays, Theosophy, and the concepts of karma and reincarnation are difficult to understand at any level, but worth the effort even if you reject all of the premises they offer. The study of these concepts and philosophies will make you more firm in your personal belief system, enable you to see what the New Age has to offer, and perhaps even open a door of further learning.

But understanding is hard. It was easier for me to pick up a calculus book in sixth grade and make sense of that than to grasp the totality of the Seven Rays. It's hard — to get the concept, to get the terms straight, and to see application in everyday life. It's hard, just really hard!

My personal exposure to the Seven Rays began in 1998, and since then I've been diligently trying to glean all I can from discussions with some very smart people. I started to read the Alice Bailey books, and while I'm an avid reader for pleasure, for news, and for education, I struggled with the language structure, the disjointed material, and all the stuff you were supposed to know before you tried to read the book. Her books are not dissimilar to a simultaneous equation; you need information from another source to get to the answer. In this case, you have to know or read another book or passage to get the gist of what she, or in reality, what Djwhal Khul has to say. Sadly, I didn't last very long as an Alice Bailey reader.

But I was intrigued by concepts that innately made a lot of sense to me. I appreciated the conversations with a number of people, especially Glenda Christian. She knows this stuff at its core; she's been doing it, teaching it, and writing about it since she was very young. My conversations usually started out with a question, her answer, my asking for a definition of a phrase she'd use, then another question about how that fit with the concept. What I found was that we could have the conversation with her speaking "Esoteric," then I'd mull it over for a few days, then I'd get back and say it back to her in my plain English, and she'd say, "Ok, that's pretty close, but did you know…" She knows how to carry on a conversation; ours has lasted for more than ten years!

Michael Robbins is a preeminent teacher, if not a master, of the Seven Rays and its teachings. He's written a number of books on the topic, his most popular is perhaps his *Tapestry of the Gods* volumes where he outlines the Ray energies and interprets Bailey's books and the Masters concepts.

He's literally amazing in his grasp and recall of the teachings. During a conversation, he'll cite a passage explaining a question on the text we're studying, then jump onto his computer, and pull up the section of the book he cited and go right to the passage, confirming a verbatim recollection of the text. Now folks, this is impressive all by itself, but when you factor in the complexity of the content, it blows me away. But, unlike most academics, he has a knack for putting complex ideas or phrases into laymen's language and he makes sure you understand what he's trying to say. He's an incredible teacher!

But the most amazing is sweet wife Diane. Did she write this stuff? She rarely talks about it, always alludes to its concepts, can answer almost any question about the Hierarchy, the Rays, and any other esoteric topic, but when you ask her to explain the purpose, she can give you an immediate application to everyday life. As she says, "I'm not a saint, but I'm working on it." She knows this stuff cold and quickly identifies cogent remedies and their rationale for those around her, as she so cryptically says, "I'm trying to help you evolve!"

I knew little of metaphysics when I met Diane, nothing of the Seven Rays, and saw little beyond coincidence when predicted events occurred. As I understand more, I see how one or all of the things I experience has application to understanding the cosmos and moving closer to ones own God. Powerful stuff!

I don't fully understand all of the concepts of the Seven Rays, much less have a practical application for them, but it is intriguing. So much so, that I relish talking to those that do know to gain these esoteric "secrets" that I find interesting, so many people have heard of, and may even be studying. This is clearly one of those topics you should at least look into; what could it hurt? And the amazing thing is, some of it actually may be in your belief system already and it may make more sense than ever before!

Chapter 4 Endnotes

[1] Bennett, Charles, *Age of the Universe*
[2] Hawking, Stephen, *Big Bang Theory*
[3] Orgel, Leslie E., *The Origin of Life on Earth*
[4] Anonymous, *Natural Selection*
[5] op. cit., *The Origin of Life on Earth*
[6] New King James Version, The Holy Bible, *Genesis, Ch. 1*
[7] Wikimedia Foundation, *Paganism*
[8] Wikimedia Foundation, *Deva (Hinduism)*
[9] Hefner, Alan G., *Devas*
[10] Findhorn Foundation, *Who are we?*
[11] Christian, Glenda, *Devas*
[12] Edwards, Dean, *Shamanism General Overview*
[13] Crystal, Ellie, *Wicca*
[14] ibid., *Wicca*
[15] Spirit Online, *Wicca*
[16] Hefner, Alan G., *Druidism*
[17] Madison, Jake, *Egyptian Gods*
[18] Xavr, *Greek Mythology*
[19] Centurion, *Roman Gods*
[20] Oosterwijk, Hugo, *Gnosticism and Christianity*
[21] Hoeller, Stephan A., *The Gnostic World View*
[22] Hefner, Alan G., *Kabbalah*
[23] Mills, Robert, *Kabbalah*
[24] Low, Colin, *Kabbalah FAQ*
[25] Mills, Robert, *An Introduction to Kabbalah*
[26] Mills, Robert, *Byzant Kabbalah*
[27] op. cit., *An Introduction to Kabbalah*
[28] Christian, Glenda, *Theosophy*
[29] Unknown, *Great White Brotherhood*
[30] Unknown, *Theosophy – A Synthesis of Science, Religion and Philosophy*
[31] ibid, *Theosophy – A Synthesis of Science, Religion and Philosophy*
[32] Hefner, Alan G., *Reincarnation*
[33] Wikimedia Foundation, *Karma*
[34] RLP, *The Seven Rays*
[35] Lindsay, Phillip, *Soul Cycles of the Seven Rays*
[36] op. cit., *The Seven Rays*

CHAPTER 5

THE NEW AGE

We've heard the term New Age for years. I heard it when I was young, songs like *The Age of Aquarius* by the Fifth Dimension, impressing on me that a new age was dawning. Well, I'm older now and we're still talking New Age. That bears a bit of explanation, don't you think?

Speaking in astrological terms, this transition to a new age is symbolized, from Earth's vantage point, by our sun moving through Pisces for the last 2000 years. That's called an astrological age — in this case, the Piscean Age. We'll cover astrology later, but for now, just know that we are in fact moving to a dawning of the Age of Aquarius.

According to my research, the Age of Aquarius begins in 2117 AD, so we might be a bit early on the dawn. So it's like 4 am. If you've been out all night, it's time to go home; if you're a working stiff, it's time to think about getting up, and if you're the privileged elite, continue your beauty sleep. Maybe that's why the meek will inherit the earth — which I don't believe for a minute; too many pushy types around to let them have it! — everyone else is sleeping or partying. Only the proletariat is left to improve our world!

So what exactly is an astrological age? It's the period of time which the Vernal Equinox Point — the point where the sun crosses the Celestial Equator, heading northward as seen from Earth — can be found in a particular constellation of stars.[1]

But it's not just the astrological position of Earth as we move through the heavens. The definition of New Age is quite liberal and embraces not only the astrology of the times, but the societal and religious changes that are occurring. Loosely speaking, the New Age is a recent, developing belief system in North America that encompasses numerous and sometimes contradictory beliefs, organizations, and events.

Generally, New Age theology stems from pantheistic Eastern religions and its practices have evolved from nineteenth century Western occultism. New Age is typically an umbrella label used to describe organizations which exhibit one or more of the following beliefs:

1. All reality is part of the whole;
2. Everything is God and God is everything;
3. Man is God or a part of God;
4. Man never dies but continues to live through reincarnation; and
5. Man can create his own reality and values through transformed or altered states of consciousness.[2]

These tenets seem to run through most New Age thinking and are the targets of religious evaluations rejecting the validity of some or all of these beliefs. There seems to be an attempt to align the religious beliefs with science and that seems to rub the religious leaders the wrong way. Perhaps both sides merit more research and study to draw your own conclusions.

The New Age movement is hardly new, since its philosophy rooted in ancient traditions often based on mystical experiences. Medicine men and Shamans were contacts used by their clans or tribes to maintain contact with the spirit world. Esoteric traditions transitioned to spiritual groups, communes, or fraternities and it became difficult for them to reconcile their beliefs with the churches. Extreme caution became the watchword and those that slipped were accused of heresy and suffered increasingly aggressive consequences from God-fearing populations.

As these mystic traditions experienced a renaissance, their religious, spiritual, and magical traditions became more accepted, then popularized in the 1960's.[3]

While Madame Blavatsky is recognized as the founder of

Theosophy, she is also credited with beginning New Age thinking, extrapolated perhaps from the coming new Age of Aquarius. Today, many spiritual people are included in the somewhat nebulous New-Age classification along with traditional mystics, magicians, and occultists.

So meditate, grab a crystal, and do a little yoga; you too, might be called a New Ager! None of it could hurt, and you might just open a new door for yourself.

Gurus

Guru is an overused word in our society, generally referring to one who has expert knowledge, is available for questions, and provides direction. Wouldn't it be nice if there were gurus at the help desks we call for our computer problems?

But here, we're referring to the guru that's a sacred conduit to self realization, usually among the Hindu, Buddhist, or Sikh belief systems. Guru is a Sanskrit word meaning a sacred place and imparter of knowledge.

In Hinduism, the guru is a respected person with saintly attributes who enlightens his or her disciples, imparting initiation mantras and giving instruction in rituals and religious ceremonies. In Indian culture, one who didn't have a guru was once looked down on as being an orphan, clearly a misfortune.

In the different sects in Buddhism, a guru can be the embodiment of Buddha, a valued and worthy mentor, and one who is essential for initiation. According to the Dalai Lama — in Tibetan, lama means guru — one should "Rely on the teachings to evaluate a guru: Do not have blind faith, but also no blind criticism."

In Sikhism, the guru is fundamental to the religion. The core beliefs of Sikhism are the belief in one God and in the teachings of the Ten Gurus enshrined in the Sikh holy book *Guru Granth Sahib.* The Ten Gurus received their "guruships" between 1469 and 1675 AD.

In contemporary India and Indonesia, guru is widely used to mean "teacher." In Western usage, the original term has been extended to refer to anyone who acquires followers, though not necessarily in any established school of philosophy or religion. The importance between a true guru and a "guru wannabe" is explored in scriptures and teachings.

Particularly in the 1960s and 1970s, many gurus acquired followers in both Western Europe and North America. It's been suggested that a major motivation may have been as an alternative to the drug culture, which had opened up transcendental experiences to them. It has also been posed that some anti-Viet-Nam-war protestors became disillusioned with changing society through politics and so turned to religion.[4] Could've happened!

Many gurus came to America during this time, making guru a household word. Some came and went quickly amidst controversy, but many settled into the American landscape introducing Hindu temples, propagating the value of meditation, and yoga. Ashrams around the country continue to provide teaching forums, spiritual opportunities, and solace to many seeking higher truths. They appear to be all about service to one's fellow man, making this world a better place, and helping individuals find or improve their place in society.

Among the first to arrive was the Maharishi Mahesh Yogi who became the guru of the Beatles and started the Students International Meditation Society in 1965. He popularized a meditation discipline he called TM, Transcendental Meditation, defining it as scientific and universal.

In 1965, Swami A.C. Bhaktivedanta Prabhupada arrived penniless in New York City, instructed to do so by his teacher in India. In Tompkins Square Park, he began chanting "Hare Krishna, Hare Rama" and within a few months opened a storefront temple on Second Avenue, the first Krishna temple of the International Society for Krishna Consciousness. The movement became know as Hare Krishna for its public chanting of Krishna's name.

Some Americans actually became gurus in the 1970s. Richard Alpert, a psychology professor at Harvard found his guru, Neem Karoli Baba, in the Himalayas and became Ram

Dass. He became a teacher, drawing on Hindu and Buddhist dharma to articulate teaching service. Joyce Green, a Jewish Housewife in Brooklyn, became Ma Jaya Sati Bhagaviti and is the spiritual teacher of Kashi Ashram in Florida. She teaches service, especially to those living and dying with AIDS.

Despite sometimes controversial histories, many Hindu teachers have attracted a following in the U.S. No one teacher or guru is responsible for yoga, meditation, and the Hindu "turn of mind" in America today.[5] Ashrams around the country provide teaching forums, spiritual opportunities, and solace to many seeking higher truths. They appear to be all about service to your fellow man, making this world a better place, and helping individuals find or improve their place in society. Not all bad!

Sri Swami Satchidananda had a more lasting impact than many. Ordained a monk in 1949, he founded the worldwide Integral Yoga® Institutes, teaching Hatha yoga, selfless service, meditation, prayer, and a 5,000-year-old philosophy that helps one find inner peace and joy. In 1969, he spoke at the Woodstock festival in Bethel, New York, urging peace and harmony for all. In 1979, he established the Satchidananda Ashram in Yogaville, near Buckingham, Virginia. He was presented the Juliet Hollister Interfaith Award at the United Nations in 1994. At the beginning of the New Millennium, he led the opening prayer for world peace to begin the United Nations new session and in 2002, he was presented the U Thant Peace Award.

Swami Satchidananda spent his life trying to bring all religions to see their common bond, and taught interfaith harmony. His physical body left this world on August 19, 2002, clearly leaving it a better place because of his presence.[6] His ashram at Yogaville is the home of the Light Of Truth Universal Shrine — LOTUS — an interfaith shrine that exemplifies the unity points of all world religions and celebrates their diversity. There, anyone of any faith or background can come to realize their essential "oneness."

Light Of The Universal Shrine (LOTUS) [7]

Swami Satchidananda, known to friends as Gurudev, is the only guru I've met personally, and he's had a profound effect on me. He was a witty, fun-loving, intellectually deep thinker who had a knack for simplifying any issue, and challenging you with a single question. That question could cause you days of introspection before you were satisfied you understood. Everything he said was a simple statement, but its dual meaning had the broadest implication for harmony and peace in our world today.

I was amazed when I found he *never* read. He appeared well-read because he could talk intelligently on just about any topic. He kept up with current affairs and truly enjoyed the latest technology. Apparently he was tapped into the Universal Wisdom, and kept current only through talking with others.

With his wonderful sense of humor, he would joke, "I don't read, I don't write, and I don't even think!"

Diane introduced me to Gurudev in 1998 and I was amazed at the feeling of having met him before. He initiated me and gave me my mantra in a private meeting on that visit. I genuinely had *fun* when I visited with him. He relished showing Diane and me around the grounds, pointing out additions since the last time we were there. He was always jovial and his wry sense of humor could keep up with the best of them. His insight was remarkable. He honed in on the crux of issues, cut through the chaff, and offered honest, executable solutions, always in the form of questions. What a talent!

Most impressive is his work that's the central theme of the LOTUS, the shrine that celebrates all religions. He was an amazing man, a guru on a clear path he showed others, and I value all the time I had with him. He focused my world on what is and what can be. His credo was "Truth is One, Paths are Many." Simply interpreted, there is no *right* way, but there is a singular goal: truth. How appropriate!

World Religions

At Gurudev's LOTUS Shrine, there is an "All Faiths Hall." The following overview is based on its exhibits, which show that "God's light" figures in all of today's world religions.

African Faiths

African Faiths have their origin in oral and cultural traditions. Kwanzaa is the time for African families and communities to come together to reaffirm their traditional values. In the traditional faiths of Africa, God is the supreme creator, planner, and procreator — the father and mother of the universe.

While not all ethnic groups follow the same beliefs, there are more similarities than differences. The emphasis is on close relationships with nature, the living, and the dead, all based on love, respect, and ancestral reverence.

There is no distinction between religion and daily life;

there are no specific ancient teachers or sacred texts. The secrets of their life/religion have been passed orally from generation to generation, instructing all to live harmoniously through rituals and practices.

"God is the sun beaming light everywhere."

- Tribal African

Buddhism

Buddhism has ten requisites of Good Behavior; Abstinence from: destroying life, taking what is not given, false speech, adultery, slander, harsh talk, senseless talk, covetousness, malevolence, and heretical views. Lord Buddha says, "My doctrine makes no distinction between high and low, or between rich and poor. It is like the sky. It has room for all; and like the rain it washes all alike."

The primary goal is described as *Nirvana*, defined as the end of change. It literally means "to blow out" as one blows out a candle. The faith gives a practical path to Nirvana and emphasizes experience rather than theory.

Gautama Buddha is the central figure in the faith, born to a royal family in the Himalayan foothills. Living a protected childhood, he renounced his world of comfort and wealth when he became a wandering monk. He practiced severe austerity without finding the answers he sought. Finally, he sat beneath a fig tree resolving to remain there until the Truth was revealed. Enlightenment was attained after seven weeks of meditation.

For the next forty years, the "Awakened One" spread the doctrine of the Four Noble Truths and the Eightfold Path. His teachings advocate a "middle path" between sensual pleasure and mortification of the flesh.

"The radiance of Buddha shines ceaselessly."

- Dhammapada

Christianity

Christianity is based on service, self-sacrifice, and surrender to God. "Love thy neighbor as thyself" sums up the philosophy; belief that Jesus Christ was the Son of God on earth is the basis of its faith.

Jesus was born in Bethlehem in Judea and grew to manhood as the son of a carpenter in Nazareth. His ministry began in earnest with his baptism by John the Baptist in the River Jordan. During the next three years, he traveled throughout Palestine with his twelve disciples and many followers, performing miracles, healing the sick, and teaching "the way, the truth, and the life." Jesus spoke truth without fear despite the ruling powers and ultimately was tried and crucified under Roman Law in Jerusalem. Three days after the death of his physical body, Jesus rose from the grave, appeared to his followers, and ascended to heaven.

Several generations after his crucifixion, the drama and lessons of Jesus' life were recorded in one of history's most influential books, *The Holy Bible*. Therein, the teachings of Jesus stressed forgiveness, love, purity of heart and mind, and the return of good for evil.

In his Sermon on the Mount, Jesus said, "Love your enemies, bless them that curse you, do good unto them that hate you, and pray for them which spitefully use you and persecute you; that ye may be the children of your Father in heaven." Today, many different sects of Christianity worship Jesus and their God throughout the world.

"I have come into the world as Light."
- Holy Bible

Hinduism

Hinduism, also known as *Santana Dharma*, the eternal religion, is rooted in the writings of the *Rig Veda*, perhaps humanity's earliest spiritual text. Ancient *rishis* — seers — heard or saw the four *Vedas* in deep meditation; no individual can be called the "author," the rishis simply discovered them.

Hindus worship the Divine in many ways, but basic to each sect is the principle of unity and the goal of achieving spiritual oneness with the Absolute. True Hinduism is true universalism; the Hindu accepts, even embraces, all paths to Truth.

In the *Bhagavad-Gita*, a core sacred text of Hinduism, we find the tenet "Howsoever people approach me, even do I welcome them; for the paths that they take from every side are mine." Whichever path you take, it leads to the Truth.

Many Hindus follow the ancient teachings of Yoga, the Sanskrit word for "yoke" or "union." Traditionally, the word Yoga refers to Raja Yoga, the science of the mind. There are yogic methods for active, introspective, intellectual, and devotional natures as well as the more commonly known system of physical postures we know in Western society that promote suppleness and dynamic health.

The concept of rebirth is a part of Hindu thought. It is necessary because of our attachment to earthly things, which creates karma. The Hindu concept of karma — the law of action and reaction — is described this way: "As is a person's desire, so is his will; and as his will, so is his deed; and whatever deeds he does, that will he reap."

> *"In the effulgent lotus of the heart dwells*
> *Brahman, the Light of Lights."*
> *- Mundaka Upanishad*

Islam

Islam means "surrender to the will of God." The Muslim religion is based on the unity of God and unity of humanity, since Islam holds all humanity as a vast brotherhood of equal beings with one all-powerful God as its Creator and Master.

God's instrument in creating Islam was the prophet Mohammed, teaching "One God" to galvanize the entire Arab world. As a successful businessman through much of his life, Mohammed was always drawn to meditation, prayer, and fasting. During a pilgrimage to Mount Hira, he was blessed with a vision of the Angel Gabriel and received the divine message that culminated in the holy book of Islam, the *Koran*. Mohammed said, "One's true wealth hereafter is the good one does in this world to his fellow man."

The Koran covers all aspects of life from the great to the small. It deals with the nature of God, his attributes, creative activity, his relationship to humanity, and prophets. Other sacred Islamic books are the *Torah* of Moses, the *Psalms* of David, and the *Gospels* of Jesus.

The mystical branch of Islam is *Sufism*, called the religion of love based on the idea of the devotee as the lover and God as the Beloved. The Sufi mystic experiences cosmic vision by seeing the Beloved everywhere in everything. They seek total unification with God.

"Allah is the Light of the heavens and the earth."
- Holy Koran

Judaism

Judaism evolved thousands of years ago in the desert areas of the Middle East. The plight of this nomadic people settled them in Canaan which they called Israel and their history of how they evolved, became enslaved, and finally delivered by God into the Promised Land is captured in the first five books of the *Old Testament*, called the *Torah*. The Torah also can be seen as a mystical pattern of thought, belief, and deed that is eternal, infinite, and fundamental to life. The Torah was revealed by God to Moses, the foremost of the Hebrew prophets, who led the people from slavery to freedom, and received the Ten Commandments on Mt. Sinai.

Judaism emphasizes maintaining a high personal code of ethics contained in the *Talmud*, a storehouse of traditions, laws, and wisdom gleaned by Jewish sages from the study of the Torah. Judaism has no doctrine of Original Sin nor is it evangelical in nature.

The religion of the Jews is inseparable from their history as a people. Jews believe in one God who is all-powerful and concerned with every individual. Through the wanderings and persecution as a minority in other lands, Jews strengthened their traditions in the face of adversity. Using the family unit as the basis for religious worship, Judaism doesn't create a division between the sacred and the secular worlds. Rather, it asserts that any and all parts of life can and should be made holy.

"The Lord is my Light whom should I fear?

- Psalms

Native American

Native American worship takes place in the cathedral of Nature, frequently in silence. The fruits of silence are thought to be self-control, true courage, endurance, patience, dignity, and reverence.

Through group rituals such as the sweat lodge, the sacred pipe ceremony, powerful chants, and dances, the Native American strives to purify the body, mind, heart, and soul in order to be an honorable and useful member of the tribe. Doing good deeds for one's people is held in the highest honor, exemplified by the words spoken by an old chief to a scout about to seek buffalo in mid-winter for the relief of starving people: "Let neither cold, nor hunger, nor pain, nor fear of them, neither the bristling teeth of danger, nor the very jaws of death itself, prevent you from doing a good deed."

A supreme being is at the core of Native American beliefs, manifested in different ways, dependent on the tribe. Polingaysi Qoyawayme of the Hopi avows "We do not walk alone; Great Being walks beside us. Know this and be grateful." White Wolf of the Crow nation asserts, "Our entire way of life will change — but it will never die, because it is of the spirit. It is a truth, and truth cannot die."

"The Light of Wakan-Tanka is upon my people."

- Song of Kablaya

Shinto

Shinto is the indigenous faith of the Japanese people; the essence of life energy in natural phenomena is deified and worshiped as Kami. Shinto is deeply connected with nature, finding healing and purifying power in mountains, streams, wind, and trees. The four elements of worship are purification, offering, prayer, and symbolic feast. The Shinto goal is to remove the "dust" which hides the divine nature of human beings.

The earliest works of Japan, the *Kojiki* and the *Nihongi*, are rich in information about early Shinto rituals and practices, but are not believed to reveal scripture. Mythology describes the formation of the Japanese Islands as a result of the union of a male and female creator, Izanagi and Izanami. Their daughter, the sun goddess Amaterasu is the central figure in many Japanese shrines including the Grand Shrine of Ise, dedicated to the highest expression of respect for the Imperial family and all that is best in the culture, history, and racial consciousness of the Japanese people.

Purification is central to Shinto, since invisible dross is believed to accumulate as a result of negative thoughts and emotions. This must be removed in the ceremony called *Misogi*, bathing for purification, ideally practiced in a calm ocean facing the sun to realize the individual's own Kami nature.

The mirror also plays an important role; the goddess Amaterasu told humans to worship the mirror which reflects their own image, as if they were worshipping Her in Her presence. The mirror, then, is the symbol of Amaterasu's spirit.

Shinto contains The Ten Precepts, holding followers to not: transgress the will of the gods, forget obligations to ancestors, violate decrees of the state, forget the profound goodness of the gods where calamities and misfortunes are averted and sickness healed, forget that the world is one great family, forget their own limitations, become angry, be sluggish in their work, bring blame to the teaching, or be carried away by foreign teachings.

"The light of Divine Amaterasu shines forever."
- Kurozumi Munetada

Sikhism

Sikhism is a monotheistic religion based on the teachings of ten gurus who lived in northern India during the sixteenth and seventeenth centuries. Today it has over 27 million followers. Sikhism emphasizes the importance of selfless service, devotion, purification, and intense repetition of God's name. The ten great gurus each embody a specific spiritual quality, and each made significant contributions to the Sikh movement.

The first, Guru Nanak, began to teach people in the fifteenth century how to find happiness and peace through repeating the name of God. The second created a language for spiritual understanding, while the third was a proponent of equality regardless of social or economic position. The fourth dug the water tank for what would become the Holy City of Amritsar; the fifth completed the most holy Golden Temple and initiated the holy book *Guru Granth Sahib* by compiling oral sayings, songs, and teachings of the four previous masters.

The last of the ten established the Khalsa Order or Brotherhood of the Pure Ones using a baptism ceremony and the five symbols: white clothes for purity, a sword for bravery, an iron bracelet for morality, uncut hair for renunciation, and a comb for cleanliness. He finished the compilation of the *Guru Granth Sahib* and at the end of his life declared that it was to be considered the Guru from that point forward. This book of song and prayer is sung daily by devout Sikhs.

Human equality is central to Sikh culture and religious practice; Sikhs are opposed to formalism and ritualism. Each Sikh is encouraged to find God in his or her own way using wisdom and common sense as well as the Guru teachings as a guide.

"God, being Truth, is the one Light of all."

- Adi Granth

Taoism

Taoism, originating in China, can be summarized by four lines from Lao Tsu, the best known Tao Master: "Reveal thy simple self. Embrace thy original nature. Check thy selfishness. Curtail thy desires." The Chinese concept of Tao means the unmanifest God from which all things spring as well as the path to union with that force. The central focus of Taoism comes from the constant change created by the interplay of *Yin* and *Yang*, the positive and negative forces of creation.

A Taoist seeks oneness with nature, because by being in tune with change, the individual becomes a quiet spot in the storm of existence. Changes still occur, but they flow through the Taoist as a ripple in water or wind through leaves.

I Ching, The Book of Changes, presents an interconnected system of relationships affecting every aspect of life showing the balance of Yin and Yang, the masculine and feminine polarities in each. The book has been used throughout the ages to "isolate the moment" and to predict the future.

The Master Lao Tsu, whose philosophy accented Wu-Wei, or non-action, wrote only one book, the *Tao Te Ching*. In only 5,000 characters, he presented the paradoxes of life; for example, "Stretch a bow to the limit, and you will wish you had stopped in time." Pithy advice that should be self evident.

The works of Confucius, the *I Ching*, and the *Tao Te Ching* as well as the works of Chuang Tsu, the greatest follower of Lao Tsu, form the backbone of Chinese philosophy. The pure Taoism of Lao Tsu and Chuang Tsu is a very individualistic faith devoid of dogma and ceremony, practiced by mystic hermits and wandering monks. The random nature of Taoism was in part a response to highly structured Confucianism.

"Following the Light, the sage takes care of all."

- Lao Tsu

Other Known Faiths

Other World Faiths have developed over the centuries as well as blossoming in more recent times. Their followers have their own approach to the Absolute One or a Supreme Being; it's important to understand that the same Truth found in one's own religion is reflected in other paths as well.

In the LOTUS' All Faiths Hall there are selected traditions that represent other known faiths. These include the Maori and Ancient Hawaiians of the Pacific Region, Jainism, Zoroastrianism, Baha'i, Confucianism, as well as Integral Yoga. Each has their own focus on God, but all respect the diversity of other religions and the peace and harmony sought by mankind through service, the heart, nature, brotherhood, meditation, purification, and ultimately love.

"Truth is one, Paths are Many."

- Sri Swami Satchidananda

The Secular World

The quest for Truth takes on a myriad of guises. Art, education, social and political ideologies, science, philosophy, psychology, humanity, and the service ethic can all be lifted to higher levels through devotion to any path followed with a pure heart. As with the world's religions, the secular paths are diverse. At their core, however, they partake of humanity's universal desire for true, lasting peace and happiness. Whenever higher good is sought in ourselves and others, the result is greater peace, harmony, and unity.

Great minds have demonstrated faith in our secular world. Here are but a few:

> *Bertrand Russell* – "Mathematics, rightly viewed, possesses not only truth, but a supreme beauty."

> *Joan Miro* – "Art class was like a religious ceremony to me. I would wash my hands carefully before touching paper or pencils. The instruments of work were sacred objects to me."

John Ruskin – "Does a bird need to theorize about building its nest or boast of it when built? All good work is essentially done that way: without hesitation; without difficulty; without boasting."

Martin Luther King, Jr. – "Everybody can be great. Because anybody can serve. . . You only need a heart full of grace, a soul generated by love."

Anne Frank – "In spite of everything I still believe that people are really good at heart... I can feel the suffering of millions and yet, if I look up into the heavens, I think that it will all come right."

Alexander Solzhenitsyn – "Nations are the wealth of mankind, its collective personalities; the very least wears its own special colors and bears with itself a special facet of divine intention."

Marie Montessori – "We discovered that education is not something which the teacher does, but that it is a natural process which develops spontaneously in the human being."

Emma Lazarus – "Give me your tired, your poor, your huddled masses yearning to breathe free, the wretched refuse of your teeming shore, send these the homeless, tempest-tossed to me; I lift my lamp beside the golden door."
                    – Inscribed on the Statue of Liberty

The LOTUS is truly a model for the precept, "Truth is One, Paths are Many."[8] Thanks to Sri Swami Satchidananda and his tireless ministration to mankind, its structures, and most importantly, every individual. The end result could well be peace and harmony!

Angels

Just a brief look at Angels here, whether they're guardian angels, divine messengers, or archangels, if not the kind of "angel" that makes plays happen on Broadway. An angel is described as an ethereal being whose duties are to serve God.

There are numerous references to angels in the Old Testament: the angels Jacob saw on the ladder in Genesis, the angel who prophesized exile in Ezekiel, the angel who warned Lot of the imminent destruction of Sodom, and the visually striking angel in the Book of Daniel, described as "clothed in linen, whose loins were girded with fine gold... his body like a beryl, and his face as the appearance of lightning, and his eyes as lamps of fire... and the voice of his words like the voice of the multitude." The number of angels is enormous. Jacob meets a "host" of them in Genesis, while Revelation reveals the number of angels to be "a thousand thousands, and many tens of thousands." So, if you haven't seen an angel, it's not because they're not out there! Keep your eyes open!

The Bible tells us angels are a medium of God's power; they exist to execute God's will. Angels apparently reveal themselves to individuals as well as entire nations to announce events affecting humans. In the New Testament angels appear frequently as the ministers of God and the agents of revelation. We have good angels like Gabriel and Michael noted in Luke and Daniel, while evil angels like Beelzebub and Satan make their way into Mark, all apparently serving a purpose in God's plan for mankind.

The belief in angels is central to Islam, since the Koran was dictated to Muhammad by the chief of all angels, Jibril — Gabriel. Angels are benevolent beings created from light and having no free will; they serve Allah, or God and carry out his bidding.

Joseph Smith, the Mormon founder of The Church of Jesus Christ of Latter-day Saints, claimed to have been visited by angels on multiple occasions. They were instrumental in restoring the gospel of Jesus Christ to Smith and his followers.[9]

Guardian angels seem to be protectors, coming to the aid

of those who find themselves in peril. A poll in Time magazine revealed that 69% of Americans believe in angels and 46% believe they have a personal guardian angel. There is no scientific evidence of their existence; only anecdotal verification is available from those who have seen them.

Guardian angels are thought to be spiritual beings assigned to assist people on Earth. They appear to interject themselves in perilous situations and inspire thoughts that spur to action, often lending us super-human strength, such as the ability to lift a car long enough to free a trapped child. Some psychics suggest that we all have guardian angels who are willing to communicate with us. They suggest that we must ask for help with a direct question, out loud, and that concise questions get concise answers.

Are guardian angels superstitious folly? We can't prove it either way, but why would you not want help? Ask. It couldn't hurt!

Science and Religion

As mentioned earlier, religion and science are not mutually exclusive. Since the beginning of time, men and later scientists have pursued the same questions: *Where did we come from? What are we made of? What is the meaning of life?*

While the questions seem spiritual, today some of the answers come from science. For instance, men of God study physics to better understand His divine rules. The laws of physics have been called "the canvas God laid down on which to paint His masterpiece." If you carry that back to the beginning of time, it becomes plausible that an all-powerful, omniscient God established the rules of nature we know as physics, and allowed his creation to evolve with those rules governing all physical interactions.[10]

One such clerical scientist was Monsignor Georges Lamaitre, who was fascinated by physics and studied Einstein's Laws of Gravitation, published in 1915. He determined that if Einstein's theories were true, the universe must be expanding. After getting his PhD from MIT in 1927, Lamaitre proposed that the expanding universe was the same in all directions, with the same composition adhering to the same laws, but that it wasn't static. In 1929, Edwin Hubble discovered that galaxies were moving away at high speeds. Lamaitre then postulated that there was once a primordial atom that contained all the matter in the universe. That primordial atom was the origin of the Big Bang.[11]

When Lamaitre first proposed the Big Bang theory, scientists deemed it utterly ridiculous; matter couldn't be created out of nothing. So when Hubble proved the theory, the church claimed victory; the Bible was scientifically accurate! It was the Divine truth.

Scientists immediately attacked the theory with mathematics, distancing it from religious implications. There was only the issue of "singularity" that remained. The exact moment of creation: where did the single atom come from? Lamaitre saw this as evidence of God.

In his fascinating book, *Angels and Demons*, Dan Brown weaves an intriguing web of science and religion into a gripping piece of fiction. He uses scions of science, like Galileo and his contemporaries as the warp and weave of a story where they were forced by religious orders to subvert their findings. They either had to frame them benignly within existing teachings or keep them underground for fear of retribution by the religious leadership of the day. These became the *Illuminati*; a secret society of enlightened ones whose research in the sciences led to discoveries they couldn't bring to the public. Those who chose to do so took on the church and inevitably were forced to flee Rome. They found refuge in another secret society, a brotherhood of wealthy Bavarian stone crafters known as *Freemasons*.

After harboring the fleeing scientists, the Masons unknowingly became a front for the Illuminati, victims of their benevolence. The Illuminati grew within the ranks and gradually attained positions of power within Masonic lodges. They established their scientific brotherhood deep within the Masons — a secret society within a secret society. The brotherhood contended that the dogma ingrained by the church was mankind's greatest enemy: They feared religion, left to its pro-motion of pious myth as absolute fact, would stifle scientific progress. Mankind would then be doomed to an ignorant future of holy wars. Interestingly there seems to be a historic corre-lation between zealous true believers and high body counts!

So, as the story goes, the Illuminati grew more powerful in Europe and targeted America, a fledgling government led by notable Masons like George Washington and Ben Franklin. These were God-fearing men, unaware of the Illuminati's stronghold on the Masons which took advantage of the infil-tration to help found banks, universities, and industry to fi-nance their quest. They saw the creation of a single unified world state — a kind of New World Order based on scientific enlightenment. They called it their Luciferian Doctrine.

The church immediately claimed Lucifer was a reference to Satan, but the brotherhood insisted Lucifer was chosen for its literal Latin meaning, "bringer of light" — thus, Illumina-tor. While the church has continued its tagging the Illuminati as satanic, the brotherhood appears to have died out over the next hundred years.

In his book, Dan Brown contends that:

• Science and religion are not at odds.

• Science is simply too young to understand.

So, science and religion support the same truth: pure en-ergy is the father of creation.

Religion is like language or dress: we tend to adopt prac-tices under which we were raised. Ultimately, though, we all proclaim that life has meaning and we're grateful to the power that created us. This would be an act of faith. As we've seen, faith is not random, it's universal. Our approaches to it are largely based on where on earth we were born. Some of us pray to Jesus, others turn to Mecca, and some of us study subatomic particles. In the end, we are all just searching for truth. The truth that is greater than ourselves.

Interestingly, science tells us God must exist. Our mind tells us we will never understand God. And ultimately, our heart says we aren't meant to.

To best illustrate the paradox of science and religion, let me quote a fairly lengthy piece from Dan Brown's book *Angels and Demons*. His book is fiction, but his comments cogent with the religion vs. science debate. This from a Roman Catholic's point of view:

> "The ancient war between science and religion is over ... You (science) have won by so radically reorienting our society that the truths we once saw as signposts now seem inapplicable. Religion cannot keep up. Scientific growth is exponential. It feeds on itself like a virus. Every new breakthrough opens doors for new breakthroughs. Mankind took thousands of years to progress from the wheel to the car. Yet only decades from the car into space. Now we measure scientific progress in weeks. We are spinning out of control. The rift between us — science and religion — grows deeper and deeper, and as religion is left behind, people find themselves in a spiritual void. We cry out for meaning... We see UFOs, engage in channeling, spirit contact, out-of-body experiences, mind quests — all these eccentric ideas have a scientific veneer, but they are unashamedly irrational. They are the desperate cry of the modern soul, lonely and tormented, crippled by its own enlightenment and its inability to accept meaning in anything removed from technology.

> "Science, you say, will save us. Science, I say, has destroyed us. Since the days of Galileo, the church has tried to slow the relentless march of science, sometimes with misguided means, but always with benevolent intention. Even so, the temptations are too great for man to resist . . . The promises of sci-

ence have not been kept. Promises of effi-
ciency and simplicity have bred nothing but
pollution and chaos. We are a fractured and
frantic species . . . moving down a path of
destruction.

"Who is this God science? Who is the
God who offers his people power but no moral
framework to tell you how to use that power?
What kind of God gives a child *fire* but does
not warn the child of it dangers? The language
of science comes with no signposts about
good and bad. Science textbooks tell us how
to create a nuclear reaction, and yet they contain no chapter asking us if it is a good or a
bad idea.
"To science I say this. The church is tired.
We are exhausted from trying to be your signposts. Our resources are drying up from our
campaign to be the voice of balance as you
plow blindly on in your quest for smaller chips
and larger profits. We ask not why you will
not govern yourselves, but how can you? Your
world moves so fast that if you stop even for
an instant to consider the implications of your
actions, someone more efficient will whip
past you in a blur. So you move on.
"You proliferate weapons of mass destruction, but it is the church who travels the
world beseeching leaders to use restraint. You
clone living creatures, but it is the church re-
minding us to consider the moral implications
of our actions. You encourage people to inter-
act on phones, video screens, and computers,
but it is the church that opens its doors and re-
minds us to commune in person as we were
meant to do. You even murder unborn babies

in the name of research that will save lives. Again, it is the church who points out the fallacy of this reasoning.

"And all the while, you proclaim the church is ignorant. But who is more ignorant? The man who cannot define lightning or the man who does not respect its awesome power?... Show me *proof* there is a God, you say. I say use your telescopes to look to the heavens, and tell me how here could *not* be a God! You ask what does God look like... Do you not see God in your science? How can you miss Him! You proclaim that even the slightest change in the force of gravity or the weight of an atom would have rendered our universe a lifeless mist rather than our magnificent sea of heavenly bodies, and yet you fail to see God's hand in *this*?... Have we become so spiritually bankrupt that we would rather believe in mathematical impossibility than in a power greater than us?

"Whether or not you believe in God, you must believe this. When we as a species abandon our trust in the power greater than us, we abandon our sense of accountability. Faith... *all* faiths... are admonitions that there is something we cannot understand, something to which we are accountable.... With faith we are accountable to each other, to ourselves, and to a higher truth. Religion is flawed, but only because *man* is flawed...

"None of us can afford to be apathetic. Whether you see this evil as Satan, corruption, or immorality . . the dark force is alive and growing every day. Do not ignore it. The force, though mighty, is not invincible. Goodness can prevail. Listen to your hearts. Listen to God. Together we can step back from this abyss."[12]

This is nothing short of brilliant! Here is argument for both sides of the science-religion contest that simply says, "Get a conscience!" Right and wrong doesn't manifest itself in rituals, it is the premise of treating *all* life — plant, animal and human — as the precious being it is. We cannot change the rules of nature and we must respect, if not revere, the power that put them in place. And we mustn't let personal bias cloud doing what's right!

So what about religion? Which one's right? Are any just wrong? My view is that your God is my God. And if you don't believe in God, then whoever or whatever is responsible for creating this universe is pretty close to my God.

Sri Swami Satchidananda's Master, Sri Swami Sivananda compared the different sects of Hinduism to a cantaloupe. He explained that the rind of the melon is divided into various sections, yet when cut open, it reveals the same, sweet, undivided flesh throughout. The analogy holds for my God as well: he or she is the same regardless how differently every individual in this world perceives him or her.

So wouldn't it be wonderful if we could resolve not to fight in the name of religion, at any level? When we realize our different "Gods" are really one and ultimately we are a part of each other, then perhaps we can resolve all our issues. Don't we all wish for the day when we can appreciate each other's differences, realizing they're simply different perspectives on the same Supreme Being?

Whether you believe in a world teacher or Savior with such names as Christ, the Lord Maitreya, the Imam Mahdi, the Bodhisattva, or the Messiah, there is a commonality in our beliefs. There are certain truths which most people innately accept — mainly, that there is a basic intelligence to which we give the name God. And there appears to be a divine evolutionary plan in the universe that revolves around love; a plan can only culminate through humanity's active participation.

Prayers are used by all religions and even by those who

might not believe in God. They're a plea for help or support from a higher authority. It may be as simple as "Oh God, help me," as one sits atop a 2000-pound bull in a rodeo chute, or as complex as the ritual invocations in most religious services. It's a plea to help from a source we believe who can benevolently respond.

While there are many invocations out there, I've personally been impressed by one, because it seems to encompass all my Lutheran, Methodist, and world experience into a simple, straightforward plea for guidance from the highest being I know, my God. Here it is:

The Great Invocation

> *From the point of Light within the Mind of God*
> *Let light stream forth into the minds of men.*
> *Let Light descend on Earth.*
> *From the point of Love within the Heart of God*
> *Let love stream forth into the hearts of men.*
> *May Christ return to Earth.*
>
> *From the centre where the Will of God is known*
> *Let purpose guide the little wills of men –*
> *The purpose which the Masters know and serve.*
>
> *From the centre which we call the race of men*
> *Let the Plan of Love and Light work out*
> *And may it seal the door where evil dwells.*
>
> *Let Light and Love and Power restore the Plan*
> *on Earth.*[13]

No one religion is better, no one worse. When we all learn to live together in harmony and work toward the same goal, we can't help but improve this planet. Care, share, love, and give. What better posture could we have?

Couldn't hurt, could it?

Chapter 5 Endnotes

[1]   Simpson, Sheperd, Dr., *Astrological Ages*
[2]   Walker, James, K., President, *New Age*
[3]   Rogge, Michael, *The Roots of the New Age*
[4]   Wikimedia Foundation, *Guru*
[5]   Harris, Grove, *The Rush of Gurus*
[6]   Anjali, Prem, *Sri Swami Satchidananda*
[7]   Anjali, Prem, *Light Of The Universal Shrine*
[8]   ibid., *Light Of The Universal Shrine*
[9]   Wikimedia Foundation, *Angel*
[10] Brown, Dan, *Angels and Demons*
[11] Sicker, Ted, PBS, *People and Discoveries,* Georges Lamaitre
[12] Brown, Dan, *Angels and Demons,* The Camerlengo's Address, pp 380-383
[13] Lucis Trust, *The Great Invocation*

CHAPTER 6

THE TRANSLATORS

Our background discussion wouldn't be complete without taking a look at those who influenced or created the theories, beliefs, or messages that are the basis for what many today think of as New Age. There are numerous sources since the beginning of time that fall into the Woo-Woo category, such as sorcerers, alchemists, shamans, witch doctors, witches, and wizards.

But we're going to deal with the modern cadre of writers, speakers, and architects. I'm sure there's many more that influence this category, but I'll just give you a smattering of what's out there and who's who at the top of the heap when it comes to New Age or Woo-Woo thinking. This is intended to be a brief overview only; you can do further reading and research on your own; there are volumes on each of these folks.

Madame Blavatsky

Born Helena Petrovna Hahn in the Ukraine on August 12, 1831,[1] Madame Blavatsky is recognized by most as the founder of Theosophy. Her widely prolific writings extend more than three feet on bookshelves, among them, *Isis Unveiled*, *Voice of the Silence*, *The Key to Theosophy*, and *The Secret Doctrine* — her magnum opus.

Her work can perhaps be summed up by one of her maxims: *Compassion is the law of laws.* She explains that brotherhood is not a mere ideal, it's a fact of nature on the spiritual plane. From that we derive a logic and binding base for morality that can guide and inspire us even when more traditional religions lose their compelling force. From that premise, she provides the means to deduce the most important principles of how to live.[2] So how did that come to be?

Her childhood was unusual; she displayed neurotic behavior from almost infancy, by walking and talking in her sleep at age four, exhibiting morbid tendencies, and loving the strange and unworldly. Among her macabre recollections was the countryside being haunted by "russalkas," green-haired nymphs living in willow trees along river banks. She often threatened her nurses with having them tickled to death by russalkas.

That threat took purchase when she was four, walking along a riverbank with one of her nurses. A boy of fourteen was annoying them when she turned and roared that she'd have the russalkas tickle him to death. The boy lost his balance, tumbled into the river, and was not seen again until weeks later when his body was found by fisherman. Helena was not a child to toy with!

At the time, Russia was a hothouse of superstition and it didn't take much for her nurses to believe that supernatural beings placated and even controlled people like Helena. While she was exorcised many times, the rituals proved useless. Even scolding and punishment didn't deter her from her belief that mighty forces could and would carry out her wishes.

Helena's mother died when she was twelve, although in later life she'd say her mother died when she was a baby. She, along with her sister and brother moved in with her maternal grandparents. Her stubbornness, fiery temper, and disregard for social norms continued unabated. These traits were apparently to be a life-long affliction.

At 17 she married General Nicephore Blavatsky, then in his forties. The marriage lasted three months before she was off to experience the world. The period between 1848 and 1858 was typically referred to as Helena Petrovna Blavatsky's "vagabond years." During this time, she traveled extensively to London, India, China, America, Egypt, and Persia; she also tried but failed to get to Tibet.[3] In 1868, however, she succeeded in surreptitiously entering Tibet and trained with the Lama and other masters. She left in 1870.[4]

In 1873, she immigrated to New York City. She impressed people with her apparent psychic powers and held out to be a medium. Throughout her career she claimed levitation, clairvoyance, telepathy, clairaudience, and out-of-body-projection as her gifts.

In 1874, Helena met Henry Steel Olcott, a lawyer by training and journalist who covered the spiritualist phenomena. They soon took up residence with one another in "Lamasery" where she wrote *Isis Unveiled*, her first book.

On April 3, 1875, she married Michael C. Betanelly in New York City. Again, it was a short-lived marriage lasting only a few months. In September of the same year, she founded the Theosophical Society with Henry Steel Olcott, William Quan Judge, and others.

The Theosophical Society was a modern day Gnostic movement that took its inspiration from Hinduism and Buddhism. Madame Blavatsky held that all religions were both true in the inner teachings and false in their external manifestations. Imperfect men attempting to translate divine knowledge had corrupted religion in the translation. She claimed esoteric spiritual knowledge and researchers consider her to be the first spark of New Age thought.

She continued to write, hold court, and minister to those seeking divine knowledge. She suffered from heart disease, rheumatism, and kidney disease, succumbing to flu complications on May 8, 1891. Her last words regarding her work were "Keep the link unbroken! Do not let my last incarnation be a failure." She was succeeded as the head of the Theosophical Society by her protégé, Annie Besant.

Madame Blavatsky's body was cremated. One third of her ashes were sent to Europe, one third to William Quan Judge in the U.S., and the remaining third to India where her ashes were scattered in the Ganges River. Today, May 8 is celebrated as

White Lotus Day by Theosophists.[5]

Miss Mabel Collins, co-editor of the Theosophical periodical, *Lucifer*, summed up Madame Blavatsky this way, quoted from Maskelyne:

> "She taught me one great lesson. I learned from her how foolish, how gullible, how easily flattered human beings are, taken en masse. Her contempt for her kind was on the same gigantic scale as everything else about her... She had a greater power over the weak and credulous, a greater capacity for making black appear white... a more ceaseless and insatiable hatred of those whom she thought to be her enemies, a greater disrespect for less convenances, a worse temper, a greater command of bad language and a greater contempt for the intelligence of her fellow-beings than I had ever supposed possible to be contained in one person. These, I suppose, must be reckoned as her vices, though whether a creature so indifferent to all ordinary standards of right and wrong can be held to have virtues or vices I know not."[6]

Regardless of her personal idiosyncrasies, she apparently had an insight to what can only be described as a glimpse into another world. She had an uncanny perception of humanity as a whole which was her guiding principle.

She expounds on understandings and natural laws that were far beyond her contemporary world at the time she wrote them. Even today, some of her observations are theories only, remaining to be proven by scientists seeking the relationships within the universe. She is credited by leaders of the esoteric and occult as the forerunner and foundation for the New Age.

Annie Besant

Annie Besant was born Annie Wood in 1847 in Clapham, London. She's reported to have an unhappy childhood probably due in part to her father's death when she was five. She was educated by Ellen Marryat, a strict Calvinist who saw to it that Annie's education — including travel in Europe — was broader than the norm at the time.[7]

Annie met and married the young Rev. Frank Besant when she was nineteen. By the time she was 23, she had two children and found that her independent spirit clashed with her husband's traditional views. She began to question her own religious beliefs. When she refused communion, her husband ordered her to leave their home; she left with her daughter while her son stayed with the father.

After the separation, she completely rejected Christianity and in 1874, she joined the Secular Society which preached free thinking. Annie soon developed a close relationship with Charles Bradlaugh, editor of the radical *National Reformer* and a leader in the secular movement in Britain. Annie worked for the paper and over the next few years wrote many articles on marriage and women's rights.

In 1877, Besant and Bradlaugh published *The Fruits of Philosophy*, Charles Knowlton's book advocating birth control. Both were criminally charged with publishing material that was "likely to deprave or corrupt those whose minds are open to immoral influences." They defended the work by arguing it was "better to prevent conception than murder children by want of food, air, and clothing." Found guilty and sentenced to six months in prison, they appealed and won. Besant then set about writing her own book advocating birth control, titled *The Laws of Population*.

The very idea of a woman promoting birth control received wide publicity. Newspapers such as *The Times* accused Besant of writing "an indecent, lewd, filthy, bawdy, and obscene book." Undeterred, Besant continued her support of women's issues and started her own newspaper, *The Link*. Like Catherine Booth of the Salvation Army, Besant grew increasingly concerned about the health and well-being of the women who worked at the Bryant & May match factory. She decided she had to do something about it.

On June 23, 1888, Besant published the article, *White Slavery*, citing the dangers of phosphorus fumes and the deplorably low wages paid to the women who toiled at Bryant & May. The three women who gave her details for the article were fired and Besant responded by helping them form the Match Girls Union. After a three-week strike, concessions were made by Bryant & May, including the rehiring of the three fired informants.

The next year, Annie Besant was elected to the London School Board winning by more than 15,000 votes, and giving her a self-proclaimed mandate for large-scale reform. Her many achievements included free meals for undernourished children and free medical exams for elementary school children.[8]

In the 1890's, Besant became a devotee of Theosophy, the movement founded by Madame Blavatsky. Upon Blavatsky's death, Annie Besant led the Theosophical Society, promulgating the belief in karma and reincarnation. In the late 1890s, she went to India and in 1898 was instrumental in founding the Central Hindu College at Benares. She became involved in Indian nationalism, established the Indian Home Rule League in 1916, and continued her support of education, women's advocacy, and Theosophy until her death in 1933. Her ashes were scattered at the seashore in India.[9]

Annie Besant continued Madame Blavatsky's New Age beliefs and established herself as her generation's advocate of women's rights. Her impact on the New Age has given it a stronger base and affords additional insight into the humanity of the universe.

Alice Bailey

Alice Bailey was born Alice Ann La Trobe-Bateman on June 16, 1880 in Manchester, England. While raised in a wealthy and orthodox Christian environment, she questioned the meaning of life and challenged the religious dogmas of her times. She was very intelligent but unhappy, and was often bad-tempered. Her curiosity on life after death led her to three attempted suicides before her 15th birthday.

On June 30, 1895, fifteen year old Alice Bateman had a memorable experience that influenced her life. Her family had gone to church, leaving her alone in the house with the servants. While in a room reading, a man dressed in European clothes, wearing a turban entered the room. She had no idea who this man was and was so startled, she couldn't say a word while he spoke to her.[10] Here's how she retells that conversation:

> "He told me there was some work that it was planned that I could do in the world but that it would entail changing my disposition considerably; I would have to give up being such an unpleasant little girl and must try to get some measure of self-control. My future usefulness to Him and to the world was dependent on how I handled myself and the changes I could manage to make. He said that if I could achieve real self-control I could then be trusted and that I would travel all over the world and visit many countries, "doing your Master's work all the time"... He added that He would be in touch with me at intervals of seven years apart."[11]

While she initially thought this man was the Master Jesus, she later discovered he was the Master Koot Humi. She received "supervision and interest" by this mysterious man every seven years as he indicated.

In 1917, Alice moved to Hollywood to be near the Theosophical Society at Krotona, working there as a vegetarian cook. She met and ultimately married a lawyer, Foster Bailey, who was devoted to ancient wisdom.[12]

In 1919, she encountered yet another Master, Djwhal Khul ("DK") who would guide her for the next thirty years. She was having a quiet time on a hillside near her house when she heard a musical note that sounded everywhere, followed by his voice. He asked her if she was willing to write some books, to which she replied no, she wouldn't be party to psychic practices. The voice gave her three weeks to reconsider. She evidently forgot about it, yet three weeks later, the voice returned with the same request.

She agreed to try it for a couple of weeks during which DK dictated to her the first chapters of *Initiation, Human and Solar*. After a month, Alice got scared and refused to do any further work. DK gave her a technique to contact her own Master, Koot Humi, who assured Alice there was no danger in that form of telepathy. She then carried on with the task of writing per DK's direction.[13]

In 1922, Bailey started the Lucis Trust Publishing Company, its purpose to establish a "New World Order." Consistent with this purpose, The Arcane School was founded by Alice Bailey in 1923 as a non-sectarian, non-political group with international scope. The school was dedicated to service and the principle that all roads lead to God and the welfare of all humanity. And in 1932, The World Goodwill, an organization that prepares the way for a one-world religion and a one-world government was founded.

In the thirty years since 1919, Bailey produced twenty four books, nineteen of which were purported to have been written by her Tibetan Master, DK — Djwhal Khul. When questioned about DK's communications, Alice commented,[14]

> "I remain in full control of my senses of perception… I simply listen and take down the words that I hear and register the thoughts which are dropped one by one into my brain… I have never changed anything that the Tibetan has ever given to me… I do not always understand what is given. I do not always agree. But I record it all honestly and then discover it does make sense and evokes intuitive response." [15]

Alice Bailey spent the majority of her time working out what she referred to as "The Plan;" the result had significant influence on other groups such as The Church Universal and Triumphant, the Tara Center, and the Robert Muller School. Each of these espouses her message of world peace, the divinity of all mankind, the unity of all religions, and service to mankind. She is recognized as a prolific author of occult writings and the mother of the modern New Age Movement.[16]

Alice Ann Bailey died December 15, 1949 leaving a legacy of spiritually occult writings that are the basis of esoteric studies today. While her writings are challenging to comprehend, they deliver her key message: God is everywhere and we are a part of God.

Edgar Cayce

Edgar Cayce was born on a farm near Hopkinsville, Kentucky on March 18, 1877. He had a normal childhood in most respects, rich with the heritage of nineteenth century farm life. He was the only boy of five children and grew up surrounded by grandparents, aunts, uncles, and cousins living nearby. He was raised in an era when much of the country was experiencing religious revival meetings. This probably accounted for his lifelong interest in the Bible; even as a child he wanted to become a medical missionary.

At age six or seven, he told his parents he, at times, could see visions, occasionally talking to relatives who had recently died. His parents didn't put much stock in these visions, attributing them to an overactive imagination and paid little attention to them.

When he was thirteen, he had a vision of a beautiful woman that influenced him for the rest of his life. The woman asked him what he most wanted in life; he told her he wanted to help others, especially sick children.

Shortly afterward, Edgar displayed talents that couldn't be explained away by imagination. He could sleep on his school books and photographically remember their entire contents. It was discovered that he could sleep on any book or document and upon awakening, could repeat back, word for word, even if those were beyond his limited education. The gift gradually faded and he left school to work on his grandmother's farm.

In 1897, his family moved into the Hopkinsville town proper where he worked in a bookstore. A few months later he fell in love and became engaged to Gertrude Evans on March 14, four days before his twentieth birthday. He decided to marry when he was able to raise enough money so Gertrude and he could begin their life together. He worked as a salesman in a dry goods store, then sold insurance, books, and stationery. It appeared it wouldn't be long before he could afford to get married.

One day after taking a sedative to relieve a headache, Edgar Cayce woke up with a severe case of laryngitis. Initially, he wasn't concerned that he couldn't speak above a whisper, but days turned into weeks and he was forced to give up his sales job. His malady persisted for months so he looked for something else to do that didn't require much talking — he was giving up on ever speaking again.

He found a job as a photographer's assistant in Hopkinsville and settled in to be near Gertrude's and his family. Although he regretted never finishing school and becoming the doctor missionary of his dreams, he was content to settle down with a wife and children.

In the early 1900's, a showman brought a comedy and hypnotism act to the Hopkinsville Opera House. He heard of Edgar's laryngitis and offered to hypnotize him and cure him. Willingly, Cayce agreed and while under hypnosis, answered questions in a normal voice to everyone's amazement. But when awakened, he remained unable to talk above a whisper. The experiment was conducted a number of times with the same results.

A New York specialist became interested in Edgar Cayce's plight and advised him to repeat the experiment, but instead of suggesting Edgar's voice return, the hypnotist, Al Layne, was to ask Edgar about his condition. Once asleep, Edgar was asked what was wrong and how could he be cured. Edgar

Cayce described his problem as a "psychological condition producing a physical effect," and went on to suggest that blood circulation be increased to the affected areas. After the hypnotist made the suggestion of increased blood circulation, Edgar's chest and throat turned a crimson red while the skin became warm to the touch. After twenty minutes, Cayce spoke again, stating that before he was awakened, it was suggested that the blood flow return to normal. When he finally awoke, he could speak normally for the first time in almost a year. It was March 31, 1901, the first time Edgar Cayce gave a psychic reading.[17]

Al Layne was amazed. He suffered from a chronic stomach problem doctors had been unable to cure. He asked Edgar to allow him to hypnotize him again and ask him about his stomach difficulties. Feeling obliged, Cayce agreed and while under hypnosis, he recommended herbal medicines, foods, and exercises for improvement. After following those suggestions for one week, Layne felt much better and encouraged further tests.

This began a career of self-induced cures described while he was in a self-induced sleep. Time and time again he would put himself to sleep, listen to a person's medical problem others hadn't been able to cure, and recommend a treatment that eased or eliminated the malady.

Edgar worked with Layne and Dr. Wesley Ketchum and became known as the "psychic diagnostician." In 1910, Dr. Ketchum submitted a paper to the American Society of Clinical research calling Cayce a medical wonder. The October 9 issue of the New York Times featured a long article on Cayce's talents with the headline, "Illiterate Man Becomes a Doctor When Hypnotized." Requests for readings increased and, often reluctantly, he conducted numerous evaluations.

In 1911, Cayce's wife Gertrude contracted what her doctor believed to be pleurisy. It hung on for months and she was eventually confined to bed. By late summer, the doctor called in a tuberculosis specialist, who confirmed Gertrude's plight was fatal and nothing else could be done; she would be gone by the end of the year. Having exhausted all medical avenues,

Cayce gave her a reading and recommended a combination of prescription drugs in addition to inhaling fumes from a charred oak keg filled with apple brandy. Following that regimen, by September her health was improving; by November, her doctors agreed she would recover, and by the first of January, 1912, she was cured.

As years passed, his psychic reputation grew. While people were helped by his readings, many had difficulty finding doctors to carry out the recommended treatments. Most doctors seemed hesitant to follow the guidance of a sleeping psychic who, in many cases, had never seen the people he diagnosed. Ultimately this led to his dream of establishing a hospital staffed with qualified doctors, nurses, and therapists who could and would carry out the recommendations of the readings. After a few false starts, a New York businessman, Morton Blumenthal, agreed to finance the hospital in Virginia Beach, Virginia.

Until 1923, most of Cayce's readings were limited to physical and medical conditions. That year, Cayce gave horoscope readings to a printer and his two nieces. The reading referred to a past life of the printer and a whole new area of research was underway.

Cayce had no doubt such information had value when dealing with health, but the readings with reference to reincarnation seemed foreign to his fundamental Christianity. He prayed, searched his soul, and obtained a few readings. He was advised to read the Bible through, cover to cover, while keeping the idea of reincarnation in mind. The underlying philosophy that emerged was one that focused on the oneness and purposefulness of life. In time, he found the concept of reincarnation was not incompatible with any religion and actually merged perfectly with his own beliefs of what it meant to be a Christian.

In the fall of 1923, Cayce hired a secretary, Gladys Davis, to take down the information in the readings while Gertrude asked her sleeping husband the questions. Gladys was careful to catalog each of the readings for access and easy reference, ultimately cataloging and indexing more than 14,000 readings on 10,000 different subjects. Her task wasn't complete until 1971 — 26 years after Cayce's death.

In September 1925, the Cayce family moved with Gladys Davis to Virginia Beach. In 1927, the Association of National Investigators was formed to research and test the information contained in the readings. On November 11, 1928, the hospital funded by Blumenthal opened its doors to patients from all over the country. Cayce's philosophy of healing was that it worked best when all the schools of medicine cooperated in the best treatment for the patient.

In June 1931, The Association for Research and Enlightenment, Inc. was formed as a research body to investigate and disseminate the information contained in Cayce's readings. The organization became interested in holistic health care, ESP, meditation, spiritual healing, the importance of dreams, and the study of life after death. Cayce was asked time and again, "How can I become more psychic myself?"

His response was simply, "The goal should be to become more spiritual, for psychic is of the soul." As individuals became more spiritual, their psychic ability would develop naturally. Rather than trying to find converts to his readings' philosophy, he encouraged people that to incorporate the information into their own religious belief systems to enable them to become better people was useful and positive. Any other end should be left alone.

As his fame grew, so did the number of skeptics. Many people came to Virginia Beach to expose him as a fraud, but in time became convinced of the legitimacy of his work. One staunch Catholic writer, Thomas Sugrue, came to investigate and debunk the trickery surrounding Cayce and ended up writing *There is a River*, Cayce's biography, published in 1943. Coronet magazine ran a feature by Marguerite Harmon Bro, "Miracle Man of Virginia Beach," and Cayce became more famous than ever.[18]

For most of his adult life, Edgar Cayce was able to provide intuitive insight into almost any question imaginable. His psychic readings comprise one of the largest and most impressively documented records of intuitive information to come from a single individual.

Nicknamed "The Sleeping Prophet," Cayce predicted the beginning and end of both the First and Second World Wars, two presidents would die in office — FDR & JFK — and in October 1935 spoke of the coming holocaust in Europe. He predicted the Austrians and Germans would take sides, later joined by the Japanese.

Cayce believed in reincarnation and past lives. Each person, he believed, existed in a self-conscious form before birth and would exist again after death. A number of his readings referred to past incarnations in the legendary lost land of Atlantis; those references totaled more than 700 over a span of twenty years.[19]

Cayce never refused a reading, although he had limited himself to two a day. During the height of WWII, Cayce was doing eight a day because he felt the obligation to use his gift to help those who were suffering and asking for help. This pace ultimately lead to collapse based on sheer exhaustion.

In September, 1944, just as he gave his first reading to himself, he gave his last to himself. The reading told him to rest; when Gertrude asked how long, the response was "until he is well or dead." He died on January 3, 1945.

Throughout his life, Edgar Cayce claimed no special abilities and never considered himself a prophet. His readings never offered beliefs that had to be embraced, but focused on the fact that each person should test the principles provided in their own life. Though Cayce was a Christian and read the Bible from cover to cover each year of his adult life, he stressed the importance of comparative study among belief systems around the world. His underlying principles are the oneness of all life, tolerance for all people, and a compassion and understanding for every major religion in the world.[20]

Corrine Heline

Corrine Heline was born Corrine Smith on August 13, 1882 to a well-to-do family in Atlanta, Georgia. Her destiny was apparent from early childhood; ultimately she authored 28 volumes of esoteric work. She demonstrated advanced consciousness and an inquiring mind as she spent many hours admiring a statue of Mary in the Catholic Church across the street from her own Methodist Sunday School. The Madonna was to be her inspiration for all her writings.

As a child of four, she said to her mother, "There is something wonderful in this Holy Book and one day I will know what it is." When she was in her teens, she discovered occult literature in the library of a Theosophist neighbor. The books she borrowed on reincarnation opened a new world for her, answering the many questions she had. The neighbor's gift of the *Rosicrucian Cosmo-conception* by Max Heindel would change her life.

When Heline was sixteen, her mother died leaving her a comfortable inheritance. She mourned her loss deeply until one night, her mother came to her telling her of the happiness in Higher Worlds and asking her to stop grieving. Heline's mother also told her to look in an old trunk where Christmas money was hidden. With the money, Heline bought herself a new Bible that she would use in her interpretation work on the *New Age Bible*.

She subsequently moved to California where she met Max Heindel and spent five years in his tutelage. Three years after his death, on Christmas Eve, 1922, Heline got her "inner commission" to write an esoteric interpretation of the Bible. She had a vision of two celebrations of the Last Supper, one for Jesus and his disciples in one room, and another room where Mary sat at the head table giving assignments to those that were to carry forward the work. Heline was told she was to write an interpretation of the Bible. Obviously overwhelmed, she asked, "Why me?"

Heline saw Mary come to her, kiss her cheek, and say, "I will help you." Heline saw this as her charter. Her works are seen as texts for understanding the plan of evolution and initiation for the Piscean and Aquarian ages as set forth in the Bible.

During this time, she had developed a strong association

with Theodore Heline who was the editor of the *Rays of the Rose Cross*, an esoteric magazine. He was a Shakespearean actor, author, and lecturer who had a knack for correlating current events to the "unfolding of man's enlightenment in the light of Ageless Wisdom." He became the editor of the *New Age Interpreter*, an esoteric periodical and started the New Age Press publishing house.

Both Corrine and Theodore Heline traveled extensively and lectured to large audiences throughout the United States. They often filled the sanctuary of the New Age Bible and Philosophy Center in Santa Monica where they were both ordained ministers. They were married in 1938.

When Corinne Heline's father died, she and her husband bought a hilltop home in California and named it Madonna Crest. It was here where Heline did much of her writing inspired by the beauty of her surroundings. Her books on the unfolding human spirit deals with flowers and the human consciousness, music as it relates to unfolding human spirit and healing. She held that she was able to visit ancient temples through her clairvoyance and extended consciousness to bring the principles used by the ancients into her writings.

She finished the seven volumes of the *New Age Bible Interpretation* in 1954, at age 72. She said, "The Bible, the supreme spiritual textbook of life, is above all creeds, dogmas, and differences in religious beliefs. It is written to meet the needs of both the wise and the simple. There are surface truths, and wisdom that is veiled. There is guidance to the spiritual life in its pages for every degree of understanding. As consciousness unfolds, its revelations multiply. It is indeed the Wonder Book of all time. The deepest wisdom contained in the Bible is accessible only to those who have attained a personal first-hand knowledge of the Spiritual world and the fundamental laws operative in them."[21]

Corrine Heline's followers believe she was divinely inspired to convey first-hand knowledge access to the wisdom of the Bible. She was a life long student of ancient mysteries and is truly one of the New Age pioneers. Her consciousness is said to far transcend that of her day, her inspiration coming from immortals overshadowing her from early childhood.[22]

Roberto Assagioli

Roberto Assagioli, born in 1888, was the first western psychologist to incorporate religion and spirituality into an overall view of the human psyche. Freud was contemptuous of religion, citing it along with spirituality to be low forms of consciousness within the child but should be left behind when one reaches maturity.

Freud's student, Karl Jung, disagreed with him, discovering that religion played a role in the human psyche through archetypical symbols like Mother. Jung made it his life's work to study these symbols to unravel the secrets of the unconscious. His perspectives of archetypes were like batteries that had the power to ignite the psyche into lofty goals, images of a better human being, and of a better world.

Roberto Assagioli was the first scientist to provide an overall map of the human psyche, offering a more accurate view of consciousness than either Freud or Jung. Assagioli defined the higher self as the core that keeps our consciousness alive when we can't control it, such as sleep or hypnosis. His goal was to have therapy build up the whole structure of the personality to bring about harmony, synthesizing the different psychological functions, after the ground for integration was laid by thorough analysis, with the methods and techniques by Freud and his successors. He called his approach *Psychosynthesis.*

So Assagioli gets the credit for introducing the *higher self* into western psychology. This concept opened up the transpersonal realms of consciousness explored today. Assagioli based his Psychosynthesis on esoteric psychology and the work of Alice Bailey, the theosophical scholar.

His concept dealt with human beings always reaching higher and beyond. He used spiritual archetypes, such as Jesus and Buddha, to internalize the qualities these people represent. He also used inner dialog, allowing the patients to connect with their issues as they saw them. At times he would use the enactment of spiritual quests, encouraging his patients to come to the same catharsis as the main character in their drama.

The effect of his methods opened the eyes of Western psychology, enabling the forgotten wisdom of both the ages and cultures to re-enter Western science. He has effectively taken away prejudices and united East and West.[23]

He recognized the spiritual longing of individuals in our present cultural wasteland. Psychosynthesis is an expansionistic psychology rather than reductionistic analysis of the psyche to a basic trauma of the past. Assagioli aimed to expand the patient's awareness to include more of who they were, connecting to a spirituality. He didn't pretend it was a spiritual teaching, but the individual could re-interpret universal spiritual wisdom into psychological insight.[24] His work continues to be a source of New Age thinking and study, enabling the individual to "synthesize" his own understanding to take it to a newer, higher level.

Manly Palmer Hall

Manly Palmer Hall was born on March 18, 1901 in Peterborough, Ontario, Canada. He was raised by his maternal grandmother who brought him to the United Stares when he was very young. Unlike his contemporaries, he concluded that wisdom was not to be found only on one path or a single religion. He saw wisdom as the highest realm, where philosophy, religion, and science come together without boundaries.

He began his speaking career when he was 20, invited to speak about reincarnation to a small group in Santa Monica, California. So began his teaching, lecturing, and writing career that would span the next sixty years. He showed thousands how universal wisdom could be found in the myths, mysteries, and symbols of the ancient Western Mystery teachings and how to embody this wisdom in their own lives.

He wrote the following in a young student's book when asked for his autograph:

"To learn is to live, to study to grow, and growth is the measurement of life. The mind must be taught to think, the heart to feel, and the hands to labor. When these have been educated to their highest point, then is the time to offer them to the service of their fellowman, not before."[25]

He felt that before a student could pursue an esoteric career, he or she must first build a sound and sane personality.

His first publications were two small pamphlets, *The Breastplate of the High Priest* and *Wands and Serpents*. He traveled extensively in 1923 and 1924, visiting many great cultural centers in Europe, Asia, and Egypt. These travels strengthened his convictions about the importance of comparative religion and deepened his understanding of significant contributions made in the interest of human spiritual evolution.

When he returned, he set seriously to work on his encyclopedic outline of the Western esoteric tradition, *The Secret Teachings of All Ages*. It took him six years to complete his work and raise $100,000 to print the first edition.

In 1934 he founded the Philosophical Research Society, dedicating it to the "ensoulment of the arts, sciences, and crafts, devoted to the single purpose of advancing the brotherhood of all that lives to enable lovers of wisdom to meet on common ground. The society still hosts a wide range of lectures, seminars, and workshops on philosophical subjects. Since its inception, a library and bookstore have been located in the Los Feliz area of Los Angeles; the location has long been a learning center for all spiritual traditions and was designated a cultural site by the Los Angeles City Council in 1994.

Hall espoused the North American continent was set aside for a great experiment of enlightened self-government by ancient philosophers. He believed that the seeds of this plan were planted a thousand years before the Christian era, revealed in part by the symbolism of the Great Seal of the United States.

Manly P. Hall was prolific in all his endeavors. He authored more than 200 books on occult topics ranging from astrology, The Bible, religion, and Tarot, to dreams, mysticism, psychology, symbols, and reincarnation as well as Eastern and Western philosophy. He gave more than eight thousand lectures, mesmerizing audiences with his extemporaneous remarks lasting as long as two hours. He always spoke to people with respect and dignity, never overwhelming them with his vast knowledge of spiritual traditions. He championed the value of an idealistic philosophical education for all, ala Pythagoras, Plato, Socrates, Lord Bacon, and all the philosophers of history who believed in a rational world soul.[26] His writings provide insight into the New Age with connectivity to ancient teachings and literature. His perspective values the individual's pursuit of knowledge and wisdom, both marks of the New Age.

Ascended Masters

It's appropriate here to talk about *ascended masters* and their role as prophets or saints as well as translators of the New Age. The term refers to those souls who, supposedly after many incarnations and life experiences, mastered the lessons of our physical realm here on earth and then ascended. So, what does it mean to have ascended?

As we'll see later, there is a belief that vibrations drive the manifestations of our body and soul. The physical body is the lowest vibration or frequency in the succession of energetic bodies, each contributing to the harmony between the body and soul. Ascension is described as consciously increasing the vibratory rate of the physical and other bodies to rise to the highest vibration, the Christ level. Supposedly the physical body loses its definition, diffuses, and then finally resembles a star-like burst of energy.

Those who have raised their bodies through ascension appear to be fully in command of the physical realm and can decelerate their vibrations to appear anyway and anywhere they desire. Ascension as such — beyond religious icons such as Jesus — is controversial to say the least. It sparks controversy and disbelief, even among those who have spent years studying esoteric doctrines.

It is difficult to comprehend beyond the Star Trek transporter that beams people and things up to the Star Ship Enterprise. Some relegate the topic to New Age myth and fantasy while others maintain it's a natural course of human evolution. Obviously there are no scientific data to support the capability to ascend, but then again, we didn't know about radio waves and x-rays two centuries ago. Regardless of the reality of today, there are a number of individuals held out to be masters who have ascended.[27]

An ascended master is a soul believed, after many incarnations, to have mastered the lessons of the physical realm and then returned to a higher consciousness of thought and light. They are thought to be able to speak or channel to us, much like Djwhal Khul did with Alice Bailey. They can also communicate on some level through dreams, meditations, art, music, synchronicities, and other aspects of the creative mind. They apparently provide higher knowledge and insight than we are able to muster, enabling us to learn more about our world and its place in the universe.

Ascended masters are a group of spiritually enlightened beings, once mortal, who have undergone a spiritual transformation and act as humanity's superintendents of spiritual growth. They can be the Great White Brotherhood or Secret Chiefs revered by various mystic organizations, and even the bodhisattvas of Buddhism or the saints of Catholic and Orthodox Christianity.

Most early references to masters describe them as Tibetan or Hindi. Various key spiritual leaders such as Jesus, Muhammad, the Virgin Mary, and Kwan Yin the compassionate bodhisattva, take their seats alongside the mystic personalities like the Count of St. Germain and Madame Blavatsky's Koot Humi when there is talk of ascended masters. Apparently the central trait is that they have put aside any differences they may have had in their earthly careers and are united to improve spiritual well-being of the human race.[28]

It bears listing a few of those and the following is by no means a complete list of those who have ascended according to religious, spiritual, or mystic authorities. But it will give you a flavor of who and what an ascended master might be.

Let's take a look at ascended masters from the Seven Rays viewpoint, that group of masters they call **The Hierarchy** — also known as The Great White Brotherhood, The Elder Brothers, and sometimes the Secret College. They've fought their way into enlightenment, understand the difficulties along the way, and the considerable effort it takes to make the major steps.

It's believed they can only watch over and guide human evolution according to karmic law. To intervene in human affairs could change the course of history, so they only inspire. It's also believed they've foregone some of their choices for their own future to serve humanity. Following is a brief overview of those I've chosen to list.

Sanat Kumara is the personality expression of the great being whose consciousness is Earth, also known as the Planetary Logos. He's the greatest of the Avatars or the "coming ones." His advisers are the three personalities called the Buddhas of Activity and together they are the embodiment of perfect love and perfect intelligence.

Buddha has left the human evolution but still returns once a year at the Wesak Festival during the full moon of Taurus where he descends no lower than the mental plane. He acts as the focal point of power and pours it over humanity; the work of Buddha is the expression of Wisdom.

The Manu is concerned with government and planetary politics. He presides over all the forces that affect the evolution of the earth's physical structure — the earth's crust and the continents as well as believed to influence the minds of politicians to create a synthesis of the past that provides a seed for the new.

The Christ or **Lord Maitreya** is the Lord of Love and Compassion, just as his predecessor Buddha was the Lord of Wisdom. He is the world teacher, the Master of the Masters and Instructor of the Angels. He's committed to the guidance of the spiritual destinies of men; he develops the realization within each human being that he is a child of God.

It is believed that he was incarnate as Krishna and later overshadowed Jesus for the last three years of his ministry on earth. The Master Jesus still works very closely with the Christ, inspiring and directing the Christian churches around the world.

The Mahachohan, the Lord of Civilization, expresses active intelligence and is responsible for the order producing energy on Earth. The Master has had numerous incarnations, the most notable are:

Roger Bacon (1214 – 1294) was a Franciscan friar, having studied at Oxford and was a philosopher and educational reformer as well as a proponent of experimental science.

Francis Bacon (1561 – 1626) was a lawyer, statesman, philosopher, and a master of English known for his literary wisdom and his power as a speaker in Parliament. He was James I's Lord Chancellor and it's been demonstrated by several writers as the author who penned Shakespearean plays. He also is purported to be responsible for the translation of the King James Bible. Through his writing and influence of the court, English history saw true democracy established. There are those that believe that he didn't die in 1626, but went on to live until 1668.

Francis Rakoczi (1676 – 1735) was born to the royal house of Transylvania. He was very difficult to follow as he covered his tracks all around Europe. He incarnated to supposedly start the cycle which changed civilization to focus on the cycle of his embodied Ray 7.

Count Saint Germain (c.1700 – 1784) never revealed his background and identity leading to speculation about his ancestry. He appeared in Versailles in 1743, enormously rich and very mysterious. He was recognized as a brilliant scholar and linguist; his talents included chemistry, poetry, music, and history. He was a skilled artist able to create luminous effects in his paintings and jewelry by mixing mother of pearl in his colors.

Master Morya is the head of all esoteric schools and responsible for the synthesis in the world of politics and government. He's acting as the inspirer of national executives around the world, reinforcing ideals that form homogenous platforms that enable them to enter the international business arena. That facilitates the synthesis of cultural, religious, and scientific elements into the whole.

Master Koot Hoomi is thought to have attended Oxford University in the 1850s, his role, to vitalize the great philosophies to stimulate the love latent in the hearts of all men. He ostensibly works with the prelates of the great Catholic Churches — Greek, Roman, and Anglican — and their educational workers throughout the world. He aligns himself with those of unselfish intent striving for the ideal and lives for helping others. A previous incarnation of Master Koot Hoomi is thought to be the Greek philosopher Pythagoras.

Master Serapis, frequently called the Egyptian, concerns himself with the great art movements of the world including music, painting, and drama.

Master Hilarion was thought to be Paul of Tarsus in a previous incarnation and works with those who are developing their intuition to strip the veil from the unseen.

Master Jesus is the focal point that flows through the various Christian churches around the world. His focus is abstract idealism. His challenge now is to steer mankind from the present state of unrest to the peaceful waters of knowledge and certitude, preparing the earth for the coming of a World Teacher.

There are those that believe Jesus came to earth a number of times and was incarnate as Joshua, the Son of Nun from 1530 to 1420 BC to experience his second initiation. Then as Jeshua for his third initiation from 536 to 456 BC, and as Jesus of Nazareth from 7 BC to 33 AD undergoing his fourth initiation. And the last time as Apollonius of Tyana for his fifth initiation, although there are some scholars who don't believe Apollonius was his incarnation.

As Jesus, he laid the foundations of modern Christianity and did much to end the Jewish dispensation in which he had played a major role. He took his fourth initiation as the crucifixion, the renunciation, or in the Buddhist tradition, liberation. The Holy Bible illustrates his ascension and appearance to those close to him three days after his physical death.

While there are a number of differing reports as to his lifetime, Apollonius of Tyana has been identified by some as another incarnation of Jesus. By one account, he was born between 37 and 41 AD, several years after Jesus' physical death.

Apollonius apparently had remarkable powers, traveling as a legislator, understanding all languages, and had the faculty of knowing what was happening at distant locations — he supposedly saw Emperor Domitian stabbed while in a city some distance away. Apollonius recommended charity and piety, traveled to almost all countries in the world and died at a very old age.

Known as the "Neo-Pythagorean," he reportedly performed many miracles in his life. As a Master of Wisdom, he used his powers to appear and disappear before large crowds and was seen simultaneously miles away in another city.

His biography portrays a Christ-like individual in both temperament and power along with the claims of performing certain miracles. The Seven Rays thinking is that Jesus has taken the sixth initiation and is now the custodian of the Sixth Ray.

Master Djwhal Khul is Tibetan and purportedly showed himself numerous times to Alice Bailey and ultimately inspired her writings. His work is to teach and spread the knowledge of the Ageless Wisdom. He works with those who heal with pure altruism and occupies himself with great philanthropic world movements and rapidly developing welfare movements.[29]

Now, there's not one religion I'm aware of that ascribes all of their teachings with all the purported "ascended masters," only the Seven Rays which I don't believe is a religion, per se. Now that doesn't make it wrong, nor does it make it impossible. There are attributes of the repeated incarnations that suggest eternal life — as a concept — can be moving closer to

God with each life time, as the soul raises its vibration level in its evolving education. Could be! Can't hurt to investigate it.

New Age Archetypes

Now, there are a number of people around the world who have positively impacted our planet with good works and good teachings. They merit note here, as they, too, can be classified as New Age archetypes. They have their own stories, their own histories, and their own influences upon our world. Take the time to read about them, each easily found on the internet or in any library. Following are but a few to get you started.

Mahatma Gandhi (1869 – 1948) was a spiritual and political leader who led the struggle for India's independence from Great Britain. His philosophy of non-violence influenced his national movement in India and to this day, his concept of non-violent civil disobedience carries weight in movements around the world.

Black Elk (1863 – 1950) was an Oglala Sioux Holy Man who fought at age 12 at the Battle of Little Big Horn and in 1890 at Wounded Knee. He was baptized as Catholic in 1903 and continued as spiritual leader to his people, seeing no contradiction in his tribal traditions and those of Christianity.

Martin Luther King, Jr., Ph.D. (1929 – 1968), was a Baptist minister, political activist, and the most famous leader of the American Civil Rights Movement promoting racial equality through non-violence. He won the Nobel Peace Prize and the Presidential Medal of Freedom before being assassinated.

Jiddu Krishnamurti (1895 – 1986) met C.W. Leadbeater on the private beach at the Theosophical Society headquarters in Adyar, India, then raised by Annie Besant within the Theosophical Society. He later traveled the world as an independent speaker and educator on the workings of the human mind. He was awarded the U.N. 1984 Peace Medal.

Mother Teresa (1910 – 1997) was an Indian Catholic nun who founded the Missionaries of Charity. Her work among the poverty stricken of Calcutta garnered her fame and she was believed by some to be the embodiment of a saint. She was awarded the Nobel Peace Prize in 1979 and in 1996 was made an honorary U.S. citizen.[30] She was beatified by Pope John Paul II in October 2003.[31]

Swami Satchidananda (1914 – 2002) was an Indian religious leader invited to the U.S. in 1966 by the artist Peter Max. Satchidananda was the opening speaker at the Woodstock Music Festival in 1969. In 1986, he opened the Light of Truth Universal Shrine in Yogaville, Virginia dedicated to interfaith harmony.[32]

Sathya Sai Baba (c.1926 – present) is a self proclaimed Indian avatar with a following of millions. He is the embodiment of love with divine powers. He preaches the foundation of Truth, Right, Conduct, Peace, and Love. He teaches the goal of unity of all major world religions and that they all lead to God.

Dalai Lama (1935 – present) is the fourteenth in the Dalai Lama lineage, enthroned as Tibet's Head of State in 1950 even as the state faced occupation by the People's Republic of China. After collapse of the Tibetan resistance movement in 1959, he fled to India where he established the Government of Tibet in Exile. Preaching peace and harmony he traveled to the West and has been instrumental in spreading Buddhism and the cause of a Free Tibet. He was awarded the Nobel Peace Prize in 1989.

Deepak Chopra (1947 – present) is a medical doctor and a writer on spirituality, synchronicity, integrative medicine, and Ayurveda, the traditional medicine of India. He taught at Tufts University's and Boston University's schools of medicine, was chief of staff at New England Memorial Hospital, and subsequently established a private practice. He became involved in Transcendental Meditation and later branched out on his own.[33]

Michael D. Robbins (1942 – present) is a renowned professor of Ageless Wisdom through the studies of the Seven Rays as well as Esoteric Astrology. He is the author of numerous books including *Tapestry of the Gods*, a treatise on the Seven Rays. He teaches and inspires students around the world, some who have gone on to form their own organizations to spread the Ageless Wisdom.[34]

So, this is but a smattering of what the New Age is based upon and what it brings to contemporary society. Belief systems appear vastly diverse as they seemingly point to a singular God that is responsible for this earth, its dynamics, and its future.

The Translators bring the New Age to a new paradigm in educating us in their perspective and the possibilities we face as we uncover new science and technology that supports a higher energy we can't yet understand. Remember, our reality of television, computers and cell phones today could scarcely be imagined 200 years ago.

Are some of these folks out on a limb? Or are they on the Path? Education, scientific breakthroughs, time, and possibly faith will tell. In the meantime, what could it hurt to satisfy our curiosity, hone our knowledge, inspect alternatives, and come to our own conclusions? Dig in! You may be in your own New Age!

Chapter 6 Endnotes

[1] Wikimedia Foundation, *August 12*

[2] Carson, Reed, *Blavatsky Net - Theosophy*

[3] Crystal, Ellie, *Helena Petrovna Blavatsky*

[4] op. cit., *Blavatsky Net - Theosophy*

[5] Wikimedia Foundation, *Helena Petrovna Blavatsky*

[6] Martindale, C.C., S.J., Theosophy: Origin of the New Age

[7] Grade, Michael, Chairman, BBC, *Historic Figures, Annie Besant (1847 – 1933)*

[8] Spartacus Educational, *Annie Besant*

[9] op. cit., *Historic Figures, Annie Besant (1847 – 1933)*

[10] Gomez, Eduardo, *Alice Ann Bailey*

[11] Bailey, Alice A., *The Unfinished Autobiography*

[12] Parker, Reba and Oliver, Timothy, *Alice Bailey*

[13] op. cit., *Alice Ann Bailey*

[14] op. cit., *Alice Bailey*

[15] Bailey, Alice A., *The Unfinished Autobiography*

[16] op. cit., *Alice Bailey*

[17] Todeschi, Kevin, J., *Edgar Cayce's ESP: Who He Was, What He Said, and How it Came True*

[18] ibid., *Edgar Cayce's ESP: Who He Was, What He Said, and How it Came True*

[19] Crystal, Ellie, *Edgar Cayce – (1877-1945)*

[20] op. cit., *Edgar Cayce's ESP: Who He Was, What He Said, and How it Came True*

[21] New Age Bible & Philosophy Center, *Corrine Heline*

[22] ibid., *Corrine Heline*

[23] Arnheim, *Roberto Assagioli*

[24] Unknown, *Roberto Assagioli*

[25] Harris, Obadiah S., *Portrait of an American Sage*

[26] ibid., *Portrait of an American Sage*

[27] Crystal, Ellie, *Ascension*

[28] Crystal, Ellie, *Ascended Masters*

[29] Lindsay, Phillip, *Masters of the Seven Rays*

[30] Wikimedia Foundation, *Mahatma Gandhi, Black Elk, Martin Luther King, Krishnamurti, Mother Teresa*

[31] Wikimedia Foundation, *Mother Teresa*

[32] Anjali, Prem, *Sri Swami Satchidananda*

[33] Wikimedia Foundation, *Sathya Sai Baba, Dalai Lama, Deepak Chopra*

[34] Unknown, *The Seven Ray Institute*

CHAPTER 7

ASTROLOGY

"Hey, what's your sign?" My first reaction to this New Age inquiry is, "Exxon?" Hey, I spend a lot of money there and figure they help get me around this world of ours. To the casual person, this gets a chuckle, to the serious astrologer, I'm but one of the proletariat that plods their way through life unenlightened. But to the proselytizing astrologer, I'm a neophyte to be educated on the spot, analyzed, and accepted or discarded on the basis of my birth date. Kind of like "I'm one of these and you're one of those. We're not compatible because you're so stubborn and uncaring. Bye."

Ok, so it's not quite that bad. Astrology certainly has its advantages in starting conversations between two strangers without a desire or perhaps the capability to talk about current events. To those educated in astrology, though, you may be giving them quite a bit of information.

Astrology has been a curiosity for me since childhood. My mother would pick up the morning paper and go directly to the horoscope and see what kind of day she was going to have. Bless those astrologers who concentrate on the positives. Those daily newspaper astrologers that throw in the negatives, I'm sure, have ruined a number of people's days. I can attest to that through second-hand horoscope, much like second-hand smoke; it doesn't affect you directly but may have adverse affects over the long term!

My guess is that more than ninety percent of the people

who read newspapers have, at one time or another, looked at the horoscope section. Suffice it to say, there are millions of people in the U.S. alone who have a daily curiosity about their horoscope, and some might pattern their day after what's read.

Well, read your horoscope. It's sorted on signs of the zodiac based on the day you were born, known as your sun sign. What you read rarely refers to you, right? Even if you go back to yesterday's paper and recall the events of the day, most of the time it's a stretch to see how it was yours.

That's because it's only a sun sign and you, astrologically speaking, are significantly more complex than that. Looking at your sun sign alone ignores at least ninety percent of your astrological composition. That's why it doesn't fit! What's your rising sign? What's your moon?

You have the sun, moon, planets, and stars that affect your astrology. On the day you were born, there was a specific position of each of those heavenly bodies that will never be in the same position again in our expanding universe. Personal astrology is understanding the difference between where everything was when you were born and where everything is today and then understanding how that affects you.

Whether or not you believe what an astrologer tells you, most people typically walk away feeling good. They just told you what your key attributes and future aspects are and you've discounted the negatives and affirmed the positives. "Boy was that guy good; pegged me perfectly" or "at least he got the big ones right." Even if he was a tad off, you still feel better than when you went in, I'll bet!

Fact or fiction? Esoteric information or entertaining pseudo-psychology? You be the judge. I'll just give you a little background on origins and a bit about the mechanics. Then when you have your first reading, or your next, you might better understand the basis of the information.

Then, understand that all the alignments, transits, progressions, and aspects that you were told are influences. That's right, *influences*. You are human with a free will. Remember that.

Any energy around you, like the stars and planets, can have an influence on you, just like the moon affects the tides. Having free will says you can take advantage of that information, if you want, or you can ignore it. But the energy is still there, just like electricity in a wall outlet. You can avail yourself of the electricity by plugging some appliance or electronic gadget into the wall socket, or you can simply ignore it. So maybe if you're armed with information, you can better cope with what life has to offer.

That, in my opinion is the advantage of any information astrology, numerology, or any other "*ology*" can provide. If you know that microwaves can affect your body, wouldn't you choose to steer wide of the source if you could? Same with astrology; look at the influence, then ignore or steer wide of pitfalls. If you choose. That's *dharma*. A Sanskrit word meaning law or way. Merriam-Webster says it's conformity to one's duty and nature. Generally, it refers to religious duty, but can mean social order, correct conduct, or simply, virtue.[1] You get to use your free will to affect your future! So if the influences are there, the signs are along the way, why wouldn't we heed their warning about holes in the sidewalk? Why not at least look for the hole? Couldn't hurt, could it?

Let's look at how astrology began.

Origins & History

Astrology has its roots deep in astronomy, the study of objects outside the earth's atmosphere and the movement of heavenly bodies. Astrology is the study of the effects these celestial movements have on human affairs. Through trial and error over extended periods, ancient astronomers were able to predict the reoccurrence of cosmic phenomena and astrologers began their forecasts which coincided with them.

Since time began, every man, woman, and child probably looked heavenward in awe at the moon and stars. The study of the heavens then gave way to being able to predict weather patterns, such as the seasons, and the best time for planting crops. Later those moving lights, the planets, were believed to be gods; the quest for understanding and divine knowledge was most likely the origin of astrology.

Astrology is believed to have begun with the Chaldeans in ancient Mesopotamia, probably in Babylon around 4000 BC. Practiced in temples, it was blended with religious elements and later spread to Egypt. Using the heavens, rulers used methods of predicting the future to forecast the fate of nations due to such events as war or peace, feast or famine.

At the same time, independent of Babylon, the Chinese and perhaps the Mayans in Central America were developing their own methods of prediction. Some experts hold that Chinese astronomy may well have begun in 5000 BC.

Stretching back even further, researchers studying the Pyramids and Sphinx suggest perhaps even more distant origins are possible. There is startling evidence that the monuments at Giza form an accurate map of the position of the three stars in Orion's belt as they appeared in 10,500 BC. Could they be that old?

Much later, after the death of Alexander the Great, astrology began to influence Greek life as Orientals mingled with Greeks in the various kingdoms, and soon spread to the Romans. Around the second century AD, Ptolemy, the Greek scientist, wrote a colossal two part work on astrology, a compilation of works from previous centuries. The first part dealt with the sun, moon, and planets, while the second interpreted how their movements affected man and human events.

During the thirteenth through seventeenth centuries, Greek, Arabic, and Medieval astrology became intricately entwined in traditional alchemy. Astrology was used for centuries by royalty, popes, scientists, doctors, and the general population alike. It was taught right along with astronomy in the schools and universities of the world.

However, in the late sixteenth century, a new scientific age was dawning and with it a demand for technical explanation. Without scientific proof, ideas and theories were rejected. Astrology suffered a distinct decline as the planets were believed to be far too distant from earth to have any influences on us.

Plus, the increasing number of charlatans out to make a fast buck caused astrology to lie essentially dormant until the late nineteenth century.

The Swiss psychoanalyst Carl Jung revived interest as he used astrology in his studies and wrote about it extensively, prompting the interest of other scientists. The English astrologer Alan Leo and Madame Blavatsky, a Russian, spurred the resurgence of astrology in England and Germany while later, American Dane Rudhyar wrote *The Planetarization of Consciousness*. Astrology was revived in America, France, and Holland as associations and schools for professional astrologers were founded in America and Britain. It spread in the latter part of the twentieth century to all corners of the globe and remains a vital segment of the New Age today.

Used to predict events, astrology perhaps is more art than science with much remaining to be discovered on the scientific docket. Today, astrology is used as a tool for personal growth, self discovery, realizing one's potential, and learning to resolve conflict with a strong trend toward spiritualism.[2]

Astronomy

Astronomy is the study of all objects outside the Earth's atmosphere, including stars, planets and their moons, as well as comets, asteroids and the like. As we delve into what astrology is and what it does, we have to understand a few fundamentals that aren't exactly easy to comprehend. So I'll spend some time here giving you the classic astrological explanation of terms and groupings, and I'll try to put them in perspective. This certainly will not be an exhaustive explanation — just know there's an application somewhere for the term, a reason for it, or a connection to other celestial bodies. Anymore than that begins an education that apparently can take a lifetime.

Astrology is based on the relationship of all stellar bodies to the earth. Its primary orientation is to those bodies in our solar system: the sun, the moon, planets, comets, and even asteroids. Secondarily, the stars and the constellations they form serve as a backdrop to the orbiting bodies in our solar system.

Our solar system is shaped like a disk, with planets revolving around the sun, all moving in the same direction. Taking a vantage point above the disk enables us to look down at all the north poles of each planet. If we divided that view into twelve parts and aligned them with the twelve constellations of the zodiac as they relate to our sun — heliocentric or sun-centered — we would have the format astrologers use to chart a specific time in our universe's development. This type of chart is used to determine the shape of worldwide or universal events.

SUN-CENTERED PERSPECTIVE

← Orbital Direction →

Then, if we oriented everything from the earth's perspective, either geocentric or earth-centered, we would have the format astrologers use to do personal charts and horoscopes. When that's the case, the earth is literally the center of the universe, so the sun appears to move through the heavens as well as all the planets.[3]

EARTH-CENTERED PERSPECTIVE

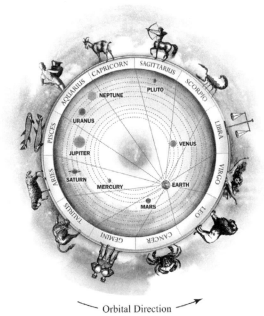

— Orbital Direction →

So, unlike the view from the sun, a view on earth gives us a perspective of other planets moving while we're moving. This means that at times, a planet we see moving across our sky might appear to stop and move backwards due to our viewing the other side of the planet's orbit, furthest away from us. That's called a *retrograde*. More about retrogrades later.

Zodiac

Let's start with the *zodiac* which is derived from the Greek meaning "circle of animals." Believed to have originated in Egypt and adopted by the Babylonians, the term has been used to designate constellations of stars. Constellations are groupings of stars that when connected by lines between them form an animal, a persona, or a design. If you're like me, it's tough to see anything beyond the Big Dipper. But for those that know where to look and use star charts, you can find these constellations in the night sky.

So, early astrologers knew it took twelve lunar cycles — months — for the sun to return to its original position and they identified constellations that were linked to the progression of seasons. So they assigned names of animals and persons to these star clusters or constellations. There was some rhyme and reason to the names. For example, when the sun was in a particular constellation during the rainy season, it was named Aquarius, meaning water-bearer.

So, the twelve signs of the zodiac are:

Aries the Ram	*Libra* the Scales
Taurus the Bull	*Scorpio* the Scorpion
Gemini the Twins	*Sagittarius* the Archer
Cancer the Crab	*Capricorn* the Goat
Leo the Lion	*Aquarius* the Water-bearer
Virgo the Virgin	*Pisces* the Fishes

These were named more than 2000 years ago and the sun entered the first sign, Aries, on March 21. This is called the vernal equinox — the beginning of spring where both night and day are twelve hours long. That was as good a starting place as any.

The signs of the zodiac are subdivided into four groups:

Fire Signs – Aries, Sagittarius, Leo

Water Signs – Cancer, Scorpio, Pisces

Air Signs – Libra, Aquarius, Gemini

Earth Signs – Capricorn, Taurus, Virgo[4]

Each of these appears to influence the general demeanor of the signs; for example, the personalities of fire signs tend to be just that: active, energetic, and perhaps impatient. A fire sign can be offset by a water sign, perhaps negating the impulsiveness of the fire sign with its calming, water-like attributes such as being intuitive, emotional, and imaginative. So two individuals might complement each other's personalities if one were a fire sign and the other a water sign.

While there is significant movement of stars relative to earth, the zodiac holds fast to Aries starting the chart. Suffice it to say that the movement of the constellations relative to the earth's position at the center of the dynamic universe is referred to as Ages. We're in the Piscean Age now and will move into the Aquarian age sometime between 2016 and 2170, depending on whom you rely. Astrologer Phillip Lindsay says it's 2117,[5] so most of us won't see it, but you can feel it coming. Yes, Virginia, this *is* the dawning of the Age of Aquarius!

Planets

Classical astrology considered the positions of the seven heavenly bodies known at the time: The Sun, the Moon, and five planets; Mercury, Venus, Mars, Jupiter, and Saturn. It was believed that these influenced the day-to-day and year-to-year attributes of a person's life.

The three remaining planets, Uranus, Neptune, and Pluto were discovered much later and were incorporated into astrological theory, but their influences tend to have effects on generations and groups rather than changes in one's lifetime because their trip around our sun is typically longer than one's lifetime.

Here are the timeframes required by each of these to orbit Earth from the geocentric perspective:

Moon	1 month
Sun	1 year
Mercury	88 days
Venus	225 days
Mars	2 years
Jupiter	12 years
Saturn	29 years
Uranus	84 years
Neptune	165 years
Pluto	248 years[6]

As you might guess, each of these "planets" have an individual influence as well.

Sun – self, will, energy, and power

Moon – the unconscious mind, habits, and emotions

Mercury – mind, intellect, and communication

Venus – love, higher emotions, and artistic sensibility

Mars – action and the expression of will through activity

Jupiter – expansion, growth, and cooperation

Saturn – structure, limitation, experience, and discipline

Uranus – innovation, nonconformity, higher intuition, and inspiration

Neptune – transcendence, higher faculties, and psychic abilities

Pluto – deep impersonal energies and transforming forces[7]

Know that each planet rules one or more signs, has a detriment, exaltation, and a fall. These are factors that are used in interpreting astrological charts and associating characteristics with where they are in a person's chart. More than we need to know just now, so if you want to know what these are, put on your research shoes.

One last item to discuss before we leave planets: *retrogrades*. As we said earlier, all the planets in our solar system travel in the same direction. Because of our perspective from earth, there are times when a planet *appears* to be moving backwards through the zodiac, therefore retrograde. All planets can enter retrograde, but it's all dependent on their orbit around the sun. With Mercury taking only 88 days to orbit the sun, we'll see it retrograde three times during a year.

Mercury rules thinking and perception, perceiving and disseminating information, commerce, and transportation. There is common thinking among astrologers that in periods of Mercury retrograde, lasting about 23 days, communications, travel, and appointments will be in disarray, snarled, or somehow disjointed. During this period, misunderstandings, flawed communications, disrupted negotiations, and missing information are believed to be rife; therefore it's best not to make critical decisions during this time unless thoroughly thought through. Unforeseen hurdles and blocks occur that bring aggravation and frustration.[8] Obviously, Mercury retrograde affects people differently depending where Mercury is in their personal chart, but for the most part, it brings delays for all the above listed reasons. But it can also bring closure to projects, plans, and actions that were well on their way prior to beginning the retrograde.

Every planet has a retrograde and it might be interesting to look them up. Then see when each goes retrograde, and determine what impact it may have on your energies.

Birth Date

As noted earlier, at the moment you were born, the position of the earth, sun, moon, planets and stars were in a position that is unique in the expansion of the universe. They've never been there before and can only get close in the future, never again to be in exactly the same place.

That's why it's critical to have the exact date, time, and location — longitude and latitude — to determine what's known as your natal chart. That's the chart that depicts the relative position of all astrological influences at the exact time of your birth. That's why it's essential to have as much information as you can. Why? Because astrology is based on mathematics and the precision of your exact time of birth drives all the astrological interpretations for your life.

Secondarily, traditional metaphysical teaching says that the soul makes its final descent into the newborn baby's body at the time of its first breath — usually within a minute or two of the time of birth. There are those that believe the newborn's soul hangs around its mother in the last weeks of pregnancy. In doing so, the soul is able to pass from the metaphysical plane into the physical plane, enabling it to begin its existence in this physical plane. Now I know some find this concept a bit hard to grasp, but what if it's true?

Some describe this as a simple lock and key. The alignment of the planets forms an energy grid which can be visualized as an ever-changing mathematical grid like tumblers in a lock. The only souls that can make their way into this physical plane are those that can match that grid, like a key in the lock. At the particular time the alignments match, the soul is allowed to move into the newborn's body.[9]

Now, I know that this may not fit some religious beliefs, but the soul has to enter a newborn in some way, so could this possibly be one way? It might not be too far-fetched. Suffice it to say, the exact time of birth is important to astrologers as well as the exact location. Have that info ready should you seek an astrology reading.

Houses

If you've had an astrology reading, you were probably given a sheet of paper which, to the untrained eye, had a target on it. That's your astrological chart. The circle is divided into twelve sections, each representing a *House*. While there are different house-systems, most astrologers use the simplest and most compelling, the Equal system that starts with the Ascendant and divides the 360 degree chart into twelve equal parts, just like a clock, except you begin at nine o'clock and move counter clockwise to number the houses.

So, first, a few terms. The First House cusp, or the line at the nine o'clock position is the sign rising on the eastern horizon at the time and location of birth and it is called the *Ascendant*. As you might guess, the sign directly opposite the ascendant is the *Descendant* on the cusp of the Seventh House. The sign overhead is the *Midheaven* on the cusp of the Tenth House, and the sign opposite is the *Nadir*, on the cusp of the Fourth House. Once the sign of one house has been determined, the rest of the signs follow in zodiac order giving you twelve possible overlay patterns in the houses.[10]

Although not critical at the introductory level, you should know that the First House is your ascendant which begins our counter clockwise trip around the circle. You should also know that the signs of the zodiac are defined by the earth's orbit around our sun, but the houses are defined by the earth's daily rotation on its axis. Probably more than we need at this point, but it's important to know your unique perspective relative to the rest of the universe.

So, your target starts out looking something like this when you number it:

ASTROLOGICAL CHART

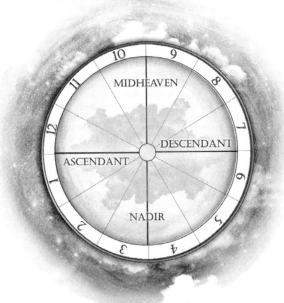

When we start with Aries as the ascendant, we have what's called the natural zodiac. So let's look at the Houses, how they're depicted, and what they can mean to an astrologer.

1st House – The *Ascendant* or *Rising Sign*. This is the most important in the chart as it shows the subject's personality and appearance and deals with formative circumstances and influences.

2nd House – Deals with material resources and possessions; concerns the ability and desire to earn a living, meet financial obligations, and acquire belongings.

3rd House – Deals with thinking and communicating; logical reasoning, getting ideas across to others, and acting perceptively are traits elicited here.

4th House – Deals with home, family, and environment that subjects create for themselves. This also includes the inner self – those things that make one comfortable and includes habits and unconscious processes.

5th House – Deals with romance, creativity, and pleasure
as well as self-expression. It governs the creative arts
and entertainment.

6th House – Deals with work and health; reveals attitude
toward work and practicality.

7th House – Deals with relationships, partnerships, and
legal matters. Can also show how one is perceived by
others.

8th House – Deals with joint resources and ventures as
well as governing sex, death, and money. Financially
it deals with business and marriage; relating to death,
it's concerned with inheritances, legacies, and rebirth.

9th House – Deals with far horizons; institutional knowledge, established systems, and long distance travel.
It deals with dissemination of knowledge through
teaching, publishing, and established systems of
religion, academia, and law.

10th House – Deals with career, reputation, and social
standing; can indicate ambition.

11th House – Deals with friendships, humanitarian activities and working together toward a common goal.

12th House – Deals with what is hidden: the unconscious
mind, psychological baggage, and mystical inspiration. This deals with deep-seated habits and emotional responses.[11]

So, each segment of the chart is a house that is influenced
by the planets in it. That's where the horoscope comes in.

Horoscope

A horoscope is simply a circular map of the zodiac depicting the houses and where all the planets are at a particular
point in time. If it's your birth date, then it's your natal chart,
if it's anytime thereafter, it's referred to as a progressed chart.
In other words, it's progressed from the origin point of the natal
chart and you'll note that the planets are in different houses
around the chart, especially the farther from the date of birth

you progress.

Once the birth date and time is computed along with the location of birth, it's converted to *sidereal time* that's measured from the vernal equinox. That basically standardizes the birth information that allows it to be used on an *ephemeris* — a table providing the positions of critical planets at a point in time — to construct a chart.

Today there are software programs that enable astrologers to quickly access this data, eliminating the tedious plotting by hand before such programs were available. The science of constructing the chart is only the first step. Interpretation of the chart is somewhere between art and science, and properly done, it defies computerization.

While the computer can be used to plot the exact locations of the planets around the zodiac chart for a horoscope, the interpretations should be done by a qualified astrologer. Some today regard astrology as superstitious nonsense without a basis in science. Others agree gravitational forces exerted on the Earth by the Sun and the Moon are measurable and planets have similar forces that can be charted through astrology. Perhaps the true measure is that ancient civilizations are gone but their gift of astrology survives. If there were none to extol the values of astrology, how could it survive so long and be so widespread?[12]

As an astrologer explains your chart to you and what the influences mean, terms may arise such as conjunction, sextile, square, trine, and opposition. These refer to angles and aspects of planets as depicted in your chart and can be accurately interpreted only by qualified practitioners. As in every facet of our world, there are charlatans everywhere, so seek recommendations from people you trust as you look for an astrologer.

It's important to understand the concept of your sun sign, your rising sign and your moon. With this combination at your time of birth, the complexity of you as an individual grows geometrically, and you can readily see with the number of permutations available, that people born at the same moment in the same location can grow to be adults and be so much alike.

The influences are there, free will allows each of them to make choices that will make them different, yet a thread runs through the energy that pulls at them from the day they were born.

Remember, your *Sun Sign* is the single most important element because it is who you are. It influences your basic character, drive, strengths, weaknesses, and your potential. Your *Rising Sign* deals with how you appear and express yourself to others. And your *Moon* reflects your past and your emotions. With these three key factors, it's surprising how close to reality an astrologer can predict an individual's aggregate behavior.

So, now you have a technical smattering of what astrology is. If you're an avid follower or a blazing skeptic, you know that coincidences are sometimes just too pat to occur randomly. I was interested at a very early age in astrology, wanting to know about the future. As the skeptics overtook the believers in my growing social circle, I thought it might be informative to do a bit of research. So while in college, I read numerous texts about astrology, avoiding the "How To" books as I really wasn't interested in process, just results — which is typical as I happen to be an Aries. I was intrigued at the coincidences that seemed to occur, but never put much stock in the various readings I got over the years.

That is, until I met Albert Gaulden, a well-known Sedona astrologer. In 1994, a friend arranged to have him give me a reading. At the time, I was a corporate executive in a Fortune 15 company and was quite used to gathering data, assessing it, asking for more, then having to make decisions in timeframes that didn't allow for total data collection. You know, just like you. You never have enough information to make a 100% correct decision. That's why hind-sight is always 20/20.

Like most folks, I loved hearing about how wonderful I was, discounted the critical watch-outs and was absorbed by the detail he purveyed. There was a single item that convinced me that smoke and mirrors were the mainstay of astrologers: he said I wouldn't be working for the company I was now with in 1998. I responded that while there may be a 2% chance, he was totally off-base.

I was with the company for more than 20 years and they valued my leadership, loyalty, and performance and had rewarded me accordingly. I told Albert the only way I would leave is if the company was to "sell out" or if I got an offer I couldn't refuse from the "outside." Having entertained a few of those outside offers, I couldn't see that happening — it was hard to match performance or potential of the company I was with. I thanked him for his time as I left and he said something cryptic like, "You'll be back."

I didn't think anything about it until the fall of 1996 when our new chairman at that time made some aggressive cash flow promises to Wall Street. Sitting at a Presidents' Meeting in London, I heard his commitment by 2000 to cash flow at $2 billion a year. He asked what each division could do. We each looked at our five year plans and our commitments were tallied. We went around the table twice, able to muster only $1.7 billion in commitments from the various divisions. We were still $300 million short. We were instructed to "go home and figure it out."

Back home, our CFO and his planning team scrubbed our five-year numbers again, and managed to squeak out a bit more, but nothing of import. Word was the rest of the divisions were tapped out as well, with no rabbits up any sleeves. As I looked for other opportunities we could pursue to grow our business without significant capital demand, I said to myself, "We're going to have to sell something."

Sorting through long term opportunities and short term values, it wasn't long before I sorted out; they're going to sell our division — *my* division. In November the decision was made and the selling of the division our folks had built from scratch was underway. It was a decision I couldn't argue with; it was the right thing to do. The only issue I had was why commit to that grandiose cash flow number? Was it because he was the new chairman and wanted to show Wall Street what he could do? Coincidentally, the stock languished over the next seven years. You can't fool the Wall Street guys too often!

Long story short, I didn't want to move to any of the other divisions, nor did I want to work for the new owners. I opted to retire at the ripe age of 50, a long term goal I'd toyed with since my late 20s. The sale actually took place in August of 1997 so I helped transition leadership to the buying company, didn't see eye to eye with their ethics, and left soon after ensuring our people were taken care of properly in the sale. I then dug out the 1994 recording Albert had given me, listened to it once again and said, "I've got to see this man."

It was February of the following year before I caught up with Albert in Sedona and asked for another reading. He was conducting a session he leads called "The Sedona Intensive" and asked if I could stay a week. I said that would cut into my ski time, but ultimately he convinced me to stay.

I asked him how he knew I wouldn't be with my old company back in 1994. He laughed, started in on a technical explanation that ended with "and so these planets and your progressed chart in your 8th House and 10th House could mean nothing less than a dramatic shift in what you were doing. It was clear as a bell to me!" Well, I didn't understand much of what he explained, but I do know that he called one of the longest shots I've ever seen for a winner.

How'd he do that? That clearly caused me to reassess my skepticism of astrology and other esoteric studies that basically say, "There are no coincidences." I still don't know how it works, but I believe I now ask very insightful questions during any kind of reading as I sort out in my own mind what's occurring on a metaphysical level I can't see.

Oh, and by the way, Albert introduced me to the fabulously talented Diane Ladd, star of stage, screen, and television. Not spending much time at the movies, I had no idea what a talent she was and asked her during a lull in the conversation, "And what do you really do?"

Key bit of advice here: don't ever, *ever*, EVER, *EVER* ask an actress what she does. Albert shrieked, Diane threw her hands up in exasperation, while Albert added, "I told him you were a movie star."

"So what is this guy some Aries with a Cancer rising?" Diane asked Albert. "He's probably even got a Moon in Capricorn." I was stunned. Albert had just given me my reading that morning, and I remembered he said I was an Aries sun sign, which I knew, and had a Cancer rising, which I had no clue what that meant. Then he added I had a Capricorn moon.

"Albert, I can't believe you'd tell someone about my astrology!" I admonished.

"I didn't say a word. I'd never discuss clients with anyone else without their permission," he sputtered.

Well, she "read" me cold. From that point forward, I saw how astute she was in understanding astrology and other things considered "Woo-Woo" in this New Age. It never ceases to amaze me how many esoteric disciplines she understands and can discuss them in enough detail to challenge experts.

I was to be even more impressed in the months to come with her insight, her clarity of mind, and her purity of heart. I fell in love with her and married this treasure the following year!

So look into astrology. Take a chance to experiment with something new if you're not familiar with it. Any book or magazine you pick up on the topic will have detailed descriptions of how wonderful you are, but remember to read the downsides as well. It's not gospel, but it's amazing how close to home astrology can hit. And remember, it's the influences the planets and stars bring, much like the moon affecting the tides — one of the strongest forces on earth. It's what you do with them that matters.

Have a reading, get a prediction of what the year ahead looks like, and then track to see what actually happens. You might just enter a New Age!

Chapter 7 Endnotes

[1] Wikimedia Foundation, *Dharma*

[2] Astro Energetics, *A Brief History of Astronomy and Astrology*

[3] Stevens, Jon, *What is Astrology?*

[4] American Federation of Astrologers, *History of Astrology*

[5] Lindsay, Phillip, *Astrology Discussions*

[6] Lofthus, Myrna, *A Spiritual Approach to Astrology*

[7] Mills, Robert, *The Planets in Astrology*

[8] Tillet, Rob, *Mercury Retrograde*

[9] Brown, Richard, *Birth Data*

[10] Mills, Robert, *The Houses in Astrology*

[11] ibid., *The Houses in Astrology*

[12] American Federation of Astrologers, *Horoscopes*

CHAPTER 8

NUMEROLOGY

"Give me full name as it appears on your birth certificate and your date of birth. I'll give you a reading," she said.

"OK. What's a reading?" was my quick comeback.

"It's a method of using the numbers contained in your name and your date of birth that identifies the influences in your life. Numerology's been around for years. It goes back to ancient times. What can it hurt? You might just find out some interesting things about your future," she explained.

Intrigued, I gave her my full name and date of birth, then promptly forgot about it. Here we were at a party, normal fare for Dallas in December. Cocktail conversation.

I didn't think anything more about it until I got a call about a week later. My "numbers" were ready and I could have them interpreted for me if I had about an hour. I agreed and set up an appointment the following week. I'd heard about others "having their numbers done" but had no clue what I would encounter. Again, made a note in my appointment book, then forgot about it until Thursday arrived and the appointment popped up on my calendar. Always intrigued by parapsychology and paranormal experiences, I was interested if not eager to see what this reading was all about. Who doesn't want to have a bit of insight for what the future holds? I know you have some interest or you wouldn't be this far into this book!

She began with "You've had some interesting times in your life. I see a significant, life-changing event that occurred at age twelve, again at age twenty-one and you had some very good career events that began at age thirty-three, again at thirty-six and again at thirty-eight. And by the way, you're going to have significant changes in your life at age forty-nine. This event at age twelve, though, probably changed your life. Do you recall anything?"

Whoa! Wait a minute! Someone told her. Had to be. "Yes, I remember distinctly. My father died suddenly and I struggled for the next few years as my mother and I didn't get along." Wow. She had no way to know.

Over the next half hour, I recounted the changes in my life, birth of children, added responsibilities and career ups and downs that coincided with the years she asked about, prefacing each with something along the lines of "This was good in 1981, what was it?"

My curiosity was piqued and I soon became interested in what she called my personal numbers: my soul number, my destiny and the rest. We delved into what the future would hold and I was warned that numbers *only identify influences, they don't predict anything.* They can only distinguish positive or negative influences; you still have free will and can minimize or maximize those influences as you live your life.

Okay, but how do they do that? During the next hour, because of my innate curiosity, she introduced me to the basic mechanics of numerology and how they are open to interpretation. Because she nailed the most significant ups and downs in my life so far, I wanted to know more.

So began my exposure and digging deeper into the mystical logic of numbers. Further visits with the numerologist and reading on my own fueled a curiosity that continues today.

Let's take a look at exactly what numerology is.
- Numerology has been described as a study of the mind where every number offers you a view into your psychological structure. It's also been described as a philosophy offering insights into existence.
- Numbers are multifaceted, offering a scientific approach to understanding and solving certain problems.

What ever way it's viewed, numerology has its followers and they believe numbers influence an individual's
life and numerology can help people understand life in
general.

• Determining the numbers is only part of the study; intuitive interpretation is another. The numbers are what
they are, but the explanation of what they mean is the
art behind the crux of numerology.[1]

• There clearly is an order to the universe, from the
smallest particles that comprise atoms to our solar system and beyond. We don't know all there is to know
about the world around us, much less the universe, but
it appears that since the dawn of mankind, men and
women have wondered about existence and how things
unfold in our world. Many theories evolved through
the ages and the science of numbers has shed light on
patterns of our existence. From simple counting from
the earliest time to complex algorithms that manage
space flight and explain things we can't see, like the
components of atoms and molecules.

• Numerology is much simpler than astrology and iron-
ically enough, doesn't require complicated mathematical calculations. It's the study of numbers and their
differing cosmic vibrations. They reflect certain
aptitudes and character tendencies as a part of the
cosmic plan.[2]

Origins

Numerology is reputed to be one of the oldest analytical
techniques in the world. It appears to be derived largely from
ancient Hindu and Arabic teachings, but it was included in
Greek, Babylonian, Hebrew and Chinese tradition. Twenty five
hundred years ago, Egyptian and Babylonian priests used
numerology to better understand their fellow man. The
Chaldeans, Mayans, Tibetans, Phoenicians and Celts are also
believed to have developed their own system of numerology
to better understand nature.

For centuries, numbers were perceived as the building blocks of the universe. Numbers were used to explain the rhythms of nature, the story of creation and sacred rituals of the Celts were often based on numbers. Greek philosophers studied numbers as an avenue to understand God, while Jewish students of the Kabbalah devised their own doctrine of numbers. Even the Bible has its book of Numbers.[3]

Remember a previous chapter on Ascended Masters? One of the incarnations of Master Koot Hoomi was thought to be the Greek philosopher Pythagoras. Well, Pythagoras was a sixth century BC Greek mathematician, widely known for his Pythagorean Theorem and is credited as the architect of what we today call numerology.

Actual origins predate Pythagoras, but he's generally credited with attributing the mystical significance numerology enjoys today. It's only within the twentieth century that the science "reappears" in a series of books published from 1911 to 1917 by L. Dow Balliett and later in the 1930s by Florence Campbell. More has been written about numerology in the last ninety years than ever before.[4]

Back to Pythagoras! He was born on the Greek island of Samos in the Aegean Sea. As a young man, he traveled to Egypt where he learned mathematics, studied with Zoraster in Persia and learned the Kabbalah in Judea, basing later teachings on Kabalistic principles. He settled in Crotona in southern Italy and established a school of the mysteries. As a prerequisite before students could study the mysteries, they had to know the four sciences of arithmetic, music, astronomy and geometry.

Pythagoras taught that "Evolution is the law of life; Number is the law of the universe; Unity is the law of God."[5] He believed everything in the universe was subject to predictable cycles; he measured these cycles with the numbers one through nine. So, using concepts defined by Pythagoras, these numbers are a way of categorizing what was happening on earth when we were born and how our current vibrations relate to what's occurring with the earth and the universe.

Many cultures have used numbers throughout the centuries and their numerology has been passed down and interpreted along the way. For example, Hindus have incorporated numerology into their beliefs through divination, a calculation of numbers to predict the time or outcome of events. Ancient Tibetan mystics used divination methods to predict the future. China has *I Ching*, the "Book of Changes," written more than 5000 years ago and it's — strangely enough — used to predict change.

Translations of hieroglyphics indicate Egyptians used numerological measurements in symmetry with the sun when designing pyramids; recall the metrics of the Great Pyramid described in Chapter 3? Ancient Greeks used a method called Sacred Geometry using circles, squares and triangles to count items like grain, recording the supply to easily determine how much was available. The Kabbalah, based on the Hebrew esoteric understanding of the Bible, used letters transcribed to numbers to provide insights about the past, present and future.[6] So we've been using numbers for a long time.

When we are born, we enter the earth's energy field marked by our time of birth. Because the earth's energy vibrations vary from moment to moment, the birth date is the discrete marker that identifies the conditions of that energy field that it is said to characterize particular actions and reactions for the rest of our lives. The basis for numerology predicates we are conditioned by the basic set of vibrations that were active when we took our first breath.[7]

Everything in life has its own rhythm, its own pace. You have your own rhythm and cycles as well. Numerologists believe lives are lived out in nine-year cycles. Knowing which cycle you're in could help you fulfill your potential. The first six years in a cycle are related to physical experiences – you are participating in life. The seventh year is for combining those experiences with wisdom. The eighth year brings a re-evaluation of the previous seven years and the previous nine-year-cycles. In your ninth year, you're completing what you're working on, beginning new ideas and situations. Often, years eight and nine bring major changes in your life. They can be emotional, mental or spiritual just as well as physical.[8]

So each person has a set of personal numbers, discreet to him or her. These are not isolated indicators, but more like interlocking pieces of the vast puzzle of existence. So the numbers, axioms, and fundamentals we'll view are the basics, open to interpretation by practitioners who have both study and experience for complete understanding. Or as close as we're going to get!

These numbers are believed to reflect a great deal about an individual's character, purpose in life, what motivates them, and what talents they possess. Experts purportedly can determine the best time for major moves and activities in a person's life. Many of those who follow numerology use their personal numbers for a variety of plans they may have: investments, partners, travel and major changes in both their personal and business careers.[9]

Some believe all life is governed by numbers, specifically one through nine. Each number has many qualities which include strengths and weaknesses as well as positives and negatives. Each person has a combination of positive and negative influences in their chart. You can be an extremely positive person but a mental or physical trauma may cause negative qualities or influences.[10]

The key to remember as we go forward: *numbers identify influences; they are neither good nor bad, but must be taken in the context they're given*. Just like the weather in a golf match. A slight drizzle may be seen as a negative. If it doesn't cancel a round, it certainly changes it: it's the same course, but the ball won't travel as far, the moisture impedes the progress of the ball, and you have to hit your putts more firmly because of the added resistance. The game must be played differently and a golfer's skills must be adapted to conditions to play his or her best.

While there are many texts on numerology, I've found one of the most comprehensive, widely used, and easily understood is *Numerology and The Divine Triangle* by Faith Javane and

Dusty Bunker.[11] It provides a soup to nuts overview and concise interpretations of more complex number combinations.

Simple numerology deals with the digits one through nine. There are, however, delineations that cover one through seventy eight, a number that isn't quite random. It represents the number twelve in combination with the basic one through nine cycle. It represents the twelve months of the year, a complete cycle, a whole circle. It also has connotations of the twelve signs of the zodiac and the twelve disciples in Christian belief. It's believed that the next step, 13, takes one to a new level of consciousness. The number 78 is attained by adding each integer, one through twelve; the result — 78 — symbolizes the complete round of experience.[12]

Interestingly, the seventy eight numbers described by Javane and Bunker as numerical vibrations are also synthesized with the seventy eight Tarot keys, planets, and signs of the zodiac. As they say, "Only a cosmic mind could have planned such an intricate pattern in which each science dovetails so exquisitely with the other."[13]

Numerologists believe that numbers represent universal principles through which all things evolve in a cyclic fashion. Orderly progressions are the rule and every word or name vibrates to a number. Every number has its own meaning.

Esoteric Numerology

Let's take a look at Esoteric Numerology. Each number has identifying characteristics, emanating from the basis of being. Every number ultimately reduces to one of these numbers, one through nine and inherently they represent characteristics that differentiate them from one another. Following are the major attributes for each number, combined from two texts.[14, 15]

1. REPRESENTS THE MALE PRINCIPLE. Original, independent, aggressive, creative, dominant. The leader, the pioneer.

Positives	Negatives
Focused	Unfocused
Pioneer	Destructive
Independent	Dependent
Courageous	Stuck Emotionally
Leader	Self-Centered

2. IS THE PAIR. Adaptable, tactful, understanding, gentle, cautious. A follower.

Positives	Negatives
Balanced	Unbalanced
Placid	Cautious
Decisive	Indecisive
Peace-Loving	Overemotional
Kind	Defensive

3. COMBINES THE QUALITIES OF 1 AND 2. Dramatic, expansive, sociable, communicative, diversified, creative.

Positives	Negatives
Adaptable	Confused
Self-Expressive	Lack of Expression
Creative	Superficial
Humorous	Chaotic
Communicative	Uncommunicative

4. IS STABILITY. Form, work, order, practicality, construction, stability, endurance, discipline.

Positives	Negatives
Responsible	Irresponsible
Down to Earth	Ungrounded
Hard Working	Lazy
Creative	Insecure
Comfortable	Dissatisfied

5. IS FREEDOM. Versatility, resourcefulness, adaptability, change, activity, travel, adventure, promotion, speculation.

Positives	Negatives
Communicative	Uncommunicative
Freedom-Loving	Restrictive
Adventurous	Impulsive
Magnetic	Addictive
Curious	Procrastinates

6. IS CONCIENTIOUS. Family, social responsibility, service, love, compassion, healing, creativity.

Positives	Negatives
Loving	Uncaring
Just	Unjust
Responsibility	Resent Responsibility for Group
Generous	Mean
Idealistic	Obsessive

7. SEEKS ANSWERS. Quiet, introspective, intuitive, analytical, inspirational, reclusive, philosophical, mystical.

Positives	Negatives
Nature Loving	Gloomy
Sensitive	Overly Analytical
Trusting	Impatient
Truthful	Dishonest
Realistic	Dreamy

8. WILL ASSUME POWER. Power, responsibility, financial rewards, good judgment, recognition.

Positives	Negatives
Inspiring	Lacking Inspiration
Strong	Weak
Powerful	Powerless
Authoritarian	Egotistical
Successful	Fears Failure

9. IS SELFLESSNESS. Love, compassion, patience, tolerance, universality, selfless service, endings.

Positives	Negatives
Selfless	Selfish
Unconditional Love	Resentful
Fair	Critical
Open	Secretive
Discriminating	Judgmental

Everyone at birth is endowed with their own four personal numbers: the *Life Lesson* number, the *Soul* number, the *Outer Personality* number and the *Path of Destiny* number. These personal numbers are determined by your birth date and the full name you are given at birth, first, middle, last.

The first step in numerology is simple. To determine the numerical vibration of names, each letter is reduced to one of the nine numbers above. Each letter in the alphabet is given a number value based on their position in the sequence. For example, A is 1, B is 2, C is 3 and so on to Z which is 26. Everything is based on 1 through nine, so all values of the alphabet can be reduced to one of those numbers. For example, Z is 26; when you add the two digits, 2 and 6, you get 8. Z's value is 8. So every number is reduced to 1 through 9, with four exceptions: 11, 22, 33 and 44. These are *master numbers* and when you arrive at one of these, you retain the master number value. We'll take a look at that below.

Listed here are each letter of the alphabet and its base number. These are the building blocks for determining your four personal numbers.[16]

A	1	J	$10 = 1$	S	$19 = 1$
B	2	K	$11 = 2$	T	$20 = 2$
C	3	L	$12 = 3$	U	$21 = 3$
D	4	M	$13 = 4$	V	$22 = 4$
E	5	N	$14 = 5$	W	$23 = 5$
F	6	O	$15 = 6$	X	$24 = 6$
G	7	P	$16 = 7$	Y	$25 = 7$
H	8	Q	$17 = 8$	Z	$26 = 8$
I	9	R	$18 = 9$		

So, to demonstrate, let's take a few words to see how this works:

L   I   B   R   A   R   Y
$3 + 9 + 2 + 9 + 1 + 9 + 7 = 40 = 4$

So, looking back at the number **4** above, we see that 4 is stability, its attributes are form, work, order, practicality, construction, stability, endurance, discipline. Sounds kind of like a library, doesn't it? If you do the same drill with the word FATHER, you'll see it equals 31, which equals **4** again; the positive attributes also sound like father, or what one is supposed to be, right?

How about the word

M O T H E R
4 +6 +2 +8 +5 +9 = 34 = 7

Look above at 7 above and we see positive attributes of intuitive, inspirational, philosophical, trusting; kind of like a good mom, right?

Now, let's take a look at the word

L I G H T
3 +9 +7 +8 +2 = 29 = 11

Eleven happens to be a master number! When we deal with a master number like 11, we acknowledge the base number of 2 but its vibrations will fluctuate between 2 and 11.

A master number is so intense and powerful in its vibration that it cannot be lived under continuously, so the base number offers respite where one can rest and collect energy before working with the master vibration number again. Master numbers demand the greatest output from an individual but in turn extend the greatest rewards.

So now that we can translate words and names into numeric values, let's take a look at the four base components of numerology. We'll start with the life lesson number, but first let me emphasize that my intent here is to familiarize you with numerology, so I will refer you from here on to the Javane and Bunker book *Numerology and the Divine Triangle* for a more thorough interpretation of the numbers you develop. I will simply summarize each numerical section so you can gain the essence of their interpretation. The book is simple, yet in-depth. Enough so that many numerologists use it regularly to help in their readings. My hope here is to pique your curiosity!

Life Lesson

The life lesson number represents the lessons you must learn in this lifetime and is most significant in your career choice. Everyone and everything has a birth date: people, businesses, organizations and even ideas. So to get your life lesson number, you simply total the month, day and year of your birth.

So, let's assume your birth date is February 14, 1967. Our addition looks like this: February is the second month – a 2 – and added to the 14, we have 16. Now add the year 1+9+6+7 which equals 23; add our earlier sum of 16, month and date, to 23, the year, and we have 39. So 39 (3+9) equals 12 (1+2) equals 3. Your life lesson then is written 39/3. Simply add all digits in the date of birth. Try it!

As an example, we're going to use the person created by Javane and Bunker, a Mrs. Ada Wynn Lunt, born November 12, 1940. So we'll add 11 for November, 12 for the day and the integers in 1940 to equal 37. That number adds to 10, which adds to 1. So we note it as 37/1. Now we can see what that means in the chart below.

So now you can check your personal number with the following from the Javane and Bunker book, *Numerology and the Diving Triangle*, as they apply to life lessons. These have been shortened for the sake of brevity. You should get the book if you want a more thorough summary.

1   Learn to be original, strong-willed, creative, innovative. You are efficient, well organized, like sports, and enjoy winning; usually at the head of social and business groups.

2   Learn to become a good mixer. You are persuasive and are good at sales. Your lessons come from groups and partnerships where you must have consideration for others as you bring people together for common cause.

3   Best in intellectual, artistic or creative endeavors. You have ambition and pride and you fight for self expression and freedom. You dislike restriction and best work alone.

4   Build a solid foundation for life; that demands well-ordered system of conduct and morals. You are a diligent worker and honestly earn your success.

5   Key word is freedom. You are a good explorer and a diligent student if interested; you have no use for subjects you deem not useful. You are eager for new experiences, shun monotony and are an avid reader, fluent talker, as well as a witty conversationalist.

6   Learn sense of responsibility for family and community. You are responsive to social needs of others and can equalize injustices. You are here to bring service, teaching and comfort to humanity.

7   Learn to use and develop mind. Your words are full of wisdom and your strong intuition gives insight; you may be an enigma. You may delve into the occult and mysterious side of life; your destiny is to use your mind.

8   Learn to work, lead, and profit by example. You have power and ambition; you are the executive, the boss who lives by brain and brawn and can push people to be successful in their own right. Learn to handle power, authority and money.

9   Be the universal lover of humanity: patient, kind and understanding. You are at the peak of life's expression, so you must show others the way. You know the true way of happiness is in service to others.

So, these are the basic numbers, 1 through 9. Then we have master numbers that aren't reduced. These are:

11   Key words are altruism and community. Must practice "love thy neighbor as thyself" and use it as foundation. This is the master number of spiritual import, bestowing power, courage and talent; fame and recognition are likely. Realize true mastership is service.

22   Must express basic building urge, accomplish things in a big way and work with large groups. You can take inspirational ideas and put them to practical use.

33   Be steady and reliable; develop a strong desire to protect others. Your talent may lie in the arts: music to bring harmony, painting to bring beauty, or literature to promote education. A 33 consciousness is almost beyond humanity; sacrifice for others may be required.

44   Stands for strength and complete mental control over your life on earth. You have high energy potential meant to further evolution by helping others set their world in order. You should promote better ethics and justice in business world. Serve as example to others through bravery, discipline, resourcefulness and courage.[17]

So these are Life Numbers. They're the vibrations that coincide with the earth on the day you were born and are the basis of what you're here to learn. So even if you don't "buy" numerology per se, any one of these numbers is a good profile of things to learn in this life. And, who knows, maybe it moves both you and humanity along the perilous path ahead. It wouldn't hurt to give it a shot!

Soul Number

So now we take a look at the soul number, your *real* personality — the you that only you know. This is the part of your personality that is not easily recognized by others unless they know you very well. It's your inner secret self; what you desire to be.

Now for a real New Age bonus. For those that embrace the philosophy of reincarnation, the soul number indicates what you've been and done in previous lives. It reveals something of the growth accumulated throughout past lives, becoming a primary energy which influences life today. So, those who believe this theory espouse that if the soul urge is suppressed by any means, it may need to repeat the same vibration in a future life until it finds true expression. So get it right this time!

The soul number is derived by adding the values of the vowels in the name. It's important to use the full name at birth — again, include your middle name. No nicknames, aliases, or shortened names. Also, disregard prefixes like Mr., Dr., Mrs. as well as suffixes such as Jr., Sr., III and Esq. They're not considered part of the cosmic name and therefore aren't counted.

So, as you do your computations, you note the values above the vowels A, E, I, O and U. The letter Y is considered a vowel when it sounds like and E, as in Mary, or it's the only vowel in the syllable, like Sybil. It is not valued in a name like May. W is tricky. It is considered a vowel when it follows D or

G as in the names Dwight and Gwen because it carries the vowel sound. Got that?

So let's go back to Mrs. Lunt. We determine her soul number by noting the vowels, adding them, then adding the sum as follows:

$$1 + 1 + 7 + 3 = 12/3$$
A D A   W Y N N   L U N T

In the listing of numbers below, you'll find an explanation of the soul number. Javane and Bunker get into a delineation of the total number and its reduction — 12/3 in Ada's name above — in their book. I'm not going there because this is only an introduction. Get their book to get a finer tuning of your soul number. I'm only summarizing the core and master numbers below.

1   Leadership won in past lives now brings a desire to strive for higher consciousness. Beliefs are independent and you yearn for free and independent thinking. You're always conscious of your inner strength and have difficulty taking second position among your contemporaries. Your inner strength is a mainstay when times are rough and you can be a tower of inspiration to others in time of trouble.

2   You have a strong desire for Peace and Harmony. You are considerate, tactful, adaptable and gentle. You are a follower rather than a leader. Overcome indecision; hesitation may allow others to forge ahead of you and claim what should be yours. Dare to do what's right.

3   You're conscientious in regard to duty. You're aware that inspiration and imagination bring results when used to help others. You bring hope and courage to those who feel depressed. Work to make your dreams come true.

4   You are well organized; practicality permeates your being. You could be a model to others in your well-ordered life. You are serious in both romance and business and can make your dreams come true in a planned and practical way.

5   You claim freedom and don't allow limitations of your ideals and thinking. Variety of self expression is essential. You need the stimulation of change and new viewpoints.

6   You respond to beauty, harmony, and peace. You are affectionate, sympathetic and loyal to those you love. Your mission could be to teach others peace and harmony to spread the Golden Rule.

7   You're quiet, reserved, a good thinker, analyzer, and mediator. You need a peaceful environment and become irritable with noise. You're refined, sensitive, secretive and usually psychic. Your true nature is to be calm, to develop depth of character, and to benefit humanity through philosophy.

8   You are ambitious; you believe in accomplishment and will allow nothing to deter you from your goal. You have the ability to organize large groups and projects. Others expect more of you than the average person so you must rely on your inner self for guidance to stay at the top.

9   You are intuitive and it plays a strong role in your life. You can think in abstract terms and are sensitive as well as imaginative. You are extremely impressionable, compassionate and generous. You're kind and forgiving with a consciousness dedicated to uplifting humanity; you could have been a master in a past life.

11 You've been on the spiritual path for a long time, perhaps many incarnations. Through spiritual evolution you've learned much about life and death. You have courage, talent and leadership and are understanding, wise, intuitive and often clairvoyant. You have extremely sensitive ESP and strong spiritual leanings.

22 You have the urge to continue tangible achievements of past lifetimes. You are a master builder and desire material fulfillment. Your aim is to leave the world a tangibly better place for your having been here, so you must maintain mental balance while expressing ideas practically. Your goals are higher than others.

33   You're prepared to sacrifice for the good of humanity.
          You see world conditions clearly and are ready to help
          in any way to bring peace to humanity. Sometimes
          your life lesson vibrations will conflict with this soul
          urge so you must practice generosity and try to see
          other's viewpoints. You're always ready to help others.
44   Universal concepts are part of your consciousness and
          express themselves as inner urges to advance world
          culture. You want to unite the practical with the philo-
          sophical. You innately solve everyday problems and
          can help others to organize their lives.[18]

So there's your soul number. It may be the urge you sometimes can't explain. That gnawing at your stomach or the back
of your mind when things don't exactly seem right or are a little "off." It may be your inner self screaming, prodding or poking you to "remember" who you are, what you stand for and
what should be done.

Maybe it's your conscience. Maybe it's the force that drives
you in all you do, that unexplainable urge to do something specific when an abstract urge propels you to "do it." The rationale we hear used many times when asked, "Why do you do it?"
is "Because it's there!" That could be your soul speaking in a
yet not fluent language, your actions speaking louder than the
words you can't find. It certainly gives us something to ponder,
doesn't it?

Outer Personality

So now that we know numerically who we are in the deepest, darkest synapses of our self, how do others see us? That
would be found in the outer personality number. It also reflects
what people expect of you based on the image you put forward.

To find the outer personality number, we simply add the
values of all the consonants — those letters that aren't vowels
— in the full birth name. We'll put those values beneath the
name and again we'll add each number then reduce the total.
Let's use Ada again:

A D A   W Y N N   L U N T
4 +   5 +   5+5 + 3 + 5+2 = 29/11

So we see that the consonants in Ada's name add to 29 which is 11 when added together. We don't reduce 11 because it is a master number. So other people see Ada as an 11, which may not necessarily be who she is! We'll look below to see exactly what others see and perceive Ada to be, her personality.

Personality stems from the word *persona* meaning façade or mask and characterizes the image we present to others. Your personality — your body language, mannerisms and traits — provides clues that others use to determine your attitude and characteristics. Put another way, it's what others use to interpret and understand you. So let's see what each number represents:

1   You represent an independent, capable and executive-like image to the world. Others expect you to take control and be able to run an organization efficiently. You can appear aggressive and domineering. You dress stylishly and exclusively, choosing not to look like anyone else.

2   You appear quiet, modest, and require a peaceful environment. You are detail oriented; neatness and cleanliness counts. You prefer balance in all you do from dress to evaluating situations. You may have difficulty in making decisions because you always see both sides of an issue so clearly.

3   You are affable, charming and sociable. Your manner is attractive and you seek pleasure and fun. Communication is a vital part of your personality and you are an ardent conversationalist. You spread sunshine and optimism everywhere you go, attracting others to your warmth. You have an artistic flair in clothing.

4   You appear conservative, self-disciplined and practical to the world through a determined and work-oriented attitude. You're honest, hardworking and respect value and industry. You can appear so disciplined that there is no time for leisure and may isolate yourself from others. Your clothes are traditional, reflecting service and you want to look neat at all times.

5   You are bright, sparkling and witty; a good conversationalist. Change and freedom are essential to you. You like constant activity and variety; you believe change is progress. You have a natural curiosity and are likely to take chances. You prefer to be among the best dressed.

6   You emanate a protectiveness and a sense of responsibility for others. You have a fine sense of balance and symmetry, able to see all the pieces separately yet as part of the whole. Your social consciousness leads you to seek truth and justice. You are careful in your clothing choices yet display an artistic flair.

7   You appear to be a loner enjoying time away from crowds. You have an air of secrecy and mystery; you seem to be the philosopher, mystic, poet, thinker, scientist, and researcher. Your keen power of observation helps you analyze any situation. You have an aristocratic air, a personal dignity and a refined manner that provides you with an unshakeable faith in the future. You are neat and well-groomed and are inclined to avoid loud colors.

8   You have a dynamic personality; people recognize your authority because you appear affluent and in control. You appear authoritative, impartial and ethical. Successful appearance is your standard, your clothing being well made of quality materials.

9   You appear to have a breadth of understanding as well as a universal personal magnetism. You're warm and charming with all those you meet and the selflessness you emanate endears you to many. You express humanitarian traits and others see you as an idealist who believes world progress justifies personal sacrifice. You dress artistically with a dramatic flair.

11   You are an inspiration to others who see you as an artistic genius which moves their soul. You appear to be the visionary that believes in true equal opportunity. Your eyes emit a spiritual light that can inspire others to achieve their potential. Your dress is original reflecting your artistic flair and inventiveness. You prefer to be different.

22   You appear as the diplomatic master who can handle anything in a practical and efficient manner. You seem to have control over the material world and have the ability to make profound changes that may alter history. You are a super power who gives finances freely to charities that affect large numbers of people. You are unusually careful about your dress opting for conservative styles of high quality.

33   You impress others as modest, charitable and humble. You gravitate to where you're needed and always give more than you receive. Generous, you don't seek rewards. You dress in dignified styles and your conduct is always proper.

44   You have a disciplined, almost military bearing that inspires confidence wherever you go. You know where you're going, what you're going to do and how you'll do it. You have a down-to-earth practicality that comforts others. You enjoy uniform-type apparel.[19]

So, that's how others see you. While there are positives listed above, please remember that every positive has a negative to maintain a balance, and it's always your free choice to follow any path you want. Should you veer into the negative aspects of these numbers, then different results will manifest themselves, each the opposite of a positive trait. For example, charm and the ability to lead others charismatically can "go to one's head" and result in cruelty while believing you're righteous. Best to watch that exterior you extend to others and ensure your "right stuff" prevails!

Destiny

Now we'll add all the numbers together to determine the path of destiny number. This number represents your aim in life: what path you are here to walk, what you should accomplish and what you must be. Although you may modify it somewhat by name changes, the birth name destiny is the power behind any change and will persist for expression throughout your life. This is what you must do this lifetime, what you are here to manifest. So how do we get this number?

So far, we've determined your life lesson number by your birth date, your soul number by the vowels in your name and your outer personality number by the consonants in your name. To get your path of destiny number, we'll take the total of your entire name. We can go through the numerics anew or we can simply add the unreduced soul number and the unreduced outer personality number. Let's take Ada's example:

$$1 + 1 + 7 + 3 = 12/3$$
$$\text{A D A   W Y N N   L U N T}$$
$$4 + 5 + 5+5 + 3 + 5+2 = 29/11$$
$$\text{Path of Destiny   } 41/5$$

So by adding the 12/3 soul number and the 29/11 outer personality number, we get a path of destiny number of 41/5. Five is her basic path of destiny. Let's look at the attributes of destiny numbers:

1   Your represent "I am," concerned with your individual desires and seeking self-preservation above all else. You use your resources for yourself and have little interest in the needs of others. You are here to develop the self. Leadership is your keyword. By demonstrating self-reliance and your ability to win, you will succeed in all cases.

2   Your role is peacemaker. You could act as ambassador of good will to other nations and benefit humanity. Use your innate tact and diplomacy to handle difficult life situations. You have a gift for creating a better world. You also have a keen sense of opposites which you can develop creatively. Expanding this awareness can not only maximize your artistic potential, but also enhance your ability as a mediator. You become an integral part of any organization with which you affiliate.

3   Your destiny is to uplift and inspire others. You should play center-stage and develop your talent for communication and expression through drama, elocution or foreign languages. Use your time wisely; promote friendship among peers by being a friend and spread sunshine through self-expression. Optimism should be your trademark.

4   Your destiny is to build useful and tangible products. This number destiny is the builder of the world. You emanate stability; others rely on you to get the job done properly and efficiently. Your keywords are impatience, honesty, determination and confidence. You demand obedience in the family and practice self-denial in your fulfillment of duties. You have a keen sense of value and know that what is worth having is worth waiting for.

5   Your mission may well be to promote progress through change, consequently there will be many changes in your life. You have the courage to let go of the old and try the new, yet you aren't a rebel; your new ideas promote enlightenment. You are fluent and expressive with words and could find writing, lecturing or selling a perfect outlet for your talent.

6   You love home and family. You are morally good, respectable, trustworthy and generous. You appreciate the luxuries of life and are a good mixer; your hosting abilities enable you to meet and greet everyone at any social gathering. Train your artistic talents to share aesthetics and beauty with others.

7   You are destined to be a teacher of ethics; you have depth of character and are serious about life. You psychically separate true from false and can discover and reveal mysteries of life to a receptive world. Your example and image could benefit both community and the world. You find strength and wisdom in solitude and are comfortable with your own knowledge. Develop your mind and the world will benefit.

8   Recognition, success and wealth are your destiny. You have courage and stamina and can attain goals through your own efforts. You must join your material forces with the spiritual to gain mastery over yourself before you can attain your ultimate visualization of your life's work. Many individuals with this number become outstanding athletes.

9   Your goal is perfection, your mission charitable. You may face many tests and setbacks; you must guard against losing balance as you are challenged with more tests. Broaden your circle of friends; your expansive philosophy must enlighten the lives of many people.

11   You have the gift of prophecy where selfless service to humanity can be expressed. You may work as a public leader promoting better standards of living for the less fortunate. Your creativity can be augmented with an inspirational touch that will affect the souls of those who come into contact with your work. You are truly inspired.

22   You have confidence in your leadership and assume great responsibility. You are a creator on the material plane; you build big. Bridges, hospitals, museums and the like are visible objects you leave to the world that aid and enlighten humanity. Rewards will be proportionate to your service.

33   Your mission is self sacrifice and service to others. Your actions are tempered by compassion and your understanding of justice. Others are drawn to you for comfort and understanding; providing these fulfills the demand for this number.

44   Your destiny is to serve the material needs of the world through productive and sound techniques. You are resourceful, have great stores of common sense and logic that serve you well when problems arise. You gain complete mastery over your body and mind and should seek to share your talents to attain universal prosperity.[20]

Now you know what numbers say about your destiny. It's what you're here to do. To learn. What you should really be. And everyone should strive to be better — for society, for your family, for yourself. It's *your* destiny!

Personal Numbers

Okay, there's more, but we're only going to mention a few of the topics and not go into detail. For instance, the first vowel in your name has significance and if it's repeated it can strengthen the influence. You can easily research the nuances of both the vowels as well as each consonant as you delve deeper into numerology.

Know that just like your personal numbers derived on your birthday, that each day of the year has its own influence, compounded by the period, month, and year. Just as we've seen above, the cycles of nine are present in each of these time divisions.

Your personal year will have a personal vibration for you and therefore, a numeric influence for the entire year. If it's a "work" year, influences throughout the year will have the overtones of work. To calculate your personal year, you simply add the month and day of your birth to the year of your last birthday.

So in Ada Wynn Lunt's example, let's assume she wants to find her personal year on March 15, 2006. Remember, her birthday was November 12, 1940, so we simply add the month and day of her birth year — 11 for November + 12 for the day, is 23 — and add that to the sum of the numbers of the year of her last birthday, which was 2005. So we add the sum of the month and day, 23, to the sum of the year on her last birthday, 7, to get 30/3; so she's in a 3 personal year.

Personal years are then divided into three equal blocks of time and can be computed as well. Each numerical influence here will span four months. While this is important in mapping our daily influences for the entire year, we won't go into that computation here. You can refer to the Javane and Bunker book for that.

The personal year is further broken down into personal months. That computation, too, is fairly easy. So if we want to find what personal month March of 2005 is for Ada, we simply add 3 — March is the third month of the year — to her personal year, 3, which totals 6. So March is a 6 personal month for Ada.

And lastly, we can compute personal days. We simply take Ada's sum of her birth month and day, 23, and add that to the sum of the date she wants to know, in this case, March 15, 2006 (March, 3, plus 15, plus the sum of the year 2006, or 8) or 26/8. It's an 8 day for Ada.

So, she's in a 3 personal year, a 6 personal month, and the March 15, 2006 is an 8 personal day. So what does that mean?

Let's first take a look at the keywords for personal numbers so we can interpret what influences Ada might be looking at on that date. Here's a quick table for fast reference:

1 **Beginnings**, new starts, action, originality, making decisions
2 **Relationships**, Harmony, cooperation, mediation, passivity
3 **Lucky**, Scattering, freedom, entertainment, self-expression
4 **Work**, Practicality, order, building foundations
5 **Selling**, Change, freedom, new intellectual interests, travel
6 **Self**, Family, health, service, listening to others' problems
7 **Planning**, Self-analysis, achievement, heath problems
8 **Power**, Business, responsibility, money
9 **Endings**, Giving to others, service[21, 22]

So if we use this chart for interpretation, Ada's in a 3 personal year, so she has no particular focus this year and is open to expressing herself freely and having fun; it'll probably be a lucky year! March, being a 6 personal month for her, will influence her toward family and service perhaps lending a sensitive ear to any issues those around her might have; it's a month of taking care of herself and personal things. And finally, the 15th is an 8 personal day for her, so she may well be responsible for a family member and may exert her power or give them money to help them.

On the other hand, it being a 3 year for her, she may be in Las Vegas having fun, entertainment, with her *family* — March being a 6 month for her — and on the 15th, may well hit the jackpot, money, while playing slots! You see how the interpretation can be in range, but may miss the actual events of the day?

That's why you should seek a numerologist that's been practicing for a number of years when you get a reading. He or she will bring the insight of experience and has probably developed a sensitivity to interpreting the numbers, their combinations, and what pluses and minuses they offer in relation to all the other components of your name and numbers.

Because numerology deals with numbers, there appears to be some precision to it. Numbers always add up the same way, especially when you're merely adding integers; what can you possibly do wrong? Maybe that's why numerology is an esoteric art or science. There are hidden meanings in the interpretation arena.

I know I was astounded at the seeming accuracy of my first reading, enough so to pursue it further. I've come to believe that there is something to the influences that numbers seem to identify. But like any choice, the same option can turn out good or bad, it's what you do with it.

So I do look at what personal day it is for me, but I treat it as I would a road sign: it depends on conditions. If there's a curve ahead, and it's dry with no visible traffic approaching the turn, I might take it a bit faster than I would if it were obscured and raining. I use it as an alert to potential issues — or goodies! It can go either way.

You might try a reading from a numerologist recommended by one of your New Age friends. You may get some insight and have it ignite your curiosity to pursue it further. Worst case, it's a bit of entertainment that can't hurt, right?

Chapter 8 Endnotes

[1] Ducie, Sonia, Numerology, *What is Numerology*

[2] McClain, Michael, Astrology-Numerology, *Numerology*

[3] Sinclair, Jim, Cyberastro, Ltd., *Numerology*

[4] op. cit., *Numerology*

[5] Javane, Faith and Bunker, Dusty, *Numerology and The Divine Triangle*, *Esoteric Numerology*

[6] Ducie, Sonia, Numerology, *Methods of Interpretation*

[7] op. cit., *Esoteric Numerology*

[8] Ducie, Sonia, Numerology, *Cycles and Trends*

[9] op. cit., *Esoteric Numerology*

[10] Ducie, Sonia, Numerology, *The Principles of Numerology*

[11] Javane, Faith and Bunker, Dusty, *Numerology and The Divine Triangle*

[12] ibid., *Numerology and The Divine Triangle*

[13] ibid., *Numerology and The Divine Triangle*

[14] ibid., *Numerology and The Divine Triangle*

[15] Ducie, Sonia, Numerology, *The Meanings of Numbers*

[16] op. cit., *Your Personal Numbers...*

[17] ibid., *The Life Lesson Number*

[18] ibid., *The Soul Number*

[19] ibid., *The Outer Personality Number*

[20] ibid., *The Path of Destiny Number*

[21] Runmark, Francie, *Numerology Discussion*

[22] op. cit., *Personal Month*

CHAPTER 9

INSIGHTS & INTRIGUE

Since the beginning of time, mankind has been curious. Curious about the world, curious about how things work, and curious about the future. And like any good entrepreneur, when he saw a need, he filled it.

That's probably how fortune telling began — sitting around their newfound fire warming their cave, someone would ask if it would rain tomorrow or if the hunt would be successful. Obviously an assertive, gambling type, one among the clan would predict rain. And it would rain. A lucky guess, or was it the ability to predict accurately?

Dealing with the real stars or actual numbers, astrology and numerology had some sense of hard science associated with them. But what about those ancients who felt, saw, or heard the future and were able, at least in their own minds, to offer portents of what would happen tomorrow, next week, or next year. Maybe they were called clerics or witches. Maybe they were able to read situations intuitively and guess correctly, or be practiced enough to be vague. Perhaps they were mere tricksters, able to convince those around them they had special talents. Or maybe they were genuinely blessed with the capability to see the future. Maybe — maybe not.

Fortunetellers

Fortunetellers have been around since day one. It's the practice of predicting someone's future through mystical or supernatural means, most often for some form of payment. Methods range from astrology and numerology to card reading, crystal gazing, and interpreting the creases in your hand. Many a future romantic association, financial prospect, or child-bearing prediction has been made by fortune tellers.

Although origins of fortunetelling are obscure, it's fairly common to associate the art of telling the future with people often called Gypsies. The term typically refers to the Roma and Sinti, a traditionally nomadic people who originated in northern India dispersing throughout the world but principally in Europe. They are known by many names and are estimated to be eight to ten million people strong with the largest concentration in the Balkan Peninsula of southeastern Europe, Romania and Hungary having the highest concentrations.[1]

Are they blessed with foresight? Can they predict the future? Perhaps in time we'll learn more, but for now, let's look at the methods and tools fortune tellers might use in this New Age.

Palmistry

Palmistry or *palm reading* is the study of the lines and signs of the hands. It's purported to be the blueprint of your life; your past, present, and future health and much more. Everything on your palm means something including the nails and the color tones of the skin.

Once you have a line on your hand, it doesn't go away. It's believed that lines are added during a lifetime through electromagnetic changes emitted by your brain. New lines typically develop on your dominant hand while the other hand is interpreted as your destiny.

This ancient practice has been recorded as far back as 12,000 to 15,000 years ago. Handprints can be found in prehistoric caves, like those in Santander, Spain displaying drawings of palms with major lines depicted in amazing detail. The emperor of China used his thumbprint to seal documents in 3000 BC. Early Hindu writings indicate the hands were a means to understand the self and relationships with others. Aristotle — 384-322 BC — discovered a treatise on Palmistry on an altar to the god Hermes, while Greek physicians like Hippocrates — 130-200 BC — were using palmistry as a clinical aid.

The first book on palmistry was written in 1477 by Michael Scott; it described all aspects of the hand with the statement, "Just as a pebble thrown into the water creates ripples, so our thoughts create similar effects on our palms."[2]

Many books written in the early seventeenth century contained early Gypsy ideas handed down since the early 1400s. The Catholic Church soon forced the practice of palm reading underground when it was branded devil worship. As a deterrent, anyone found to have any interest in palmistry was promptly murdered.

In the early 1600s a certain propriety returned, and writers began to pen their research, creating an interest that overcame the Church's suppression. Eighteenth century publications blended scientific information of the age with a bit of mysticism. It was opined that a person read the hand with a scientific eye, then spoke from intuition.

Advances in genetics, psychology and forensics have thrust palmistry into the modern age. In 1901, Scotland Yard adopted fingerprinting in criminal investigation and identification. Medical researchers soon found correlations between genetic abnormalities and unusual markings on the hand. Certain fingerprint patterns are even linked to heart disease.

Those that can "read" the palm look for patterns in the lines of the hand that denote lifespan, love capability, empathetic qualities, and some even purport to be able to tell if a person is homosexual. Karmic relationships are supposedly revealed as well as your fate, career, and destiny. There are travel lines, money lines, scattered lines, deep lines, and lines that make stars, triangles, and circles, all depicting certain aspects about an individuals life depending on their location.

The fingers also play a role, dependent on length, alignment, and spaces. Your fingers can indicate leadership, self-esteem, organization, and teaching capabilities. They are also a gauge of your creativity, health, and communications abilities. The fleshy lumps are called "mounts" and are the high spots on the plane of your hand and can depict both traits and talents, like inventiveness and artistic bent, as well as what might be called attitude: indifference and respect.[3]

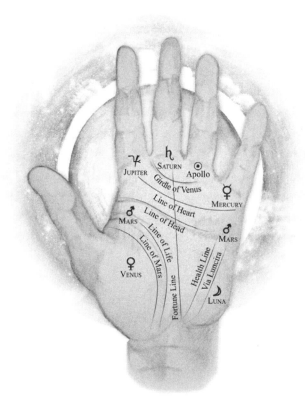

The Palm [4]

There are a multitude of websites and books that are as basic or advanced as you'd like. Many are "how to" guides to enable you to do a first-brush at palm reading and can well offer you an insight to yourself and others.

Is palmistry real? Well your hands and their unique lines certainly are! Can you tell your past and future? Only you can determine that. Like most analytic tools, it's only as good as your interpretation and confidence in the results. It's a great way to have fun and perhaps gain more insight into who you are and where you're going. And what if, by chance, you were able to see something you'd like to change?

Now, there are a number of "tools" that psychics, seers, and fortune tellers may use to help them align with your thinking, intuition, subconscious, or vibrations. They are simply items or methods that make the reader more comfortable with communicating with you, the person getting a "reading." Let's take a look at some of the most popular of these tools.

Tarot Cards

Tarot Cards have been around for quite some time and their origin a bit foggy. Myth has it that the cards were created in ancient Egypt, India, or China and is based more on a sense of romance than any hard evidence. One popular origin offered by the Court de Gebelin in the 1781 printing of *Le Monde Primitif* was that the cards were brought from India by Gypsies who were thought to have come from Egypt as the root of their name implies. The true origin of Tarot cards remains a mystery because the first cards known today originally appeared in Italy and France in the late fourteenth century.

The earliest known cards date from 1392 and only 17 of the original deck exist today. The earliest surviving full deck was painted by the Italian artist Bonifacio Bembo in 1422, and is known as the *Visconti* deck after the Duke of Milan's family name who commissioned the deck.

While early decks depicted several different structures, today's modern deck consists of 78 cards in two sections: the 22 archetypal Tarot cards in the Major Arcana and the 56 cards of the Minor or Lesser Arcana. Four suits of fourteen cards numbered from one to ten with four court cards. Perhaps initially used to play games, the Tarot cards eventually found their way into the hands of fortunetellers, their main application today.

The cards, especially the 22 cards of the Major Arcana, have strong esoteric associations and have been explored since the eighteenth century. They've been linked to areas of mystical study including the Kabbalah, ritual magic, and divination.

Whether true or simply lore, many authors in the nineteenth and twentieth centuries wrote about the occult applications of Tarot cards.

Arthur Edward Waite was a prominent member of the Golden Dawn, an English Rosicrucian society founded in 1888. In his book, *The Key to the Tarot*, published in 1910, he wrote, "the true tarot is symbolism; it speaks no other language and offers no other signs."[5] He directed a fellow member, Pamela Coleman Smith to design a deck known as the Rider-Waite deck, Rider being the publisher. Another member, Aleister Crowley designed the Thoth deck, painted by Lady Frieda Harris. Both these decks are replete with esoteric symbolism, combining important symbolic aspects of earlier decks with Kabbalistic and astrological references.[6]

The *Major Arcana* is composed of 22 cards. While there are differing styles and artists, the components typically are the same. They represent forces or actions that face overcoming positives and negatives to attain a certain end or goal. It's beneficial to have a deck as you go through the cards of the Major Arcana to better see the symbolism reflected in each card. Here are the twenty two cards, their names, and what they represent:

The Fool represents the super-conscious, symbolizing we never attain the limit to our potential.

The Magician represents the conscious mind; focus on a goal and the conscious mind will bring it to fruition in the material world.

The High Priestess, represents the subconscious mind; the balancing force between pairs.

The Empress is another aspect of the subconscious, the memory which evolves in creativity and imagination.

The Emperor is an older, wiser version of the Magician using conscious elements in the material world. His knowledge of handling affairs systemically gives him his seat on the throne.

The Hierophant represents our inner being, the teacher, and intuition. Intuition is a collection of facts from the conscious mind sent to the subconscious which assesses and sends it back to the conscious mind for action.

The Lovers, symbolic of relationships and partners. Use the subconscious, the conscious, and the superconscious to reach the source of our power to gain insight and inspiration.

The Chariot, symbolizing the soul and the physical shell. The driver expresses his will to control the direction the chariot without reins; speech and words are used to set ideas into motion.

Strength, represents control over material forces.

The Hermit, having mastered the elements, he stands at the peak of attainment, set apart from the rest. He must enlighten others, because knowledge has no meaning unless we show others what we have learned.

Wheel of Fortune represents the grasp on the persona by understanding who you really are, enabling you to never be without material possessions.

Justice is balancing the wrongs of the past and setting them right, cutting out negative thoughts.

The Hanged Man represents reversal of view: everything is not as it appears on the surface.

Death represents transformation and rebirth of the consciousness to higher planes.

Temperance is balance. Higher knowledge gained through introspection and following truth can lead us to wisdom.

The Devil represents blindness and misconception.

The Tower is symbolic of the jolt of actual understanding. True knowledge enlightens one, enabling power for your own use.

The Star represents the subconscious mind gathering knowledge from the universal subconscious and pouring it over humanity.

The Moon represents the evolution of the spirit, identifying the positives and negatives we must face to complete our time here.

The Sun is the giver of life; it shines for all, good and bad alike. All things must be achieved without bias.

Judgment represents understanding of spiritual things. When achieved, our conscious is ready to bond with the universal consciousness.

The World represents continuance of the never ending cycle of life. All things emerge from a supreme being.

The remainder of the deck, the *Lesser Arcana* consists of 56 cards in four different suits: wands, cups, swords, and pentacles. Each of the suits contains cards numbered from ace to ten, followed by four "court" cards. Each of the cards values has a direct relationship to numerology, therefore one, for example, signifies a beginning. Let's take a look at what each suit symbolizes.

The *Suit of Wands* – clubs, fire, creativity – is the realm of the spirit. Representing ideas, it's the original idea and the primary element of growth. So Wands point to ideas, ambition, and growth.

The *Suit of Cups* – hearts, water, emotions – is the mental realm. This represents the next step towards manifesting ideas, the next step in the order of things. Cups point to desires and feelings that we may be aware of, but not show outwardly.

The *Suit of Swords* – spades, air, intellect – is the astral realm, representing action. This is the focused attempt to make intent reality, often times indicating struggles as it's difficult to bring an idea into reality.

The *Suit of Pentacles* – diamonds, earth – is the realm of the physical or material. This represents true product of one's labors. Pentacles typically point to realization of goals.[7]

So, the Tarot cards are used by the psychic or fortune teller to provide insight as they read the cards. Typically, they'll ask you to shuffle and cut the deck, then select a number of cards for what's called a spread. There are a number of different spreads used, but basically they represent the past, present, and of course, the future. So the reader turns over each card in order and explains the implication of the specific card as it pertains to you or a question you might have had.

Does it work? I can't really say, although some readings I've had are eerily close to past and present while the future somehow manifests itself in the days, weeks, or months following the reading. But not always!

Is your subconscious affecting the selection of the cards at some subatomic level? Or are you simply open to the power of suggestion and able to link whatever comes up to something that's happened to you in the past or is currently affecting you? Is the future prediction going to happen? Maybe you really want it to come to fruition and you simply live out a self-fulfilling prophecy.

Who knows? But I do believe if you remove the negatives and concentrate on positives, good things happen. Fate, destiny, or blind dumb luck? Only you can tell for yourself. What about other methods of trying to see what the future holds?

Tasseomancy

Tasseomancy is a fancy word for *reading tea leaves*. It's believed to have originated in the Middle Ages and stemmed from the practice of pouring molten wax or metal into water, then interpreting their shapes.

In the seventeenth century, the West Dutch Indies merchants introduced tea from the Orient. The drink became popular, and reading the leaves that remained in the bottom of the cup supposedly held signs and omens for the drinker.

As in most fortune telling, the inquirer asks a specific question regarding the future. Of course you need psychic intuition to interpret the tea leaves' remnants, and the reader looked for patterns and designs formed by the inquirer drinking all the tea from a cup. There could be, as one would guess, a myriad of possible shapes, patterns, and designs. And I suppose you could get lucky and have a word actually spelled out. Well, okay, maybe not.

There are some standard symbolisms in the interpretation, such as a snake represents enmity or falsehood, a spade bodes good fortune through industry, and a mountain indicates a journey or hindrance. So it boils down — okay, pun intended — to the "talent" of the reader. Tea bags, as you would guess, put a crimp in the reading, but that's circumvented by simply cutting the bags open.

Tasseomancy is currently conducted in England, Ireland, and Europe. You may find "Gypsy Tea Rooms" in larger U.S. cities,[8] but it's not a mainstream method of fortune telling.

Psychometry

Psychometry is the ability to perceive the character, surroundings, and events connected with a person by holding an object that belongs to an individual in one's hands. The term is credited to J. Rhodes Buchanan, an American scientist, who in 1842 derived the term meaning "soul measuring" or "measurement of the human soul."

Buchanan's premise is based on the belief that every thought, action, and event that has ever occurred since the beginning of time has left an impression on the ether. He also extended his belief to concrete objects such as trees and stones.

Many people, especially occultists, believe that psychometry is connected to animism, the acceptance that all objects possess an inner or psychological life which enables them to receive from and transmit impressions to other objects. In other words, inanimate objects have a memory of their own.

There are those who believe that the human mind radiates an aura in all directions around the body which impresses everything within its orbit and has a connection to psychometry. It has been suggested that psychometry is perhaps the mind's eye, enabling the mental faculties to receive impressions or visions in the same cerebral center where dreams are registered.[9]

So the ability to tell something about an individual, object, or location is an entertaining talent. Many magicians and seers have entertained audiences with their holding an article owned by someone in the audience, then identifying something about that individual that few people would know.

Can it be done? Do you feel impressions in your mind's eye when you pick up historical objects or someone else's possessions? Do you have visions of being in other places where the object has been? If so, perhaps you have the talent.

Scrying

Scrying is a method of predicting the future by means of anything shiny, such as crystal, a mirror, or water — anything that the reader can use to enter an altered mind state. The Gypsy fortune teller and her crystal ball is the stereotype for scrying.

Scrying works on the principles of the Ganzfeld effect. If you've ever stared at a blank wall until you're dizzy, begin hallucinating, and see patterns, then you've experienced the Ganzfeld effect. The degree of success is directly proportionate to one's ability to concentrate.

Typically, when using a crystal ball, the seer clears her mind and gazes intently into the crystal, supposedly linking her third eye to the crystal, visualizing a ray of light coming from between your eyes and entering the crystal.

At that point, the crystal appears to cloud up and precise patterns and pictures arise within the cloudy mass. A practiced scryer can then relate the images to the person getting the reading and attempt an interpretation for the future.

Shell scrying — using a sea shell over your ear — supposedly picks up sounds and conversations. Smoke scrying is used by certain American Indians in their sweat lodge ceremonies where water is poured over hot rocks. Combined with the humidity and temperature, visions may be seen in the steam.

Water scrying is an ancient method used quite often by the Celts. They collected water from a stream at night, preferably by the full moon, and filled a bowl made from glass, silver, or brass. Using a branch from a bay, hazel, or laurel tree, they wet the tip of the branch and the rim of the bowl and drew the branch around the bowl causing it to resonate. The circular ripples formed visions that were interpreted.

There are a number of other scrying methods using mirrors, clouds, and oil, all conjuring images to be interpreted as to future events.[10] Clearly, this method of fortune telling is open to critique, as it is very personal and relies on the reader having some sort of clairvoyant insight and analysis trained into their methods. Should you come across a practiced scryer, you may well be surprised at their talents.

Divination

Divination is the art or practice that seeks to foresee or foretell future events or discover hidden knowledge usually by the interpretation of omens or by the aid of supernatural powers.[11] So, divination is the search for knowledge or advice by a means that lacks any satisfactory scientific information as to how it might work.

While divination covers a considerably broad arena of methods — some are still used today by forecasters of the future — some have gone by the wayside. It is more reliable today to look at a map to find your way to San Jose than it is to cast goat entrails on the ground, something our long lost ancestors might have done. Today, we use a map. Besides, it's cheaper to buy a map than a goat, *and* considerably less messy, even if you can't refold it when you're done.

There are an amazing number of things used for divination. On one website alone, there are more than 75 "mancies." You'll recall our earlier discussion of tasseomancy or reading tea leaves as one type of "mancy."

There's *alectryomancy* where a bird — usually a black hen — is used. Here, the diviner sprinkles grain on the ground and the patterns left on the ground after the bird has finished is interpreted.

Then there's *pessomancy*, where beans or stones are marked with symbols relating to health, success, travel, love, and the like; the stones are then thrown out of a bag after shuffling for the interpretation.

Or *bibliomancy*, divination using a book. This usually involves using a sacred book like the Bible, Torah, or Koran. The person seeking guidance closes his eyes, opens the book, and points to a passage interpreted by the diviner.[12]

Human concerns haven't changed much over the centuries. People today still want to know the same things as their ancestors. Everyone still wants a peek at the future and sometimes unscientific or folk remedies appear to work.

Take *dowsing*. It's a technique that may deliver practical results, yet no one can explain how it works. Using a pendulum over a map or a forked branch as a dowser walks over a field to find the best place to sink a well is one practical example. Does it work, or was there water everywhere beneath the property? I've met farmers and ranchers that swear by dowsers and wouldn't think of drilling for water without using one.

So, if divination is the collective term for using unscientific means to seek knowledge, then one could conclude that some forms deliver better results than others. So we use what seems best.

Do you use divination? You certainly are exposed to it every day through forecasting, whether it's stocks or weather. *The Fortune Sellers*, a book by William A. Sherden examines what he calls the $200 billion a year business of buying and selling predictions. In a study of seven different types of forecasting, he concludes that most of what goes on in them is of little value! Only demography and short-term weather forecasting does he see limited return of the huge investment, and only meteorology has any scientific foundation.

In the areas of economics, investments, technology assessment, and organizational planning, the predictions offer no firmer a platform for decision making than does a coin toss — originally a form of divination! All of them are often as wrong as right which means the 50-50 chance of a coin toss has as much chance of coming up right as often as the expensive forecasting models used by business today. Yet for reasons that are sometimes difficult to understand, these professions are respected and well paid. Are those who trust them more or less credulous than those who sought omens in the entrails of goats?

Obviously, some forms of divination are more believable than others. For instance, prayer is a rational activity for those who believe in a God and believe that divine contact is possible. For those who don't believe in God or contact with the divine, prayer is not rational. So, being irrational is not the same as being wrong.

Modern experts don't always get it wrong and neither did the ancient oracles when they made their predictions. But it's hard to base an expertise on a platform of "not always getting it wrong." The point is that success rates of experts are sufficiently low that one should question the rationality of trusting their judgment. Those that would mock the ancients for their faith in oracles might keep that in mind.[13]

My only experience with divination — at lease one of which I was aware of — came from a visit to a psychic in San Diego. She was an elderly Mexican lady whose Mayan features belied her ancestry. She spoke no English and worked out of her house.

The friend who told me about her translated for me as the lady began a rapid-fire stream of Spanish telling me that she uses a fresh egg to tell me what my future holds and that I'd have to lie on my back on the table. She would touch me over my entire body — fully clothed, thankfully — then she would crack the egg into hot water and read it for me. Simple and straight forward, no participation necessary from me, and no intrusion on my person. I laid down and she began.

She continued her flood of Spanish, a plea to god, angels, and spirits to help her in the reading according to my friend. She started on my head, pressing and rubbing the egg around my face, around the ears, over the top, then around my mouth. From there she went to my chin, my throat, my shoulders, arms, chest, and on down the body, all the while continuing her pleas to those I couldn't see.

All was going well until she pressed the egg to the outside of my right knee — the egg broke and her voice went up two octaves and the words came twice as fast. "What's happening? What's she saying?"

"She's saying you've got big problems in your knee. The egg almost never breaks but it did!" said my friend.

"Tell her not to worry," I said. "Tell her I broke it about eight years ago, but it's okay now," as she quickly translated, as the lady dropped the broken egg into the water filled glass. She studied it in silence as she turned it around and around to get a better view of the gelling glob of egg suspended in the water. She promptly put down the glass, picked up another egg, and completed her scanning of my body as she whipped off another comment to my friend.

"She says it was a bad injury, there's still some damage to the cartilage, but she says it should be okay and only cause pain occasionally," the translator said.

Now, I don't remember the rest of the reading; it was probably the usual. You know, "big things in your future, you're going to do well, and live a long life." But the thing that blew me away was the fact that she was dead-on with the knee thing.

I'd cracked my fibula, had a 5mm compression fracture of the tibia, and had torn the posterior cruciate ligament when I found a stray tree while skiing. And it only hurt once in a great while, but when it did, it was debilitating. How'd she do that? I don't limp, it's not swollen, and there's no way she could have known! Maybe it was the egg, maybe it was her, or maybe there's more to this divination than we know or can prove! I was duly impressed.

Oftentimes we can't explain how others have insight that we can't comprehend. It certainly doesn't make it wrong, however irrational it may seem. It does make it a bit Woo-Woo, but maybe there's more out there we'll learn in the New Age to come!

Graphology

Graphology or *Handwriting Analysis* is the study of hand-writing, its connection to behavior, and supposedly gives us insight into an individual. I guess that works as long as the individual can write. Supporters cite extensive anecdotal evidence such as testimonials to use handwriting analysis, while critics say there is no sound empirical evidence available. The premise that handwriting can indicate behavior or traits is one that is clearly debatable. But it is impressive that certain characteristics consistently appear and most people that have readings, even short ones at parties, see that their handwriting reveals so much about them.

There are three basic tenets that are the basis for why handwriting analysis works:

- First, the writing movement is under direct influence of the body's central nervous system and is modified by the coordination of muscles and nerves that connect the hand, arm, and shoulder.
- Second, any mechanisms that contribute to the written movement are related to the central nervous system and will vary as it is affected. Therefore, the writing strokes will reflect changes such as development, the influence of alcohol, and diseases, such as Parkinson's disease.
- And finally, handwriting examples are evaluated on quality, overall size, regularity, and consistency of the graphic stroke. These are then interpreted under varying theories by an analyst as a component of many different clusters open to different psychological interpretations.[14]

So there you have it; a concise if not stiff definition. But what does it mean? How does a graphologist delve into your handwriting?

Well, your brain and body combined drive your handwriting. Remember when you learned to write cursive, maybe third grade? Mine always looked like a flock of chickens helped me, while Sally's handwriting — it was always a girl — looked like she worked evenings for Hallmark!

Graphology is the combined result of how you literally make and connect every letter of the alphabet. How you cross your *T*s, dot your *I*s, and how large the loops are in your lower case *B*s, *D*s, and *L*s. The slant of your letters, spacing between words, the roundness of letters, and the connections between letters, as well as the height and depth of letters like *H*s, *T*s, *P*s, and *Y*s. Plus many more criteria, a lot specific to certain letters.

There are three major "schools" of graphology — The Integrative, Holistic, and Symbolic Analysis. Each one is based on similar criteria but differing emphasis. We won't take time to enumerate the subtle differences, but each is easy to research further if you have interest.

While there are no reliable figures on the use of handwriting analysis, many organizations have at least investigated the use of graphology. While there are a number of legal considerations such as privacy, EEOC, and ADA issues, there seems to be claims by practitioners that handwriting analysis is used by a number of establishments around the world.

Employment profiling and compatibility are services usually offered by handwriting analysts. The focus is to identify desirable traits and analyze applicants and work groups to determine probability of success in their assignments.

Psychological aspects are used by some analysts to reveal personality traits, while some tout marital compatibility capabilities. There's even a controversial position taken by some that cancer can be detected using handwriting. Apparently John Wayne's signature shows a blackened out portion that supposedly represented his cancer. Not totally conclusive!

There are, however, a number of handwriting analysts that testify in court hearings around the world. While not always considered graphologists, they do provide their opinion as to the comparison of documents or the authenticity of a person's writing. They are precluded from testifying to an individual's physical or mental condition based on a handwriting sample.[15]

So the handwriting is on the wall, so to speak. I've found that handwriting does follow patterns and certain characteristics can be surmised when looking at someone's handwriting.

The first caveat is to disregard a person's signature, because experts say that a person's signature rarely matches directly with their handwriting. They've practiced their name, have written it innumerable times, and have probably developed an affectation with the way they sign their name.

I've read a couple of books on the subject and I'm the first to say I'm not even close to being proficient, but I do believe you can make some assumptions that are generalities about our population. Such as, a right handed person who writes with a backward slant tends to be an introvert while an aggressive forward slant usually signifies a gregarious, extroverted person.

There are a number of other things I look for in people's writing, and although I know they don't always hold true, I'm consistently impressed at how often the trait identified comes to the fore.

The crux in handwriting analysis is not the ability to profile a person, to predict how they'll handle a situation, or even delve into their sexual proclivities as many analysts would purport. In my opinion, the key is to have fun with it!

The best application I've seen is to have a graphologist at a party and have everyone who wants to have some fun, allow a brief analysis of their handwriting. It's a lot of fun to gain a new insight to what you project to the world, and it's even more fun to hear comments like, "By golly, that fellow's right on in his assessment of me." And, "Wow, I'm amazed how accurate he was!"

Woo-Woo? Probably. Fun? Absolutely!

So are the people who tell fortunes psychics or hoaxes? Or something in between? It's included here just to have you know that many psychics use some of the above as tools of their trade. Tarot cards, palmistry, and the numerous forms of divination are methods psychics may use to gain their insight into you and perhaps the future.

Are psychics for real? Many believe there is something to it—whether it's the voices they hear or their track record of predictions that have come true. And as long as you're not betting the farm or risking lives with their predictions, what can it hurt? Are they Woo-Woo? They certainly are from my side of the hill!

So if you have the opportunity to try anything we've covered above, give it a shot. Be skeptical but open; let your mind guide you, and perhaps your intuition. It can't hurt, and you may be intrigued enough to do more research; then you may discover *you're* psychic!

Chapter 9 Endnotes

1   Wikimedia Foundation, *Fortune-Telling*
2   Crystal, Ellie, *Palmistry*
3   ibid., *Palmistry*
4   ibid., *Palmistry*
5   Mills, Robert, *History of the Tarot*
6   ibid., *History of the Tarot*
7   Crystal, Ellie, *Tarot*
8   Hefner, Alan G., *Tasseomancy*
9   ibid., *Psychometry*
10   Maudhnait, *An Overview of Different Type of Scrying*
11   Merriam-Webster, *Divination*
12   Unknown, *Divination*
13   Curnow, Trevor, *Philosophy & Divination*
14   Wikimedia Foundation, *Graphology*
15   ibid., *Graphology*

CHAPTER 10

OTHER WORLDS

Are we alone? Not now, I mean in the whole, entire universe? What are the probabilities of life as we know it on another rock floating around a sun making its way through the universe? There have been stories and tales handed down throughout the ages that speak of or refer to life from other worlds; you know — *aliens*. What are the possibilities?

Well, let's use my "mother-in-law" logic to start. There are more than 125 billion galaxies in the universe.[1] And according to the latest estimate of total stars in the known universe, there are 70 sextillion stars — that's 70,000 million million million. That means the number written out is 7 followed by 22 zeros.[2] So, let's operate on a diminishing 1% scenario — that is, we take 1% of the 70 sextillion stars, then we'll take 1% of that number, and then take 1% of that number, and so on. So,

- Let's assume: there are only 1% of all stars that emit radiation in the range to support life as we know it, so that leaves 700 quintillion stars.
- Only 1% of those are large enough, so that's 7 quintillion stars.
- Only 1% of those are small enough, giving us 70 quadrillion stars.
- Only 1% of those have planetary systems, resulting in 700 trillion stars.
- Only 1% of those have planetary gravity capable of holding an atmosphere, leaving us with 7 trillion stars.

- And of those, only 1% actually has a planetary atmosphere that can support life, resulting in 70 billion stars.
- Only 1% of those have a planet with oxygen as a major component, giving us 700 million stars.
- Then only 1% of those have water on the planet, resulting in 7 million stars.
- Only 1% of those have a planet with a temperature range that will support life as we know it, leaving us with 70,000 stars.
- Then, if take only 1% of those as being old enough to have developed life as we know it, we're at 700 stars that could contain an earth-like planet.

Not rocket science, but plausible, right? Which doesn't prove anything other than mathematically, there might be at least a few planets that could be just like ours.

As an article from *Space Daily* suggests, the factors determining earth-like planets are probable according to British astronomers. So far, 105 planetary systems within our galaxy, the Milky Way, have been qualified, having the attributes of what they call the Goldilocks Zone — not too hot, not too cold, just right — that would sustain life.[3]

So, if life on other planets could be similar to ours here on earth, there probably are less advanced as well as more advance life-forms.

Using that logic, *aliens or extraterrestrials* just might exist. If we keep an open mind, we might find some connections to those phenomena some of us witness that can't be explained.

Foggy History

Erich von Däniken postulates the Earth could have been visited by extraterrestrials in the remote past. His first book, *Chariots of the Gods*, began his career as the world's most successful non-fiction writer. He's written 26 books and has sold more than 60 million worldwide. He challenges thinking by comparing ancient symbols, hieroglyphics, and writings that resemble what could be depictions of spacecraft and alien beings.

He poses challenging problems such as sand vitrifications — sand turned to glass — found in the Gobi desert resembling those produced by atomic explosions in the Nevada desert. Or cut crystal lenses found in Egypt and Iraq which can only be made using cesium oxide produced by electro-chemical processes. Or a piece of cloth in Helwan, the fabric so fine it could only be woven today in a special factory with great technical know-how. Or ornaments smelted of platinum — with a melting point of 1800°C — found on the Peruvian Plateau. Or in Delhi, India, an ancient pillar made of iron that isn't destroyed by phosphorous, sulfur, or weather effects — a feat we can't replicate today. Or parts of a belt made of aluminum — refined from bauxite under exacting chemico-technical steps — found in a grave at Yungjen, China.

He points out the coincidence in the content of the Mahabharata, the Bible, the Epic of Gilgamesh, and the texts of Eskimos, the Scandinavians, the Tibetans, and others that chronicle the same stories of strange heavenly vehicles, flying "gods," and frightful catastrophes connected with these apparitions. How could they have the same ideas all over the world? Did they have help from extraterrestrials?

He points out the apparent miracles in Egyptian society. Experts estimate there were 50 million inhabitants of the Nile Delta during the time the Great Pyramid was constructed — contradicted by the fact that the total population of the world was considered to only be 20 million in 3000 BC. Could that many people have "lived off the land" at that time?

Then, where did they get the wood for the rollers they ostensibly used for moving the great blocks of stone used to build the pyramids? Not until around 1600 BC were horse-and-carts used to transport people or goods. How did they carve the stone? How did they manage the craftsmanship that would be a challenge today?

He asks if it's really a coincidence that the height of the pyramid at Cheops — 479 feet — multiplied by one billion is approximately 91 million miles – the distance to the sun at its nearest point? And is it just a stroke of luck that a meridian running through the pyramids divides the continents and oceans into equal halves? Is it a fluke that the area of the base of the pyramid divided by twice its height gives us 3.4159, the celebrated π?

He also questions how they leveled the rocky terrain, how they drove tunnels downward in the rock and how they illuminated them given that there are no blackened ceilings or walls and not the slightest trace of a torch. And how were the stones cut with sharp edges and smooth sides? More than 2,600,000 gigantic rocks were quarried, transported, and then fitted together to the nearest thousandth of an inch.[4]

So more than 35 years ago, Von Däniken challenged the status quo thinking of our history books. He also stepped into the realm of alien life, connecting hieroglyphics and pictographs as well as unexplained structures around the world to images of flying machines and astronaut garb. He espouses no proof, only circumstantial evidence of baffling coincidences that have no clear justification. He simply asks, "What if?"

What if, indeed! Now, while Von Däniken isn't a scientist, per se; he's studied ancient holy writings and is a world-class researcher. His concept of intelligent life beyond Earth though, is not outside the scientific community's thought arena, as evidenced by a formula developed in 1961.

In November of that year, a conference was held at the National Radio Astronomy Observatory in Green Bank, West Virginia to discuss the search for extraterrestrial life. The gathering attracted a worldwide array of prominent astronomers intent on attempting to theoretically quantify the extraterrestrial intelligence within the galaxy. The result was an equation, driven by Frank Drake's proposal of the core premise that seeks to quantify the number of technical civilizations in the galaxy.

The formula is now known as the Green Bank equation or simply, the Drake equation. Now, I won't bore you with the actual equation or the values they argued before arriving at their conclusion; you can find that on the internet or in most any library. The conference participants' considerations were constrained to the Milky Way, our galaxy, and included the following step parameters:

- The mean rate of star formation
- The number of stars which form planetary systems
- The number of planets in those systems ecologically suitable for life forms to evolve
- The number of those planets on which life forms actually develop
- The number of those which evolve to an intelligent form
- The number of advanced intelligent life forms which develop capacity for interstellar radio
- The lifetime of those technically advanced civilizations

Their conclusion was that at least one world existed and that would be us! Are those guys good, or what?

The thought among the group was assuming advanced civilizations could avoid self-annihilation, and if 1% of developing galactic nations made peace with themselves, then our nearest neighbor would be a few hundred light years away. Carl Sagan, a member of the group, concluded there could be *106* technologically advanced extraterrestrial civilizations in our galaxy![5] They're even more aggressive than my Mother-in-Law logic used at the beginning of this chapter!

There are too many descriptions in both lore and recorded history of "fiery chariots," strange descriptions or pictographs of hooded entities, and "iron thunderbolts" to fully understand their meaning. But with today's technology, our imagination can run wild with these reports being flying life forms, some with armament. Ancient astronauts? One can only wonder.

Egyptians have been meticulous through the years, carefully recording the history of families, the life of the Pharaohs, and their wars. Isn't it interesting that there are no descriptions, plans, or accounts that have survived the years on how the Sphinx, the pyramids, or their obelisks were conceived, planned, or erected? There are plenty of hieroglyphics that depict unknown, unexplained items, but some are genuinely mind-boggling. Take the Seti I Temple in Abydos, where a ceiling beam has some very interesting pictoglyphs.

Here are the images found on that beam:

Abydos Closeup[6]
Abydos Egypt Photographed 5 Nov 1992 by Bruce Rawles

What could the images possibly be? They look just too close to flying craft we have today. A helicopter, jet, tank, or submarine could have taken their design from one of these!

Other civilizations have unexplained mysteries as well. Indian history cites the Emperor Ashoka starting a "Secret Society of Nine Unknown Men," great scientists who were to catalog their science knowledge. They apparently wrote nine books, the first, *The Secrets of Gravitation*, supposedly dealing with gravity control. While these books have not been seen, historians continually refer to them. Presumably they contain knowledge of "futuristic weapons" that had destroyed the ancient Indian Rama Empire thousands of years earlier.

Potentially connected to these books, the Chinese recently discovered some Sanskrit documents in Lhasa, Tibet. They sent them to the University of Chandrigarh to be translated by Dr. Ruth Reyna; she indicated the documents, thought to be thousands of years old, contain directions for building craft for interstellar travel.

Dr. Reyna said they were propelled by anti-gravitational means based on a system analogous to *laghima*, the Hindu Yogis explanation of the energy that enables levitation. Called *Astras*, the Indians purport to be able to send a detachment of men to any planet.

Indian scientists didn't take the translations seriously, but reacted more positively when the Chinese announced they were studying certain parts of the data for their space program. This is the first indication of a government admitting to anti-gravity research.

The Rama Empire in Northern India and Pakistan developed at least fifteen thousand years ago and included many large cities, many still found in the deserts of the area. Cities in the empire were governed by "Priest-Kings," the seven greatest cities were known in classical Hindu texts as "The Seven Rishi Cities."

According to ancient texts, the people had flying machines called *Vimanas*, a double-decked, circular craft with portholes and a dome, much as we envision a flying saucer today. They supposedly flew like the wind and emitted a melodious sound, powered by some form of "anti-gravity." There were evidently many texts on Vimanas, even including flight manuals.[7]

Even if we discount the description of a flying machine in the story about the prophet Ezekiel "rising into the heavens on a chariot of fire" about 600 BC as being just a vision, what about the designs of aircraft by Leonardo da Vinci in the early sixteenth century? Some of them bear close resemblance to the devices described in ancient texts from Knossos and Syracuse. Did he have access to ancient documents, now lost, about flight? Did he only need the secret of their propulsion to make them fly again?[8] Unanswered questions, yet again. Flying machines!

Dropa Stones

What about something a bit more tangible? In the barely accessible mountains along the border separating China and Tibet, a 1938 archeological expedition happened onto some caves. Obviously occupied by a primitive people long ago, the pictograms carved into the walls illustrated the sun, moon, and stars along with the earth; lines of dots connected these celestial bodies. Buried in neatly arranged graves within the caves were skeletons of a strange race of humans with spindly bodies and large overdeveloped heads. Initially, the skeletons were thought to be an unknown species of ape, but as the leader of the expedition, Professor Chi Pu Tei, a Chinese archeologist, pointed out, "Who ever heard of apes burying one another?"[9]

While studying the skeletons, a team stumbled over a large round disc half buried in the dirt floor of the cave. The stone looked like a gramophone recording, nine inches in diameter and three quarters of an inch thick with a hole in the center, and a fine groove spiraling out from the center to the rim.

Under closer inspection, it was found that the groove was in fact a continuous line of strange hieroglyphics. The almost microscopic characters were in a language heretofore never encountered. All in, 716 plates were found, each exactly the same. The discs, which became known as the *Dropa Stones*, were taken to what is now Beijing and stored while many attempted to translate the inscriptions.[10]

All experts at translation failed until Dr. Tsum Um Nui broke the code in the late 1950s. His translation of the "speaking grooves" and conclusions were so controversial they were suppressed. In fact, the Peking Academy of Pre-History forbade him to publish his findings. In 1965, the professor and four of his colleagues were given permission to reveal their theory under the cumbersome title, *The Grooved Script concerning Space-ships which, as recorded on the Discs, landed on Earth 12,000 years ago.*

The text revealed an astonishing tale of inhabitants from another planet, the Dropas, crash landing on earth with no way to rebuild their craft and return home. In the years since the discovery of the first disc, archeologists and anthropologists delved into the area around the cave. Local lore seemed to corroborate the story recorded on the discs — small, yellow-faced, gaunt men with large heads and puny bodies who "came from the clouds, long, long ago." Interestingly enough, the descriptions substantiated the skeletal findings in the caves.[11]

In 1968, Dr. Viatcheslav Zaitsev, a Russian philologist published extracts from the stone-plate story in *Sputnik* magazine. Subsequent research by the doctor found that the stones contained high concentrations of cobalt and other metals, making the stones extremely hard, making carving the minute hieroglyphics especially difficult for any primitive people. When the stones were tested, an oscillation rhythm — a humming or a vibration — was recorded as if they had once been electrically charged or had served as electrical conductors of some sort.

In 1974, an Austrian engineer, Ernst Wegerer, took four photos of two discs he came across in Banpo Museum in Xian. Twenty years later when German scientists Hartwig Hausdorf and Peter Krassa visited the museum, they were told that the director's superiors had ordered the discs destroyed and that officially, they never existed! A dead end to what might have been ancient CDs that had a link to our planet's past, and who knows, perhaps a Woo-Woo record of New Age extraterrestrial visitation!

Oklo Reactor

The *Oklo Fossil Reactors*, perhaps a natural phenomenon or the remains of some help by unknown benefactors, are in Gabon, West Africa. In the early 1970s, scientists discovered an inordinately low amount of the isotope U-235 in the uranium they were extracting from underground mines at the Oklo mine. The isotope levels in the uranium ore was comparable to percentages found in used nuclear fuel produced by modern reactors.

Scientists around the world asked, "How could fission reactions happen in nature, when such a high degree of engineering, physics, and acute, detailed attention went into building a nuclear reactor?"[12] Their calculations determined that the nuclear reaction that occurred in the Oklo mine probably occurred 1.7 billion years ago, and functioned intermittently for a million years or more. The chain reactions stopped when the uranium isotopes became too sparse to keep the reactions going.[13]

While considered a natural nuclear reaction, the Oklo mine would appear to have had a coincidentally precise amount of water trickling through the sandstone above a granite substructure to even start such reaction, much less to keep it going.

The imagination struggles with a reactor degrading on the site, or perhaps it was a dump site, much like the proposed Yucca Mountain project. Then, the question becomes, "who built the reactor?" or "who dumped the nuclear waste?" Some help from others in the cosmos? Do we need this kind of help?

So, the question remains, are there aliens in the universe? And if so, have they visited planet earth? Proof is marginal, but many phenomena have been observed and deemed to be UFOs. By definition, if you see a flying object you can't identify, it's an Unidentified Flying Object. As we've cited earlier, there appears to be an abundance of myth, lore, and history of extraterrestrial alien life as well as their flying machines. Just look at the number of hits you get on an internet search engine when you type "aliens" or "UFOs;" more than 51 million and 10 million respectively. There are some who believe and a healthy group of skeptics. Those of us who don't really know comprise the balance, but, how do we know for sure?

UFOs

According to recent polls, almost 50% of Americans and millions of people worldwide believe that UFOs are for real. Peter Jennings did a special on February 24, 2005, "UFOs — Seeing is Believing." He concluded that after more than 150 interviews with scientists, investigators and those who claim to have witnessed unidentified flying objects, "There are important questions that have not been completely answered — and a great deal not fully explained."[14] So, let's acquaint ourselves with how this all began.

The official history of UFOs in the United States probably began with Kenneth Arnold on June 24, 1947. Arnold was a U.S. Forest Service employee searching for a missing plane, sighted nine bright, saucer-like objects flying at "incredible speed" at an altitude of 10,000 feet. He said they appeared to weave in and out of formation between Mt. Rainier and Mt. Adams in Washington State, at an estimated speed of 1200 miles per hour.[15]

Arnold's sightings prompted a flurry of UFO reports that the Army Air Force began studying. In a letter dated September 23, 1947, Lt. Gen. Nathan F, Twining, Chief of Staff of the U.S. Army directed the establishment of the study of UFOs.

Not surprisingly, many public as well as military individuals responded with somewhat emotional positions. Some believed from the beginning that UFOs were interplanetary or interstellar visitors while others deemed UFOs were secret weapons of a foreign power, most often mentioned was Russia. Still others contended the UFOs were hoaxes or honest misidentification of ordinary phenomena. Within the Air Force, leadership factions filled the spectrum: from "the subject should get no attention" because it was absurd, to "we are at risk being invaded by weapons unknown" either from foreign powers or visitors from outer space.[16]

So began the reporting, categorizing, and research by the Air Force of UFO's. Since 1947, there have been thousands of reports, many explained, many debunked, but a fair number remain in the realm of "could o' been." As you might guess, there are stories, compilations, reports, as well as books on the topic of UFOs, their history, the sightings, and theories. Dial up the internet to read incident after incident, some with very interesting photos of unexplained objects in the sky.

What do the experts say about UFOs and the probability of extraterrestrial or alien life? While you can sort through the witness accounts of UFO sightings, I believe it may bear more weight if we reviewed what those who are trained to deal with both flying and military situations to see what they believe about UFOs. Here are a few comments by supposedly reliable individuals.

> *These UFOs are interplanetary devices systematically observing the earth, either manned or under remote control, or both.*
> - Colonel Joseph J. Bryan III,
> Founder of the CIA's Psychological
> Warfare staff

Of course UFOs are real — and they are interplanetary... The cumulative evidence for the existence of UFOs is quite overwhelming and I accept the fact of their existence.
> - Air Chief Marshall Lord Hugh Dowding, Commanding Officer of the Royal Air Force during WWII. Stated in August of 1954.

Reliable reports indicate there are objects coming into our atmosphere at very high speeds and controlled by thinking intelligences.
> - Rear Admiral Delmar Fahrney, U.S. Navy Missile Chief

That movie Close Encounters of The Third Kind is more realistic than you believe.
> - Steve Lewis, Former Air Force intelligence officer after his retirement when he announced that he was convinced UFOs were intelligently controlled, extraterrestrial vehicles.

Flying saucers are real. Too many good men have seen them, that don't have hallucinations.
> - Captain Eddie Rickenbacker, medal of honor-winning commander, 94th Aero Pursuit Squadron in WWI

I can assure you that flying saucers, given that they exist, are not constructed by any power on earth.
> - President Harry S Truman, 1950

I am convinced that UFOs exist because I have seen one.
> - President Jimmy Carter during his campaign

*I believe that these extra-terrestrial vehicles
and their crews are visiting this planet from
other planets... Most astronauts were reluc-
tant to discuss UFOs.*
　　　　　- Major Gordon Cooper, NASA
　　　　　astronaut, to the United Nations

Probably the most widely known UFO event in history is the July 1947 incident in the desert near Roswell, New Mexico. The now famous "UFO crash," with its numerous witnesses, press releases, quick removal of remnants and remains, along with the disappearance of key witnesses has long fueled suspicions of a widespread cover-up.

There have been and still are a number of researchers who spend their waking hours attempting to solve the mystery of the crash, whether or not there were beings on board, and why the official story changed so quickly. Books have been written about the incident, museums established, and an annual UFO Encounter festival held every year in July.

The incident has clearly energized the Roswell economy, as alien gift shops are evident around the city, and signs display flying saucers while announcing "Aliens Welcome" to all visitors.[17] The now famous encounter with supposed alien debris and possible alien life-forms prompts many questions. What happened?

In the summer of 1947, there were numerous reports of UFO sightings throughout the U.S. In early July, 1947, something crashed near Roswell.

While there is some discrepancy in sighting dates, July 2 or 3, Dan Wilmot, respected business owner, and his wife observed a bright, saucer-shaped object estimated to have a diameter of 20 to 25 feet, glowing with lights, and moving across the sky from the southeast to the northwest at 400 to 500 miles per hour. He reported this unusual sighting to the local newspaper, the *Roswell Daily Record*.[18]

After a night of intense thunderstorms, W. W. "Mack" Brazel, foreman of the J.B. Foster Ranch rode out with the son of neighbors Floyd and Loretta Proctor, to check his sheep and discovered a large amount of what appeared to be metal debris scattered over a wide area. Closer inspection revealed a shallow trench several hundred feet long gouged into the desert. Mack drug a large piece of the metal to a shed where he later showed the Proctors what he'd found. The Proctors suggested he might have the wreckage of a UFO or some sort of government project and he should report it to the sheriff. A day or so later, he drove to Roswell and reported his finding to Sheriff George Wilcox, who then reported it to the Intelligence Officer at the Roswell Army Air Force Base, Major Jesse Marcel of the 509 Bomb Group.[19]

According to research by Don Schmitt and Kevin Randle in their book, *A History of UFO Crashes*, the military had been watching an unidentified flying object on radar in southern New Mexico for four days. On the night of July 4, 1947, radar indicated that the object was down between thirty and forty miles northwest of Roswell. An eyewitness, William Woody, who lived east of Roswell, remembered being outside on the night of July 4 and seeing a brilliant object plunge to the ground. A couple of days later when he and his father tried to locate the area of the crash, they were sent away by military personnel who had cordoned off the area.

After Sheriff Wilcox's call to Major Marcel, the Major and the Senior Counterintelligence Corps agent, Captain Sheridan Cavitt, followed Mack Brazel off-road to his place and inspected the large piece of debris Mack had dragged from the pasture.

The next morning, July 7, Major Marcel took his first step onto the debris field and remarked later that "something… must have exploded above the ground and fell."

Marcel, Cavitt, and Brazel inspected the field and the Major reported the debris was "strewn over a wide area, I guess maybe three-quarters of a mile long and a few hundred feet wide." Picking up a piece of the small metal bits, Marcel lit his cigarette lighter to the thin pieces and found they didn't burn. Marcel also described weightless I-beam-like structures that were three-eighths of an inch by one-quarter inch and not very long; they would neither break nor bend. Some had indecipherable characters along the length in two colors. He described other metal the thickness of tin foil as indestructible.

After gathering enough wreckage fragments to fill his staff car, Major Marcel stopped by his home on the way back to the base. He showed his family the unusual pieces.

In May of 1990, under hypnosis by Dr. John Watkins, Jesse Marcel, Jr. remembered being awakened by his father that night, helping him carry in a large box filled with metal parts he described as lead foil and I-beams. He recalled the writing on the I-beams as "purple." "Strange. Never saw anything like it." "Different geometric shapes, leaves and circles." Questioning revealed the symbols were shiny purple and small; there were many separate figures.

Major Marcel was back at the base the next morning and at 11:00 a.m., Walter Haut, public relations officer gave the press release he was ordered to write to the two radio stations and both newspapers. By 2:26 p.m., the story was on the AP Wire:

> "The Army Air Forces here today announced
> a flying disk had been found"
>
> — Roswell Newspaper [20]

On the morning of July 8, Major Marcel reported his findings to Colonel Blanchard, showing him pieces of the wreckage. Blanchard had never seen anything like it; he sent Marcel to see General Ramey, Commanding Officer of the Eighth Air Force at Carswell in Fort Worth.

Marcel stated years later that he'd taken some of the debris into Ramey's office, displaying the pieces on Ramey's desk. General Ramey wanted to see the exact location of the debris field and took Marcel to the map room down the hall. On their return, the pieces on the desk were gone and a weather balloon was spread out on the floor. Major Charles A. Cashon took the now-famous photo of Marcel with the weather balloon in General Ramey's office.

It was then reported that General Ramey recognized the remains as part of a weather balloon. Brigadier General

Thomas DuBose, Chief of Staff for the Eighth Air Force said, "[It] was a cover story. The whole balloon part of it. That was the part of the story we were told to give to the public and news and that was it."[21]

Courtesy of the Roswell Daily Record

Interestingly, back in Roswell, Glenn Dennis, a young mortician working at the Ballard Funeral Home, received a call from the Mortuary Officer at the airfield. The officer needed some hermetically sealable coffins and asked for information on how to preserve bodies that had been exposed to the elements for a few days, without contaminating tissue.

Curious, Mr. Davis drove out to the base hospital later that evening and observed large pieces of wreckage with strange engravings on one of the pieces sticking out the back of a military ambulance. He went inside and visited with a nurse he knew, but was quickly confronted by the military police and forcibly escorted from the building.[23]

The next day he met with the nurse at a coffee house;

Marcel with
Weather Balloon [22]

she told him she was in attendance during autopsies performed on "several small non-human bodies." She sketched pictures of them on a napkin or a prescription pad, depending on the account.[24] Within days, the nurse was transferred to England where she was killed in a car accident a few months later.[25]

July 9, 1947 found clean-up crews busy clearing the debris field while news reports indicated that the crashed object was actually a weather balloon. The wreckage was brought to the base in Roswell and crated.

Back in town, Mack Brazel was escorted to the *Roswell Daily Record* offices by three military officers where he changed his story. He claimed, now, to have found the debris on June 14 and mentioned he'd found weather observation devices on two other occasions. Later that afternoon, an officer from the base retrieved all of Haut's press release from the radio stations and newspaper offices.

The *Las Vegas Review Journal* along with dozens of other newspapers carried the AP story:

"Reports of flying saucers whizzing through the sky fell off sharply today as the army and the navy began a concentrated campaign to stop the rumors."

The story also reported that the Army Air Force Headquarters in Washington had "delivered a blistering rebuke to officers in Roswell."[26]

Evidence and records indicate that there was another crash site west of Socorro, New Mexico, about 150 miles WNW of Roswell, in an area known as the Plains of San Agustin. Witnesses there supposedly discovered not only a damaged metallic craft resting on the desert, but also dead, human-like bodies.

The first witness on-site was Grady L. "Barney" Barnett, a civil engineer with the U.S. Soil Conservation Service on military assignment at the time. He related to friends that in early July 1947, he encountered a metallic disk shaped aircraft about twenty to twenty five feet in diameter. While examining it, a small group of people arrived claiming to be part of an archeological research team from the University of Pennsylvania.

Barnett told his friends that the group was standing around looking at dead bodies that had fallen to the ground and believed there were others in the metallic disk. The machine looked like it was made of stainless steel and had been split open by either explosion or impact.

He described the bodies in and outside the vehicle as "human, but not humans." Their heads were round, with small eyes, oddly spaced. They had no hair and were small by our standards, their heads disproportionately larger than their bodies. Their clothing seemed to be a gray, one-piece suit without zippers, belts, or buttons.

While looking about the wreckage, a military officer drove up and advised everyone the Army was taking over. Military personnel cordoned off the area; everyone at the site was told to leave and not talk to anyone about what they'd seen. They were advised that it was their patriotic duty to remain silent.

There is no way of knowing if the craft and its occupants allegedly witnessed by Barnett were connected with the debris found in Roswell. There is no clear connection between the two sites. Some believe two flying saucers collided, one crashing in Roswell, the other making it to the Plains of San Agustin before smashing into the desert.[27]

Enough has been written about the 1947 New Mexico incidents to fill a library. Researchers have attempted to reconstruct the finding, investigation, and the resultant reports by the military of both the Roswell and the San Agustin discoveries. Are they extraterrestrial crashes? Were they "covered up?" Only a hand full of people knows for sure, but the conjecture goes on.

UFOs are sighted almost daily. An almost guaranteed sighting can be seen near Marfa, Texas. West of Alpine, the topography around Marfa is flat with sparse vegetation; the Chianti Mountains rise in the distant south. A phenomenon known as *The Marfa Lights* appears southwest of the Chianti Mountains on Mitchell Flat. A roadside plaque on US-90 eight miles east of Marfa, near an abandoned Air Force base commemorates the lights.

The lights are yellowish green and appear above the horizon at dusk. They show up almost nightly and move, divide, merge and brilliantly flicker as they dance in the sky south and southwest of Marfa. Explanations vary, from ball lightning, radiant gasses released along fault lines, car headlights, and swamp gas, although there's not a swamp for five hundred miles in any direction.[28] And of course, many insist they are alien related UFOs.

If they are UFOs, one has to wonder why they're around every night and our military hasn't bothered to confront them. Probably just an unexplained natural phenomenon.

Many have concluded that perhaps UFOs are directly related to covert military operations. *Area 51*, also known as Paradise Ranch, Dreamland, and simply, Groom Lake, lends a bit of credence to that possibility. At almost 5000 square miles, even in Nevada, the military installation is tough to conceal.

Groom Lake was used for bombing and artillery practice during WWII. It was then abandoned until 1955. It was selected by a skunkworks team at Lockheed for the ideal test site for the U-2 spy plane. The location with its runways and dry lake bed afforded a functional test area situated between two mountain ranges that isolated it from prying eyes. Since then, it seems to be used for testing top secret aircraft as well as a permanent home for a number of Soviet designed aircraft, reportedly analyzed and used for training purposes.

While buildings and runways are clearly observable in satellite photos and from surrounding mountain vistas, the Groom Lake facility doesn't appear on U.S. government maps, nor does the government acknowledge its existence. *But*, they don't deny its existence, either! The area is permanently off limits to civilian and regular military air traffic as well as any ground access. The area's protected by radar stations, buried movement sensors, and other sensing devices. Uninvited guests are met by helicopters and armed private security guards, then handed over to the Lincoln County Sheriff's department.

The section of Nevada Highway 375 near Rachel has been officially named "The Extraterrestrial Highway." Obviously people work there and have to commute. A number of un-marked aircraft operated by a defense contractor, EG&G, from a private terminal at McCarran International Airport in Las Vegas provides a daily shuttle service to area 51. These aircraft reportedly use the radio call sign JANET, said to be an acronym for "Joint Air Network for Employee Transfer," while others say, perhaps tongue-in-cheek, "Just Another Non-Existent Terminal." Estimates of thousands of commuters daily have been made by observers counting departures and cars in the private EG&G parking lot at McCarran.

Fueling UFO and alien rumors, a number of conspiracy theories about Area 51 abound. Some think it's a repository for the storage, examination, and reverse-engineering of crashed alien spacecraft, the study of their living or dead occupants, and the manufacture of aircraft based on alien technology. Some also believe there is an extensive underground facility in which meetings with extraterrestrials are held, exotic weapons are developed, weather control technology tested, and concepts related to a shadowy world government are fleshed out.[29]

My personal contact with Area 51 activity is limited to one interesting event. I was on a commercial jet traveling from Dallas to Los Angeles and the pilot had been chatty about points of interest along the way. As we were passing over Henderson, Nevada he came on the intercom to say, "For those of you on the right side of the aircraft, you'll notice two dark specks moving from near the desert below to well above us. They're quite far away, near a location you may have heard of, Area 51. I believe they're F-117 aircraft, the Air Force's newest tactical fighter, performing exercises that I'm estimating from 10,000 feet to about 60,000 feet."

Not usually one to peer out at every landmark, I stared intently at what seemed to be two gnats skittering after one another. Down, then what appeared to be straight up, then straight down, then zigging and zagging before they did it all again. Incredibly fast and fascinating. I wanted to be in one of those babies! If we hadn't been told what they were, most of us on board would have certainly thought "UFO."

There are numerous organizations around the world reporting and researching UFO sightings. Google alone identifies 53.5 million sites when you enter "UFO." Jump in and determine for yourself if UFOs have merit.

Aliens

Extraterrestrials or extra density beings, are purported to be in our midst, living in the ocean, inside the earth, and of course, on the earth. According to one resource, [30] there are numerous types of *Reptilians*, requiring a balanced environment because like reptiles, they're cold-blooded. They have scales to protect them from moisture loss and have long, thin arms that end in three webbed fingers with an opposing thumb. These beings are supposedly from the constellation Orion; there are conflicting stories as to whether these are good guys or bad guys.

A crossbreeding of Reptilians and humans gives you *Grays*, who are used as slaves by the Reptilians. There are three different species of Grays, ranging in height from three to five feet, four to five feet, and from six to nine feet. The more negative and dangerous of the Grays have manipulated humans into developing sources of nuclear power that emit radiation so they can "feed" on the energy.

The Grays

But, the first Grays were highly intelligent, living around 1,000 years and left on earth to guide humans. They were vegetarian and given a high metabolism to offset heat-loss. They have been able to inter-breed with humans to develop a full spectrum of awareness.

The small benevolent Grays are the most often encountered aliens. They're said to be about four feet tall and get their name from the color of their skin. They appear insect-like with large heads, large black eyes, small noses, and a slit for a mouth. Some people say they are here to help humans evolve.[31]

Next we have Men in Black or MIBs. They usually show up to harass or intimidate witnesses to UFO activity. They've been known to make vague threats to stop witnesses from sharing UFO information. They are typically hairless, wear their trademark black coat, whiter than white shirt, and black tie. Their body mechanics seem robotic, their voices are monotone, and devoid of emotion. Sort of like the old FBI stereotype. Of course, anything they use must be black, like their Cadillacs and their helicopters. Although they are quick to threaten, there is no documented case of the threats being carried out.[32]

The next type of alien is *The Ancients*. They resemble a Praying Mantis or Grasshopper with large eyes. They are reported to be superior to Grays and may be malevolent to humans.[33]

The last type of alien is *The Nordics*, appearing similar to humans except they're a little taller and a bit heavier. The Nordics are here to watch over humans and help guide them into a new plane of existence.[34]

Thoroughly whacked out? How about a theory or two on how Grays operate? Here we go!

One theory is that Grays are connected to the U.S. Government. This is the "Alien-United States Government Technological Exchange Theory." This theory explains why the government continuously keeps information secret and dispenses misinformation to discredit eyewitness accounts. How else could the U.S. have made the technological progress that resulted in the F-117 stealth fighter and the B-2 stealth bomber?

Another theory held by New Age proponents is that the Grays are a truly benevolent race here to guide humanity with spiritual understanding. They are here to help humans save themselves by saving their planet.

Yet another theory holds that Grays are descended from a

dolphin- or cetacean-based life form. First, the skin appears to be the same in color and texture. Next, the skull shape of Grays is similar to dolphins, both skulls having a large rounded area on the upper front and back. The eyes of Grays are described as large with what appears to be a protective shield covering a black eye — which may be conducive to low-light conditions. Aquatic mammals have developed protective eye shields they use underwater where they use sound to navigate.[35]

Other theories abound, but get a bit too strange for this writer. Too Woo-Woo for me! Now for some contact with aliens; let's look at alien abductions… and of course, how to avoid them!

Alien Abductions

As you might expect, there is considerable controversy when someone reports being abducted by an alien. Many psychologists believe the experience is psychological rather than physical. Those reporting an alien abduction typically tell similar stories. So one would surmise one of three things: the same aliens are taking specimens in the same manner, the same part of the psyche is affected generating similar experiences, or people are simply adopting for themselves a story they've heard or read from another person.

Abductees usually claim to have been taken from their own homes or cars. Sometimes they've seen a UFO or an alien entity prior to the experience. In many cases, the abductee claims to have been examined by the extra terrestrials, most remembering the experience only under hypnotic regression. Many psychologists think that such a process in itself may prompt memories not connected with a physical abduction.

Some abduction experiences seem to correlate to other incidents or occasions dealt with by the subject. One renowned case involved a woman who claimed she was abducted, then seated in a chair enveloped in a large structure that was filled with a clear fluid. During the experience, she was fed a sweet tasting liquid through a tube in her mouth. While she apparently believed this abduction was real, a popular theory holds she surfaced memories of being in the womb.[36]

Researchers and hypnotherapists who've worked with people claiming extraterrestrial abductions indicate some of the reported experiences may be caused by dreams, mental problems, media indoctrination, or a misinterpretation of what the person has seen. Clearly, all experiences leave an indelible imprint on the person involved.

Abductions are reported in all countries around the world, large cities and rural areas, as well as day and night. Many abduction experiences go unreported because the individual fears ridicule, especially if they've been sexually violated.

There have been numerous ways people deal with the purported abductions. They may keep journals, seek ways to protect themselves from being abducted again, and even attempt to take photos or video of the experience — usually without result.

There's been much written about abductions. There are lists to determine if you have been abducted with such items as being paralyzed in bed with a being in your room, a waking memory of being inside a UFO or interacting with its occupants, missing or lost time, channeled telepathic messages from extraterrestrials, or my personal favorite, unexplained foreign objects lodged in your body.

Researchers report abduction agendas involve physical rather than spiritual motivation or crossbreeding attempts. The aliens are reported to use various types of implants as well as insertion of wires and tubes into the chest, kidneys, wrists, knees, and brain.

Many abduction experiences revolve around the same scenarios. Here's what's termed a "classic abduction" experience:

You are driving in your car or are at home in bed. You see a light following your car or outside your bedroom window. You see alien beings coming toward you, but you can't do anything — you're paralyzed — all you can do is watch. The aliens may speak to you or communicate telepathically. They "float" you out of the room and transport you to their craft. You find yourself in some sort of examination room, like your doctor would have. The aliens remove your clothing, laying you on a hard metal or ceramic table, and examining you, paying close attention to your head and genitals. They may stick probes into you and take sample tissue from various parts of your body. And, they may place tiny implants in your body to track or monitor you. Then, they return you to where ever you were taken, they disappear, and you are "missing time."

One of the most publicized alien abduction experiences occurred on September 19, 1961 on a road, US 3, in New Hampshire. Returning home from a Canadian vacation, Barney and Betty Hill saw a light in the sky; it was unusual and moved erratically. The light grew larger and followed them on a parallel course.

As they neared Indian Head, the light moved directly in front of them and Barney stopped the car, got out, and looked at the glowing object in front of them through binoculars. He reported seeing five to eleven figures moving behind a double row of windows. Betty heard her husband repeating, "I don't believe it! I don't believe it! This is ridiculous!" She didn't see the figures or the descent of the UFO.

When the craft was about 100 feet away and 70 feet overhead, Barney ran back to the car exclaiming, "They're going to capture us!" He sped away at break-neck speed. All the while, Betty was unable to see the object; Barney thought it was directly overhead. They both heard a loud beeping noise similar to a tuning fork and felt very drowsy.

When they awoke, they found themselves driving near Ashland, two hours later, 35 miles south of Indian Head. They drove home but were confused about the missing two hours.

The following day, they reported their experience to officials at Pease Air Force Base. A few days later, an investigator from the National Investigations Committee on Aerial Phenomena documented their stories.

Within ten days, Betty Hill began having nightmares where eight to eleven beings would stand in the middle of the road and stop their car. They would then lead the Hills to a disk-shaped craft and examine them, taking samples of skin and hair. Continued anxiety led both Barney and Betty to Dr. Benjamin Simon, a Boston psychiatrist specializing in treating personality disorders and amnesia.

Their hypnotherapy during the ensuing six months revealed many details about their encounter. The details of her nightmares matched with both their descriptions of being abducted and examined. Under posthypnotic suggestion, Betty drew a star map of the alien abductors origin. It wasn't for some years that the significance of her map was realized.

Information unavailable in 1961 produced a controversial match between Betty's star map and a cluster of previously unknown stars near two stars called Zeta Reticuli.

Dr. Simon later stated that in his professional opinion, the Hill's abduction was mere fantasy. Perhaps he was protecting his image within his professional community. His premise was "people do not necessarily tell the factual truth while they are under hypnosis — all they tell is what they believe to be the truth."[37] But what about the unfound stars on the star map Betty drew?

Another widely publicized "abduction" occurred on November 5, 1975 in the Apache-Sitgreaves National Forest near Snowflake, Arizona. A brush-clearing crew of seven men was going home after a day's work when a light in the forest caught their eye. On closer inspection, they saw the light came from an object hovering near the ground. One of the men, 22-year old Travis Walton, got out of the truck to get a closer look.

As he approached what appeared to be a lighted saucer hovering just above the pines, he heard what seemed to be turbines spooling up. As he looked up at the wobbling craft, he was struck by a bolt of intense blue-green light. His cohorts panicked and drove away, returning later to find that Walton and the object had vanished. They reported the disappearance to the authorities, a search of the area was made and no trace of Walton was found.

The authorities suspected that the crew had killed Walton and were investigating that possibility when Walton turned up five days later near Heber, Arizona. He told a sketchy tale of alien abduction.

When he groggily awoke after the bolt of light, he believed he was in a hospital, a large light above him and doctors wearing orange surgical gowns. As he struggled to focus on the doctor nearest him, he found he was staring into huge, luminous eyes the size of quarters. Frantically looking around he sees there are three of them and he flails at the two on his right and staggers to a wall. His legs too weak to support him, his head wracked with pain, he wields the nearest item he can grab, an eighteen inch tube, too light to do any damage.

Crouching, ready for an attack, he notices his "doctors" are a little less than five feet tall, and had human-like arms, legs, and hands with five digits each. Their skin was smooth, chalky; their hands thin, without fingernails. Their facial features were almost infantile, small ear lobes, miniature noses with oval nostrils, their eyes large with no lashes or eyebrows.

Walton screamed at them, questioning their intentions. The three never said a word. After reaching out to Walton, perhaps to calm him, they leave hurriedly as he crouches to defend himself.

As he explores the small room and the hallway, a tall human-like, muscular man wearing a transparent helmet and a blue velour-like, skin-tight, bright blue suit, appears in the doorway. He silently leads Walton down a hallway into a larger room with clean, cool air wafting through it. The "room" he'd just left was shaped like the saucer he saw in the woods, but larger, about 60 feet in diameter. There were two or three other oval-shaped saucers, forty or fifty feet wide. He led Walton to a white room, about 15 feet square, eight feet ceiling with three other humans resembling the escort, all clad like him without the helmet.

They silently take Walton by the arms to a table and easily lift him on it, not responding to his barrage of questions. They gently pushed him to a lying position and the woman placed a clear plastic mask on his nose and mouth. As he tried to push it away, he felt the room fade to gray, then to black.

When he awoke, he found himself on the cold pavement just west of Heber. Light faded from the forty foot saucer about four feet above him, the saucer streaked vertically out of sight without a sound. He managed to get himself to an Exxon station and use the phone to have his brother-in-law pick him up. When he arrives, Walton babbles on about the saucer, the beings, their lack of speech, and their horrible eyes.

When he calms down, he finds he's got a healthy growth of beard, amazed that it could have grown in the few hours he was in the saucer. Walton is stunned to find he's been missing for five days![38]

There are a number of apparently credible incidents that purport to be alien abductions. The one-offs are easy to discount; they could simply be dreams, hallucinations, or memory aberrations. There seems to be a bit more credence in the multiple witness scenarios like the two above. As the subjects and witnesses try to explain their stories, there is remarkable continuity to their experiences.

One of those is recapped in Budd Hopkins' book *Witnessed*, where four people were abducted in lower Manhattan in November of 1989. A UFO sighting around 3:15 in the morning lasted one to two minutes. Beams of white light came from a glowing red UFO, beings moving around inside, seen through its windows. While it took a while to garner all the witnesses to the event — two policemen that saw the abduction came forward fifteen months afterward — the similarity between observations was remarkable.

Apparently road lights went out and cars stopped on the Brooklyn Bridge, a woman floated out of a window with small beings or children floating above and below her, implant and surgical scars were found on subjects not having medical procedures, and according to one car clock, an hour was unaccounted for.[39]

Could these accounts be a hoax? They could well be, but

there are so many people involved that collaboration and secrecy would have to have been so finely tuned that flaws in each individual's story would surely have been found. That's the trouble I've found with most conspiracy theories; we give too much credit to the people involved to pull it off and then not brag about it! So let's take a look at known hoaxes.

Hoaxes

As with everything, there are hoaxes; people elaborately creating illusions to lead the naïve and gullible to outrageous conclusions. Here are a few I found while compiling the background for alien, extraterrestrial, and UFO information and sightings.

The Lolladoff Stone: Purported to be a 12,000 year old stone plate found in Nepal depicting a disc shaped UFO and an apparent alien.[40] It was first shown in a book from the 1970s, *Sungods in Exile* by Karyl Robin-Evans. The book was actually written by David Agamon, real name Gamon, who admitted to the magazine *Fortean Times* that this was a hoax.[41]

Another was the film of an alien on an autopsy table, covered with white fabric, with its pallid gray skin and expressionless eyes. Two people are obviously cutting and removing what appears to be internal organs while a person in a long coat fleetingly appears in the shadows. The shadow person, according to those that know, was President Harry S Truman. After little more than a minute, the black and white film ends, some versions containing a security code in the corner: "Restricted Access, A01 Classification, subject 1 of 2, July 30th 1947."

The film purports to be an examination of an alien recovered from a spacecraft that crashed near Roswell in 1947. This footage first appeared in 1994 and has been shown, copied, and debated on countless TV stations and subject to detailed scrutiny and analysis, including the types of lamps and clocks on the walls.

It appears as if Ray Santilli, a London-based video producer came across film he wanted enhanced and brought it to

Keith Bateman and Andy Price-Watts. Santilli indicated it was a film of aliens; the enhancement produced nothing.

Except the idea by Bateman and Price-Watts that if Santilli wanted alien footage, perhaps they should get him some. They researched the Roswell Incident and decided to make a version for Santilli.

They shot the footage in a barn in the quiet village of Ridgmont in Bedfordshire, U.K. They cobbled the props, used a wig holder for the head and painted orange peels for the eyes, while chicken guts were used for internal organs. It was shot in color, processed in black and white and animators in the studio added the scratch lines to overlay on the film; it was then transferred between video formats to make it as grainy as possible.

They took the finished film clip to Santilli, saying they'd bought the clip in the U.S. He told them it wasn't very good, mentioning the fact that it should have a restricted notice on it. Bateman added the classification message and sent it back to Santilli, who told the men he couldn't use it.

In the summer of 1995, Bateman and Price-Watts were going to integrate the clip into a film they were making. Santilli by that time had secured an alien autopsy video and was planning a huge media launch in about twelve countries. He paid Bateman and Price-Watts to hold off releasing their film for ten weeks so as not to detract from his launch.

Santilli claimed the film came from a scrap reel from an army cameraman, processed by friends. He continued to hold out he didn't know any of the people in the clip, and they hadn't yet been identified. While confusion over the origin of the clip continued, a colleague of Bateman and Price-Watts confessed some details of the hoax on the internet.[42]

Alien Conspiracies

There are those, of course, who insist they have access to alien communication and encounters. Not too surprisingly, though, there are those that take a stab at protecting themselves and others from alien abductions.

One of those is the individual who provides free information on the internet on how to make a "thought screen helmet" complete with pictures and step by step instructions. When you're done, you'll be the proud owner of a device that protects you from alien mind control and telepathic communication between aliens and humans. It must work, because "Only two failures were reported since 1998."[43]

Interestingly, there are a number of websites that have laundry lists of ways to check if you've been abducted by an alien being. You may ask yourself if you:

- Have unexplainable missing or lost time.
- Have unusual scars or marks on your body.
- Have had a shocking UFO sighting.
- Have the feeling of being watched all the time.
- Have channeled telepathic messages from extraterrestrials.
- Have many of the indicators but can't remember anything about an abduction.[44]

The mind goes wild with the apparent cover ups and conspiracies revolving around UFOs and Aliens. From the supposed government cover up at Roswell and today's Area 51 tales, we are led to believe by the conspiracy mongers that there are in fact aliens and they probably control our government; that's why they won't admit to the reality of these extraterrestrial phenomena.

Imagine NASA secreting pictures from space that prove there are aliens. There are those who believe the reptilian aliens are seeking to take over the world through high-profile government leaders. We supposedly have been visited by extraterrestrials for eons and a few of them have even crashed. Our government has the wreckage and won't divulge its existence or its origins. There are those who hunt aliens, seeking to find those among our population who are undercover, covert operations. Some believe the extraterrestrials are here to help, others believe they are positioning earth for takeover.

Regardless of your point of view, it's darned interesting to conjecture that there may be life out there, and apparently smarter than us. Although, all it takes to hope for our future is to watch some of the brilliant things we do as earth's population — I do believe some planets may have rocks more intelligent than some of the people we have here on earth!

Nevertheless, we all have wondered at some point, "Is there anybody out there?" Who's to say yes or no? And who knows, what could it hurt? It doesn't shake the foundations of any of my beliefs. As I said earlier, my God has the capacity to do anything.

What about hard proof? That's what it takes to convince most people. So let's look at the agricultural phenomena of late night work.

Crop Circles

Crop circles, for the most part, are unexplained patterns found in fields of wheat, corn, or other grains. They appear to be a worldwide phenomenon with a significant concentration in the southern English countryside.

While crop circles may have been around since time began, they have largely been a phenomenon reported in the last forty years. Perhaps the reason we have only learned of this phenomenon in the latter part of the twentieth century has something to do with the advent and proliferation of the aircraft. Typically, crop circles go unnoticed and unreported unless the viewer has a vantage point high enough to allow viewing a design in the field, such as a hill or from an aircraft.

Very often, crop circles are formed where powerful ley lines intersect — that is the earth's magnetic energy lines. They often are created at night between the hours of 11 pm and 4 am, although there have been daylight formations.[45]

The earliest recorded formation was in 1647 in England and academic texts mentioned them in the late seventeenth century. Slightly more than 200 cases were reported prior to 1970, while thousands of reports per year are now common. There are some eighty eyewitnesses that report crop circles forming in less than twenty seconds, describing balls or shafts of light responsible for the crop circle.

Remarkably, ninety percent of the designs are reported in southern England and it wasn't until the 1980s that they were critically pursued. Early designs were basic circles and rings but by the late 1980s straight lines were reported, resembling petroglyphs found at sacred sites throughout the world.

After 1990, the designs developed exponentially in complexity. Today, it's not unusual to come across glyphs that mimic computer fractals and fourth dimension expressions in quantum physics.[46]

The physical aspects of crop circles are quite intriguing. In genuine formations — those thought not created by humans — the stems of the crop are bent, not broken. If a plank or garden roller were used to flatten the crop, the plants would be broken near ground level and the plants would be damaged.

Apparently to bend rather than break the crops, the plants appear to be subjected to a short, intense burst of heat which softens the stems — like wilting — just above the ground at 90° where they re-harden into their new, permanent position without damage.

Plant biologists are baffled by this phenomenon which is the singular method of identifying real phenomena. From a scientific perspective, sound below 20 Hz is capable of developing pressures capable of boiling water inside the stems in less than a second, expanding the water, resulting in tiny holes in the plant's nodes and causing a surface charring along the stems.

The localized heat also appears responsible for altering the surface and ground water, causing evaporation and a shift in the soil structure, seemingly baking it. Even short life radio isotopes are noted inside the genuine crop circles, dissipating after three or four hours. These attributes tend to discount the human creation element with the degree of difficulty in replicating the infrasonic sound necessary to accomplish the resultant evidence.

The electromagnetic energy that seems to be associated with the causal sound energy is known to produce dizziness, disorientation, and nausea. The localized electromagnetic field in and around crop circles tends to dislocate compasses, cameras, and cellular phones. Fresh batteries are drained in minutes and the frequencies noted have affected aircraft navigational equipment. Radio frequencies are markedly different within the space.

Moreover, local farm animals appear agitated hours prior to a crop circle's appearance as well as avoiding them after their formation. Car batteries in an entire village may not operate the morning after a circle is found. Some instances have left entire villages without power.

Colin Andrews is one of the critically acknowledged experts on crop circle origins and has compiled more than 15 years of research. His analyses include *flux gate magnetometer* — electromagnetic — surveys that demonstrate increased magnetic field intensity within the formations. Similar to hotspots on an infrared photograph, we see areas in the design of the crop circles studied that indicate upwards of three times normal readings of the surrounding area. While he's concluded that 80% of all circles studied show clear signs of being manmade, the remaining 20% lack any signs of human interaction.

Interestingly, after the crops are cut, the area can still register increased readings. A dowser can generally find the energy imprint of the crop circle design long after physical traces have faded away.[47]

So, we've talked about *genuine* crop circles, so what other kinds are there? Why the hoaxes of course! Whenever we deal with anything that is less than a "hard science," there are those who try to replicate the events and pass them off as "other worldly." Poor form to say the least, but let's look at what the potential causes of crop circles are, starting with the human element and the hoax.

It all began one summer evening in 1978 when Doug Bower and Dave Chorley started the craze when they conjured up the idea in a pub in Winchester, England. Bower related a story he'd read while living in Australia about mysterious circles appearing in a Queensland corn field and the conjecture that it was an alien spacecraft landing site. They were determined to see if they could fool the locals into believing that a flying saucer had landed nearby.

It worked. For the next twelve years, many scientist and spiritualists were attracted to their surreptitious work. Eventually, they "came out" and formed a group called *The Circlemakers*, whose members have made many increasingly intricate patterns as an art form. They use planks, ropes, and other paraphernalia to create crop circles, normally trying to execute them overnight. So while they are tangible, they're not a phenomenon, therefore, not "real."

What about the real crop circles, then? Certainly one way to explain them is that they're caused by natural conditions, such as weather and wind. One explanation is the Plasma Vortex Theory, postulated by meteorologist Dr. Terence Meaden, where a constant stream of air over hilly areas produces small, electrically charged whirlwinds that build into columns, break down, then build up again. The resultant patterns can be complicated in design and accompanied by light and sound during their formation. Believable, but the existence of plasma vortices has not yet been proven.

And finally, we have the theory that the crop circles are created by aliens, other-dimensional energy, or just plain magic. There are those who believe the crop circles truly are landing sites of alien spacecraft. They might also be messages from extraterrestrials to us or simply for navigational purposes for use by them. Or they might be trying to introduce us to an advanced form of physics we don't yet understand.[48]

Perhaps the alien angle is plausible. We don't yet know all there is to know about our universe and certainly at this point we can't explain many phenomena.

Take the crop circle known as the 2001 Milk Hill Formation. John Lundberg, a member of the *Circlemakers* suggests that this particular crop circle couldn't have been made with known techniques.

Lundberg says, "If this formation was man-made allowing for time to get into and out of the field under cover of darkness the construction time left should be around four hours. Given that there are over 400 circles, some of which span approximately 20 meters in diameter, that would mean that one of those circles would need to be created every 30 seconds. And that's not even allowing any time for the surveying, purely flat-

Milk Hill Formation [49]

tening, this formation pushes the envelope and that's a MAS-SIVE understatement."[50]

So it would appear that if humans had anything to do with the creation of this crop circle, they had to have some help — just like the Pyramids! Sometimes we can't do it all ourselves, even if we don't know who helped!

Time Travel

Ok, we won't spend a lot of time on this topic, because we have little to no evidence that such concept as time travel is possible. It probably belongs in a category beyond Woo-Woo, but some information is appropriate here.

H. G. Wells published *The Time Machine* in 1895 and it would be ten years before Albert Einstein would publish his first treatise on his Theory of Relativity. Man has been fascinated with time travel since the beginning of time, even if it was just a wish to go back in time to take the other path away from the T. Rex!

To those who believe time travel is impossible, they typically use the classic example of the "granny paradox." This is where a person travels back in time and inadvertently causes the death of his granny when she was a small girl. The obvious result is the time traveler's mother and consequently the traveler himself was never born. So he couldn't go back in time. Sounds logical, right?

Well, to those that believe, a smattering of quantum theory comes into play. First, we are dealing with not one universe, but a number of them, let's call them *multiverses*. In quantum theory, particles — and our time traveler — have multiple options at any point in time to travel down one of any number of these multiverses. So, as our traveler in the granny paradox goes back in time, his granny is inadvertently killed, and time moves forward, but up a different branch, multiverse. In this branch of the time traveler's reality, the traveler was never born, but no problem: "next door," in a parallel universe, granny is alive and well, so the time traveler is in fact born to go back in time to instigate granny's demise.[51]

So, some scientific phenomena to keep us on our toes! Just because you don't understand it or it runs counter to all the science available at the time, doesn't mean it can't happen. Remember, "it can never be" was the point of view that people held when they said flying wasn't possible or that space travel was impossible. Maybe time travel is possible but perhaps we just don't yet know how!

Energy

While we'll talk more about energy later, let's take a peek at one type of energy that may have played a role in our world's long past and what may be the propulsion system of the future: antigravity. By definition, antigravity is a reducing, canceling, or reduction in the force of gravity. So if you had an antigravity device, you could reduce the force of gravity on yourself, and if you could control it, you could float just above the ground and move about effortlessly. Not to mention the fact that you could lighten yourself up a few pounds to not weigh what you do just now. You won't look any better, but you'll weigh less!

The concept of antigravity or said another way, magnetic levitation, has been around since the ancients. There are allusions to vehicles propelled by antigravity, like the previously mentioned *Vimanas* of ancient India.

But we also posed the possibility of the ancients having a bit of help in moving large masses of rock and constructing wonders like the pyramids. While many of these building materials and artifacts could have been moved with brute force on rollers as many archeologists opine, the prospect of higher intelligences harnessing and controlling gravity is a distinct possibility. Witness the fact that using the supposed methods of transporting these large stones and objects, even with today's technology, it would not be possible to move them.

So we mentioned the ancients may have had help. Some legends have magic spells making huge stones move through the air like birds by Olosopa and Olosipa who built the megalithic city of Nan Madol on the Micronesian island of Pohnpei. Or the tales of magicians or priests using mind power to make the stone statues of Easter Island "walk" or float through the air.

The list goes on: Greek historians say the stones in the walls of ancient Thebes were moved by Amphion to the music of his harp. The Egyptians moved granite beams — weighing more than 70 tons — for the King's Chamber of the Great Pyramid 200 feet above the ground. Or what about the placement of the 1,000 ton foundation platform in the Roman Temple of Jupiter at Baalbek in Lebanon?[52]

And there are many more stories of levitation or moving objects with sound, psychokinesis, or "heavenly fire" that aren't understood. Whether it be the lost continent of Atlantis, the ancient Greeks and Egyptians, or the Tibetans and islanders throughout Micronesia, it would appear they either had better machinery than we have today, or they had a bit of help beyond our comprehension and replication today. How did they do it?

And what about antigravity's application and potential existence in UFOs? Of course, if we can't identify the object, it's really hard to ascertain its propulsion system. But technology teams in India are simulating UFO flight patterns and attempting to reverse engineer a propulsion system that can accelerate incredibly fast, turn sharply, hover, and travel at virtually any speed. They're working with electromagnetic waves and the change of intensity of these waves — known as electromagnetic flux — to accelerate or decelerate a vehicle.[53] Their research and study is most intriguing and may well provide a propulsion option for us in the near future. Maybe UFOs aren't that New Age after all!

Finding Other Worlds

So with all the legend, lore, and sightings of UFOs, the possibility of intelligent extraterrestrial life, as well as witnesses to events we can't comprehend, it makes sense to determine if there is life beyond earth. Probably the best known resource for searching out intelligence beyond our world is the *SETI Institute*. SETI stands for Search for Extraterrestrial Intelligence. Its mission is to explore, understand and explain the origin, nature and prevalence of life in the universe.

The SETI Institute was founded in 1984 and today employs more than 100 scientists, educators, and support staff in two distinct groups: the Center for SETI Research, and the Center for the Study of Life in the Universe. The Institute has been sponsored by a number of prestigious organizations including NASA, the Argonne National Laboratory, the Jet Propulsion Laboratory, and the Department of Energy among many others.[54]

The amazing diversity of their projects and studies is constrained only by the universe. There are other groups that pursue the unknown with scientific research, collaborating with others in the world of science, and challenging the status quo. In time, maybe we'll get explanations to all the questions we have. When we know, then it won't be so New Age anymore!

So let's see what we have now that we didn't have before.

Chapter 10 Endnotes

[1]   Murray, Topaz, *Number of Galaxies in the Universe*
[2]   CNN.com, *Star Survey reaches 70 Sextillion*
[3]   Agence France-Presse, *Galaxy holds dozens of other Earths, astronomer suggests*
[4]   Von Däniken, Eric, *Chariots of the Gods*
[5]   Warrington, Peter, *The Drake Equation and Extraterrestrial Life: A Brief Overview*
[6]   Rawles, Bruce, 1992 Photograph
[7]   Childress, D., *The Anti-Gravity Handbook*
[8]   op. cit., *Ancient Flying Machines*
[9]   Sedona, Rick, *The Dropa Stones*
[10] ibid., *Dropa they came from the sky*
[11] op. cit., *The Dropa Stones*
[12] US Department of Energy, *Oklo: Natural Nuclear Reactors*
[13] ibid., *Oklo: Natural Nuclear Reactors*
[14] ABC News, *The UFO Phenomenon – Seeing is Believing*
[15] Associated Press, *Kenneth Arnold Sighting*
[16] Condon, E.U., *UFOs: 1947 -1968*
[17] American International Consultants, *UFO Incident*
[18] ibid., *1947 Roswell UFO Incident*
[19] International UFO Museum & Research Center, *Roswell Incident*
[20] ibid., *Roswell Incident*
[21] ibid., as published in *UFO Crash at Roswell* by Kevin D. Randle and Donald R. Schmitt. Photo courtesy of Fort Worth Star Telegram Photographic Collections division, University of Texas at Arlington Libraries
[22] ibid., *UFO Crash at Roswell*
[23] unknown, *Roswell Story*
[24] op. cit., *1947 Roswell UFO Incident*
[25] op. cit., *Roswell Story*
[26] op. cit., *Roswell Incident*
[27] Coverups.com, *The Roswell Incident, 1947*
[28] Crystal, Ellie, *Marfa Lights*
[29] ibid., *Area 51… Groom Lake… Dreamland*
[30] Shapiro, Joshua & Desy, *What are Extraterrestrials?*
[31] ibid., *The Greys*
[32] ibid., *Men in Black*
[33] ibid., *Ancients*
[34] ibid., *The Nordics*
[35] Dragonbane, *Alien Harvest*
[36] Unexplained Mysteries, *Alien Abduction*
[37] Crystal, Ellie, *Alien Abduction Case Histories*
[38] Walton, Travis, *Travis Walton's Home Page*
[39] Crystal, Ellie, *Alien Abduction Case Histories*

40 Cooke, Patrick, *Ancient Art*

41 ibid., *Ancient Art*

42 Felding, Nick, *Hoaxes – How We Faked Alien Autopsies*

43 Menkin, Michael, *Stop Alien Abductions*

44 Leslie, Melinda, *Are you an alien abductee?*

45 Crystal, Ellie, *Crop Circle Theories*

46 Silva, Freddy, *So it's all done with planks and bits of string, is it?*

47 op. cit., *So it's all done with planks and bits of string, is it?*

48 BBC, *Crop Circles*

49 Alexander, Steve, BBC, *Crop Circles*

50 op. cit., *Crop Circles*

51 Gribbon, John & Mary, *Is Time Travel Possible?*

52 Pratt, David, *Gravity and Antigravity*

53 India Daily Technology Team, *Reverse Engineering intense electromagnetic waves for antigravity propulsion of a space module from Extraterrestrial UFO technologies*

54 The SETI Institute, *Search for Extraterrestrial Intelligence*

CHAPTER 11

ARE YOU READY FOR THE NEW AGE?

We've now been exposed to the *origins* of things called *New Age*. Did you take a deeper look at any of the topics? Did you learn anything you didn't know? Did you think about things you've never before thought of? Do you "buy" any of the ideas you didn't before believe?

We've sorted through a lot of stuff in this book. Stuff you knew, stuff you didn't know, stuff you might find interesting, and stuff you find unbelievable. Stuff. Prehistoric guesses. History. Science. Religion. New Age. Woo-Woo?

Tangible stuff we don't know about, like pyramids, cities, and structures that used techniques that we can't replicate. How'd they do that?

Mysteries. Petroglyphs and pictographs we can't rationalize. Stuff that happens but we can't figure out why. Phenomena that we see but can't explain. Theories that are mathematically explained but hard to believe.

Our world is a living paradox. Just when we think we've got it figured out, something happens to change our mind, our environment, or our belief system. Technology drives progress today and we've got plenty of it. It's amazing how far we've come. Did you ever stop to take a look at how we've changed over the last hundred years? Here's what 1905 looked like in the United States:

- The American flag had 45 stars.
- The population of Las Vegas, Nevada was 30.
- The average life expectancy was 47 years.
- Only 8% of homes had a telephone while 14% had a bathtub.
- With 8,000 cars, there were only 144 miles of paved roads.
- The average wage was 22 cents an hour.
- More than 95% of births took place in the home while ninety percent of all doctors had no college education.
- The leading cause of death was pneumonia and influenza, followed by tuberculosis and diarrhea.
- Twenty percent of adults couldn't read or write and only 6 % had graduated from high school.
- Crossword puzzles, canned beer, and iced tea weren't yet invented.
- There were 230 reported murders in the entire U.S.

Can you believe the progress we've made? Or is it progress? Certainly not in the murder statistic, but the others are arguably progress. Imagine how difficult it is for us to correctly fathom what life was like 500 or 1000 years ago. Just can't do it. Don't even try to imagine the million or billion year old lifestyle — you couldn't even get close, *Jurassic Park* not withstanding! The heavens have moved significantly, the ecosystems have changed radically, and surviving then may well have taken up the entire day.

If you're holding this book, you're probably in the top 2% of the socio-economic strata of the world's population. We're fortunate to live in a society that values education and hard work. Both drive discovery and advancement. Like my Grandmother used to say, "The harder you work, the luckier you get." I consider myself lucky.

Religious beliefs hold people together, as do communities, organizations, families, and even companies for whom you work. We're here to learn, to grow, and hopefully to teach those around us. We should evolve. The only way to do that is to help others, help the group, help the community, help the world. I believe we should willingly pass along the wisdom we've gained to better improve and evolve this world.

What's out there in the heavens beyond what we can see? Closer to home, what's next to us we can't see? Will we explore other dimensions in the near future? Or has humanity progressed as far as it can? Are there benevolent aliens out there? Or will we have to defend our world some day? How different will our world be 100 years from now?

All these are cogent questions that no one I know can answer. Perhaps the answers lie in the path to the answers. Perhaps the journey is our lesson and we should take our wisdom from everything around us as we "progress" to our individual, collective, and ultimate goals.

The New Age and its implications probably depend, as does most things, on your perspective. For instance, wouldn't a missionary be a New Age phenomenon to the aborigines who've never seen one? Of course, so would a pilot, or heavy machine operator if you've never seen a plane or a bull dozier, so it's all relative.

Approach those things you don't understand with an open mind – probe, challenge, ask questions and then make up your own mind. Ask people who are non-judgmental what they think. Do they discount your observations or do they ask questions that prod your curiosity? Delve into the unexplained, seek the rationale for phenomena, and probe esoteric practices. Find the reasons that make you comfortable. But push your envelope to learn, to seek, to understand the wisdom that awaits all of us.

I believe a poem from *The Tibetan Book of Living and Dying*[1] is cogent in anyone's pursuit of the esoteric and certainly the New Age. Imagine the following:

I walk down the street.
There is a hole in the sidewalk
I fall in.
I am lost... I am hopeless.
It isn't my fault.
It takes forever to find a way out.

I walk down the same street.
There is a deep hole in the sidewalk.
I pretend I don't see it.
I fall in again.
I can't believe I'm in the same place.
But it isn't my fault.
It still takes a long time to get out.

I walk down the same street.
There is a deep hole in the sidewalk.
I see it is there.
I still fall in. . . it's a habit
My eyes are open
I know where I am
It is my fault.
I get out immediately.

I walk down the same street.
There is a deep hole in the sidewalk.
I walk around it.

I walk down another street.

Eventually I learn to be more careful
about the streets I choose to walk down.

Can this be progress? My hope is that I've brought you an entertaining read that perhaps sparks some interest in what many consider "a little out there." As in most things, there is a logical path through most of what we sometimes consider beyond this world. You don't have to believe it, you don't have to buy it, but it can't hurt to be aware of it. It will at least give you a start point if you're confronted with someone who works at Ghostbusters, or a rocket scientist, or someone who wants to know your sign at your local watering hole.

Or maybe you have a banging in your wall you can't find. Or things that have moved during the night. Or something's stomped a pattern in your grass overnight.

As you find rationale for what you see, do, and experience, perhaps the novelty of the New Age will fade.

But be careful!
It's the New Age.
You, too, might be called Woo-Woo!

And just so you don't come away with nothing to show for your New Age education, let me introduce you to a drink I call a Woo-Woo. I found this on the beach at the Four Seasons in Nevis. You can order what they call a Woo Hoo[2] – equal parts of vodka and peach schnapps filled with cranberry juice and garnished with a lime. Wonderful summer drink. And you'll find as you order your third, all that comes out is "Canna have 'nother Woo Woo?" Surely you're on your way!

Chapter 11 Endnotes

[1] Brown, Richard, *Autobiography in Five Chapters*
[2] Jones, Makishma, Four Seasons Resort, Nevis

EARTH TIMELINE

Estimated Timeline of Significant Development [1]

Millions of Years Ago

4800 - 4600   Formation of the Earth by planetesimal accretion.

4300   Molten Earth due to radioactive and gravitational heating which leads to its interior structure as well as out-gassing of molecules such as water, methane, ammonia, hydrogen, nitrogen, and carbon dioxide. Atmospheric water is photo-dissociated by ultraviolet light to produce both oxygen atoms and hydrogen molecules.

3800   The Earth's crust solidifies forming the oldest rocks found on Earth. Atmospheric water condenses into oceans.

3500-2800   Prokaryotic cell organisms develop. Photosynthesis by blue-green algae releases oxygen molecules into the atmosphere and steadily strengthens the ozone layer, changing the Earth's atmosphere from chemically reducing to chemically oxidizing.

2400   Rise in the concentration of oxygen molecules stops the depositing of uraninites, soluble when combined with oxygen, and starts the deposition of banded iron formations.

2000   The Oklo natural fission reactor in Gabon, Africa begins operation.

1600   The last reserves of reduced iron are used up by the increasing atmospheric oxygen. The last banded iron formations are formed.

1500   Eukaryotic cell organisms develop.

1500-600	Rise of multicellular organisms.
580-545	Fossils of Ediacaran organisms are formed.
545	Cambrian explosion of hard-bodied organisms.
500-450	Rise of the fish, the first vertebrates.
430	Waxy coated algae begin to live on land.
420	Millipedes appear, the first land animals.
375	Appearance of primitive sharks.
350	Primitive ferns emerge, first plants with roots. Primitive insects appear.
350-300	Rise of the amphibians.
300	Winged insects appear.
300-280	Rise of the reptiles. Beetles and weevils appear.
250	Permian period mass extinction.
230-200	Roaches and termites appear, as do modern ferns, bees, primitive crocodiles and the first mammals.
145	*Archaeopteryx* walks the earth.
136-90	Primitive kangaroos, primitive cranes and modern sharks appear.
65	Extinction of the dinosaurs; beginning of the reign of mammals.
60-20	Rats, mice and squirrels appear as well as herons and storks, rabbits and hares, primitive monkeys, koalas, parrots and pigeons.
20-12	The chimpanzee and hominid lines evolve.
4	Bipedal hominids appear.
2	Widespread use of stone tools.

Thousands of Years Ago

2000-10	Most recent ice age.
1600-200	*Homo erectus* exists.
1000-500	*Homo erectus* tames fire.
200-30	*Homo sapiens neanderthalensis* – Neanderthal Man – exists.
50-0	*Homo sapiens sapiens* – Modern Man – exists.
40-12	*Homo sapiens sapiens* enter Australia from southeastern Asia and North America from northeastern Asia.
25-10	An ice sheet covers much of the northern United States.
12	*Homo sapiens sapiens* have domesticated dogs in Kirkuk, Iraq.
10	First permanent *Homo sapiens sapiens* settlements. *Homo sapiens sapiens* learn to use fire to cast copper and harden pottery.
6	Writing is developed in Sumeria.

Earth Timeline Endnotes

[1]   Brandt, Niel, *Evolutionary Timeline*

GLOSSARY

or Words We Thought We Knew!

Ageless Wisdom Esoteric knowledge passed down through the ages, describing initiations necessary to gain the understanding of the universe and its creator. Perhaps, your grandfather's back teeth?

Ashlars Cut, rectangular stone used in walls. Patterns are made of cut stones that fit together either in a random pattern — Random Ashlars — or placed in rows — Coursed Ashlars. Fancy name for really nice cut-stone walls!

Astrological Age The time the Earth spends in a particular constellation. We are currently in the Piscean Age, moving to the Age of Aquarius. May refer to what's showing when you ask someone, "What's your sign?" and strike out yet again — Get a better line!

Atlantis The "Lost Continent," according to Plato; a civilization developed some 11,600 years ago, having technologies advanced beyond what we know today — e.g. electro-magnetic propulsion used for flight — that sunk beneath the seas. Proving yet again, it's not nice to fool Mother Nature!

Avatar The embodiment of a concept or philosophy in human form. Could be misconstrued as what cigarettes have besides nicotine.

Crop Circles Unexplained patterns found in fields of wheat, corn, oats, rapeseed, or barley; origins may be natural or alien, often believed to be man-made. Do not confuse with the welts left on your legs by the inappropriate use of a riding crop.

Cuneiform The earliest writing; Mesopotamian picture writing invented by the Sumerians writing on clay tablets using long reeds. This pictorial writing developed into a more abstract series of wedges and hooks, looking a lot like golf tees strewn in a line across the page!

Dharma A Sanskrit word meaning law or way. Generally, it refers to religious duty, but can mean social order, correct conduct, or simply, virtue. Can also be Greg's wife.

Dowse To use a divining rod, typically to locate water. Not to be confused with dousing, which always finds water on the person in question.

Elementals Similar to other nature spirits, they are raw forces of nature not having a definite form or appearance – think sparks, wind, fire, warmth, etc. Elementals have extraordinary power and cannot be tamed or controlled. This *is* Mother Nature!

Esoteric Only understood by the specially initiated. Ss and Os by terrorists confuse their targets.

Essential Oils A class of volatile oils that gives plants their characteristic odor typically used in perfumes and flavorings. Could be the oils that cause sensuous feelings.

Ether A medium that permeates all space and transmits transverse light waves. Also can be a moveable holiday wherein a large rabbit hides eggs for children to find.

Exoteric Suitable to be imparted to the public; relating to the out circle. Use of Xs and Os to scare the public.

Great White Brotherhood Believers in a presence of "only love and light and knowledge of All That Is;" a "collective of loving energies which is termed 'white' because they are of the light which lies closer to the Creator than the vibration of dense matter and negative forces."[1] *NOT* the KKK or similar white supremist groups!

Hierophant The fifth card in the Major Arcana of the Tarot cards representing intuition; an advocate. Similar to a sycophant, except they kiss higher up the body.

Horoscope An astrological forecast. Might refer to a device to see things that scare the hell out of you.

Karma An influence or force generated by a person's actions; the cumulative burden of good and bad deeds that each of us carry with us. Careful not to let your karma run over my dogma!

Lemuria A vast hypothetical sunken continent, believed by some to be the actual birthplace of man. Its civilization is said to have begun approximately 75,000 BC. Also known as Mu. And you wondered where lemurs came from!

Ley Lines Alleged alignments of ancient sites or holy places, such as stone circles, standing stones, cairns, and churches. Also lines that connect vortices. Not to be confused with your opening line in a singles bar.

Mantra Mystical formula of invocation or incantation. Don't confuse with sea life found in the Caymans.

Megalith A very large stone used in prehistoric cultures as a monument or building block. No, it's not a dramatic speech impediment.

Metaphysics Abstract philosophical studies: a study of what is outside objective experience. The study of matter and energy beyond the physical plane to other dimensions. The study of Woo-Woo in socially acceptable pseudo-scientific terminology.

Mu A lost culture, the center of civilization 25,000 years ago that sunk into the ocean, lost forever. Also known as Lemuria. And you thought it was a bovine language!

Occult Not revealed; secret; mysterious; hidden from view; concealed. It can also be a winter condition where sneezing and stuffy nose is prevalent.

Petroglyph A carving or inscription on a rock. Often the guttural sound heard at the Exxon station during a fill up, directly related to the cost of gasoline.

Polytheism The belief in or worship of more than one God. It is not the deifying of parrots.

Psychokinesis Moving objects with the mind; the older term is telekinesis. This has nothing to do with the legendary football player Crazy Legs Hersh.

Pythagorean Theorem Developed by the Greek mathematician Pythagoras, it states *the square of the hypotenuse of a right triangle is equal to the sum of the squares of the other two sides.* Not to be confused with organic greens used in tossed salads.

Reincarnation The rebirth of a soul in a new body. Not the flowers near the Tack Room.

Scrying The technique of predicting the future by using shiny objects such as crystal balls. Also a response for the question, "What's the baby doing?"

Sidereal Time An astrological calculation of time based on the hour angle of the vernal equinox at a place. Don't confuse with the time you spend leaning on the railing trying to balance yourself after a few drinks.

Skunkworks A small often isolated facility for engineering research and development with minimal supervision within a company. Could also be the working mechanism that produces the incredibly foul smell in the aft section of a skunk.

Soul The immaterial essence, animating principle, or actuating cause of an individual life. Or sometimes, the ability to catch the rhythm of a tune and let your body flow with it.

Synchronicity The coincidental occurrence of events that seem related but are not explained by conventional mechanisms of causality; a connection without links to a common cause. It's not the timing of your sins!

Theosophy The teachings of a modern movement originating in the U.S. in 1875 following theories of pantheistic evolution and reincarnation. Not the study of Teddy Roosevelt.

Vedas Any of the four canonical collection of hymns, prayers, and liturgical formulas that comprise the earliest Hindu writings. Also might be those guys coming over the top of the castle walls!

Vibrations All matter resonates with a vibration, atoms moving at certain speeds on certain paths. Combinations of these atoms affect the vibrations and their affects on other elements in our environment. This does not refer to the household appliance kept in nightstands around the world.

Vimanas Vedic Indian literature: flying machines – and other advanced devices are said to have been in use in the Uiger civilization. Probably an early form of *vamoose* or let's fly outta here!

Yin & Yang In Traditional Chinese Medicine, Yin is the essence of the passive feminine principle in Chinese cosmology while Yang is the masculine active principle. They are opposites and cannot exist without each other. Don't confuse with Scandinavian bells.

Woo Woo The evident but unexplainable. A little beyond reality. A little too New Age. Also is a wonderful summertime drink — see end of Chapter 10!

Zodiac An imaginary band in the heavens that is divided into twelve constellations each given a name that emanates from seasonal activity. Could be a maniac on Zoloft®.

Glossary Endnotes

[1] Bear, White, www.white-bear.org

BIBLIOGRAPHY

Books

Brown, Dan, *Angels and Demons*, Pocket Books, a division of Simon and Schuster, Inc., ©2000, pp 25-383.

Ducie, Sonia, *Numerology*, Thorsons 2000, Harper Collins Publishers, London, ©2000, pp 1-86.

Free, Wynn with Wilcock, David, *The Reincarnation of Edgar Cayce*, Frog, Ltd., Berkeley, California, ©2003.

The Holy Bible, New King James Version, Thomas Nelson, Inc., ©1990.

Javane, Faith and Bunker, Dusty, *Numerology and The Divine Triangle*, Whitford Press, A Division of Schiffer Publishing, Atglen, PA., 1979.

Lindsay, Phillip, *Soul Cycles of the Seven Rays*, Apollo Publishing, Auckland, New Zealand, 2003, P. 11.

Lindsay, Phillip, *Masters of the Seven Rays*, Apollo Publishing, Auckland, New Zealand.

Lofthus, Myrna, *A Spiritual Approach to Astrology*, CRCS Publications, Sebastopol, CA, 1983, p. 16.

Merriam-Webster Collegiate Dictionary, tenth edition, Merriam-Webster, Inc., ©2000; eleventh edition, Merriam-Webster, Inc., ©2003.

Von Däniken, Erich, *Chariots of the Gods*, The Berkley Publishing Group, a member of Penguin Putnam Inc., New York, NY, ©1968, 1999.

Interviews

Christian, Glenda, Spiritual Leader, Author; Devas, Theosophy, Wicca.

Jones, Makishma, Four Seasons Resort, Nevis

Lindsay, Phillip, Author, Esoteric Astrologer; Age of Aquarius.

Runmark, Francie, Numerologist; Numerology.

Periodicals

Lovell, Jeremy, *Explorers in Peru Find Lost Inca City*, The Globe and Mail, Bell Globemedia Publishing Inc., Friday, November 7, 2003, p. A14.

Pictures & Photographs

Alexander, Steve, http://www.temporarytemples.co.uk/shop/pictures-big.html, The 2001 Milk Hill Formation.

Anjali, Prem, http://www.lightoftruthuniversalshrine.org/images/lg/A1810RW.jpg, LOTUS.

International UFO Museum & Research Center, *Roswell Incident*; as published in *UFO Crash at Roswell* by Kevin D. Randle and Donald R. Schmitt. Photo courtesy of Fort Worth Star Telegram Photographic Collections division, University of Texas at Arlington Libraries, Marcel with Weather Balloon.

Jupiterimages Corporation, pictures ©2008, Great Pyramid, Great Sphinx, Machu Piccu, Moais on Easter Island, Stonehenge.

Rawles, Bruce, bruce@brucerawles.com, Abydos Egypt, photographed 5 Nov 1992, Close-up of hieroglyphics in Abydos.

Roswell Daily Record, July 8, 1947, page 1.

Websites

ABC News, http://abcnews.go.com/Technology/Primetime/story? id=468496: The UFO Phenomenon – Seeing Is Believing.

Agence France-Presse, http://www.spacedaily.com/2004/040401171808.gnp jy4di.html: Galaxy holds dozens of other Earths, astronomer suggests.

American Federation of Astrologers, http://www. astrologers.com/: History of Astrology, Horoscopes.

American International Consultants, http://www.roswell-online.com/comunity/history/ufo.htm: 1947 Roswell UFO Incident; http://www.roswell-online.com/ comunity/history/index.htm#ufo: UFO Incident.

Anjali, Prem, http://www.swamisatchidananda.org/docs2/home. htm: Sri Swami Satchidananda; http://www.lightoftruthuniversalshrine.org/docs/ taoism.htm; LOTUS.

Anonymous, http://www.open2.net/sciencetechnologyna-ture/worldaroundus/evolution_p.html: Natural Selection.

Arnheim, http://home.wxs.nl/~brouw724/Assagioli.html: Roberto Assagioli.

Ashmawy, Alaa K., http://ce.eng.usf.edu/pharos/wonders/pyramid.html: The Great Pyramid of Giza.

Associated Press, http://www.ufoevidence.org/History.htm: Kenneth Arnold Sighting near Mt. Rainier, WA USA; Pendelton, Ore. June 25.

Astro Energetics, http://www.astroenergetics.com/HTML/History.htm: A Brief History of Astronomy and Astrology.

Bailey, Alice A., http://www.watchman.org/profile/bailypro.htm: The Unfinished Autobiography, Copyright 1951 by Lucis Trust.

Bayuk, Andrew, http://www.guardians.net/egypt/gp1.htm: The Great Pyramid of Khufu.

BBC, http://www.bbcco.uk/science/space/life/aliens/cropcircles/human.shtml: Crop Circles.

Bear, White, www.white-bear.org.

Bennett, Charles, http://map.gsfc.nasa.gov/m_uni/uni_101age.html: Age of the Universe.

Brandt, Niel, http://www.astro.psu.edu/users/niel/scales/ geohist1.pdf: *Evolutionary Timeline.*

Brown, Amy, http://www.geocities.com/comet_97_1/
faetypes.html: Fairies, pixies, elves, leprechauns
and sylphs.

Brown, Richard, http://www.karmastrology.com/index.shtml:
Autobiography in Five Chapters, Birth Data.

Brown, Thomas, http://www.geocities.com/Athens/Forum/
4611/fairyG2.html: Gnomes.

Campbell, Wayne, http://www.echoedvoices.org/Feb2002/
Elementals.html: Basics of Magick: Elementals.

Canadian Museum of Civilization,
http://www.civilization.ca/civil/maya/mmc01eng.
html: Maya Civilization.

Carson, Reed, http://www.blavatsky.net/, Blavatsky
Net – Theosophy.

Centurion, http://www.roman-empire.net/index.html:
Roman Gods.

Childress, D.,
http://www.crystalinks.com/ancientaircraft.html:
The Anti-Gravity Handbook.

Childress, David Hatcher,
http://www11.brinkster.com/code10v2/civilization/
advanced_ten.html: "10 Ancient Civilizations with
Advanced Technology".

Clark, Liesl, www.pbs.org: Easter Island.

CNN.com,
http://www.cnn.com/2003/TECH/space/07/22/stars.
survey/: *Star Survey reaches 70 Sextillion.*

Condon, E.U.,
     http://ncas.sawco.com/condon/text/s5chap02.htm:
     UFOs: 1947 – 1968.

Cooke, Patrick, http://www.bibleufo.com/anamisc2.htm:
     Ancient Art.

Coverups.com, http://www.coverups.com/roswell/index.htm:
     The Roswell Incident, 1947.

Crystal, Ellie, http://www.crystalinks.com: Alien Abduction
     Case Histories, Area 51…Groom Lake…Dreamland,
     Ascended Masters, Ascension, Helena Petrovna
     Blavatsky, Bolivia, Edgar Cayce, Crop Circle
     Theories, Easter Island, Machu Picchu, Marfa
     Lights, Nazca Lines of Peru, Palmistry, Tarot,
     Tiahuanaco, Wicca.

Curnow, Trevor,
     http://www.philosophynow.org/issue42/42curnow.
     htm: Philosophy & Divination.

Dimitrakopoulos, Sandra,
     http://exn.ca/mysticplaces/enigma.asp: Stonehenge.

dos Santos, Dr. Ansio Nunes, http://www.atlan.org/faq/:
     "Frequently Asked Questions".

Dragonbane, http://www.abovetopsecret.com/pages/greyori-
     gins.html: Alien Harvest.

Edwards, Dean, http://deoxy.org/shaover.htm#1: Shamanism
     General Overview.

Felding, Nick,
     http://www11.brinkster.com/code10v2/hoax/main/
     ufo/alien_autopsy.html: Hoaxes – How We Faked
     Alien Autopsies.

Findhorn Foundation, http://www.findhorn.org/about_us/
display_new.php: who are we?

Fisher, Diana M., www.clexchange.org: Easter Island
Population.

Fox, Seth, Managing Editor, Britania.com, http://
www.britannia.com/history/h7.html: Stonehenge.

Gomez, Eduardo,
http://www.innerlab.com/atmanet/index.cfm?artID=
594: Alice Ann Bailey.

Grade, Michael, Chairman, BBC, http://www.bbcco.uk/
history/historic_figures/besant_annie.shtml:
Annie Besant.

Gray, Martin, http://www.sacredsites.com: Machu Picchu.

Gribbon, John & Mary,
http://www.lifesci.sussex.acuk/home/John_Gribbin/
timetrav.htm#Time_travel_for_beginners:
Is Time Travel Possible?

Groves, Colin, http://www.geocities.com/tasosmit2001/
flying.htm: Ancient Flying Machines.

Harris, Grove, Managing Director,
http://www.pluralism.org/about/people.php:
The Rush of Gurus.

Harris, Obadiah S., President and Chairman of the Board,
PRS, http://www.prs.org/about.htm: Manly P. Hall,
Portrait of an American Sage.

Hawking, Stephen, http://www.pbs.org/wnet/hawking/
universes/html/bang.html: Big Bang Theory.

Hefner, Alan G.,
    http://www.themystica.com/mystica/info/contents.
    htm: Devas, Druidism, Kabbalah, Psychometry,
    Reincarnation, Tasseomancy.

Hoeller, Stephan A., http://www.gnosis.org/gnintro.htm:
    The Gnostic World View.

India Daily Technology Team, http://www.indiadaily.com/
    editorial/2890.asp: *Reverse Engineering intense
    electromagnetic waves for antigravity propulsion
    of a space module from Extraterrestrial UFO
    technologies.*

International UFO Museum & Research Center,
    http://www.iufomrc.com/incident.shtml:
    Roswell Incident.

Jenks, Kathleen, Ph.D., http://www.mythinglinks.org/ct~
    NatureSpirits.html: Author's Note;
    http://www.mythinglinks.org/2Workshop~FAQ~
    PastLives.html: Explore Your Karmic Roots.

Ladatco Tours, http://www.ladatco.com/NAZgate.htm:
    Nazca lines.

Leslie, Melinda, http://anw.com/aliens/52questions.htm:
    Are you an alien abductee?

Low, Colin, http://www.digital-brilliance.com/kab/faq.htm:
    Kabbalah FAQ.

Lucis Trust,
    http://www.lucistrust.org/en/service_activities/the_
    great_invocation__1: The Great Invocation.

McClain, Michael, http://www.astrology-
    numerology.com/numerology.html: Numerology.

Madison, Jake, http://www.ehs.pvt.k12.ca.us/ehs/pro-
jects/9798/AnCiv6/Egypt/acjake: Egyptian Gods.

Martindale, C.C., S.J.,
     http://www.ewtn.com/library/NEWAGE/THEOSOP
     1.TXT: Theosophy: Origin of the New Age.

Maudhnait, http://realmagick.com/articles/56/2056.html:
     An Overview of Different Type of Scrying.

Menkin, Michael, http://www.stopabductions.com/:
     Stop Alien Abductions.

Mills, Robert, http://www.byzant.com/kabbalah/introduc-
     tion.asp: Byzant Kabbalah, An Introduction to
     Kabbalah, The Houses in Astrology, An Introduction
     to the Kabbalah, History of the Tarot, Kabbalah,
     The Planets in Astrology.

Murray, Topaz, http://hypertextbook.com/facts/1999/
     TopazMurray.shtml:
     Number of Galaxies in the Universe.

New Age Bible & Philosophy Center, http://newagebible.
     tripod.com/corinneheline.htm: Corrine Heline.

Oosterwijk, Hugo, http://www.theosophy-
     nw.org/theosnw/world/christ/xt-oost.htm:
     Gnosticism and Christianity.

Orgel, Leslie E.,
     http://www.geocities.com/CapeCanaveral/Lab/2948/
     orgel.html: Origin of Life on Earth.

Parker, Reba and Oliver, Timothy,
     http://www.watchman.org/profile/bailypro.htm:
     Alice Bailey.

Perrault, Charles,
    http://www.geocities.com/ssesbo/fairies.html:
    The Origin of Fairies.

Pomona College, http://www.astronomy.pomona.edu/
    resources.html: Stonehenge construction.

Pratt, David,
    http://ourworld.compuserve.com/homepages/dp5/
    gravity2.htm: Gravity and Antigravity.

RLP, http://www.skepticfiles.org/mys1/7rays.htm:
    The Seven Rays.

Rogge, Michael,
    http://www.xs4all.nl/~wichm/newage3.html:
    The Roots of New Age.

The SETI Institute,
    http://www.seti.org/site/pp.asp?c=ktJ2J9MMIsE&b=
    178025: Search for Extraterrestrial Intelligence.

Sedona, Rick, http://www.meta-
    religion.com/Paranormale/Ancient_mysteries/
    ancient_discoveries.htm: The Dropa Stones.

Shapiro, Joshua & Desy, http://www.v-j-enterprises.com/
    alitype.html: Ancients, Greys, Men in Black,
    The Nordics, What are Extraterrestrials?

Sicker, Ted, Sr. Producer, http://www.pbs.org/wgbh/aso/
    databank/entries/dp27bi.html:
    Georges Lamaitre.

Silva, Freddy, http://www.lovely.clara.net/education.html:
    So it's all done with planks and bits of string, is it?

Simpson, Sheperd, Dr., http://www.geocities.com/astrolo-
gyages/ageofaquarius.htm:
Astrological Ages.

Sinclair, Jim, http://www.cyberastro.com/online/num.asp?
action=origin: Numerology.

Spartacus Educational,
http://www.spartacus.schoolnet.co.uk/b5.htm:
Annie Besant.

Spirit Online, http://www.spiritonline.com/files/
messages/9/30.html?964401125: Wicca.

Stevens, Jon, http://www.astrologyguidance.com/instruct/
what-is.shtml: What is Astrology?.

Stone, Joshua David,
http://www.crystalinks.com/nature_spirits.html:
Devas; elementals.

Tillet, Rob, http://www.astrologycom.com/mercret.html:
Mercury Retrograde.

Todeschi, Kevin J., http://www.edgarcayce.org/
edgar-cayce2.html: Who Was Edgar Cayce?

Unexplained Mysteries, http://www.unexplained-
mysteries.com/articleabduction.shtml:
Alien Abductions.

UFO Area, http://www.ufoarea.com/aas_dropa.html:
Dropa They came from the sky.

Unknown, http://aliens.monstrous.com/roswell_story.htm:
Roswell Story.

Unknown, http://www.ascendedmasters.ac/gwb.html:
The Great White Brotherhood.

Unknown, http://www.geocities.com/Athens/Olympus/3987/
theosop.html: A Synthesis of Science, Religion and
Philosophy.

Unknown, http://www.geocities.com/little_pagan_gurl:
Animal Guides.

Unknown, http://www.paralumun.com/divination.htm:
Divination.

Unknown, http://www.revelation37.freeserve.co.uk/
contents/assag.htm: Roberto Assagioli.

Unknown, http://www.sevenray.net/sri_education_schedule_
robbins.html: The Seven Ray Institute.

US Department of Energy, Office of Civilian Radioactive
Waste Management,
http://www.ocrwm.doe.gov/factsheets/doeymp0010.
shtml: Oklo: Natural Nuclear Reactors.

Waldron, Ian, http://www.geocities.com/Athens/
Delphi/3499/sphinx.htm: The Sphinx.

Walker, James, K., President,
http://www.watchman.org/cat95.htm#New:
New Age.

Walton, Travis, http://www.travis-walton.com/:
Travis Walton's Home Page.

Warrington, Peter,
http://www.geocities.com/bororissa/ext.html:
The Drake Equation and Extraterrestrial Life:
A Brief Overview.

Wikimedia Foundation, Jimmy Wales, founder, http://en.wikipedia.org/wiki/Main_Page: Angel, August 12, Black Elk, Helena Petrovna Blavatsky, Dalai Lama, Deepak Chopra, Deva, Dharma, Fortune-Telling, Graphology, Guru, Karma, Krishnamurti, Mahatma Gandhi, Martin Luther King, Mother Teresa, Paganism, Sathya Sai Baba.

Xavr, http://www.messagenet.com: Greek Mythology.